PRAISE FOR EYEWITNESS

"A chilling personal account of the atrocities committed by the Serbians during the 1992-1995 Bosnian War as experienced by Gaši and told by debut author Koos. The history of Yugoslavia, created after World War I, is complicated. In the early 1990s, it broke apart into separate republics: Slovenia, Croatia, Bosnia, Serbia, Montenegro, and Macedonia. Beyond that, there was a mélange of ethnicities and religions within each of the Republics. Gaši, who has always thought of himself as Yugoslavian, is the son of an ethnic Albanian and a Bosnian Muslim. His wife is the daughter of a Croatian Catholic and a Bosnian Muslim. When the Soviet Bloc crumbled, the individual republics vied for independence. This is the story of the Serbian attempt to take over Bosnia, an endeavor enthusiastically supported by the Bosnian Serbs, which led to horrific violence among neighbors. Gaši's hometown was Brcko, next to the Sava River, which was the border between Bosnia and Croatia. It was also the site of a warehouse converted into the dreaded Luka prison, a torture chamber in which Gaši spent three weeks and was put on the Black List, scheduled for execution. After his release, he spent the next two-plus decades working to bring attention to the ethnic cleansing perpetrated by the Serbians and to testifying in the war crimes tribunals at The Hague.

Readers not already familiar with the history should expect to get lost periodically in the weeds of geographic details and hard-to-pronounce names (although plenty of reference sources are provided), but this careful attention to specifics, and the precision with which he recalls the unspeakably brutal events he endured or observed, is exactly what has made Gaši such a good witness. A reportorial tone makes the gruesome tale even more powerful: 'Looking…into the hotel parking lot, I saw a dumpster. It was filled to overflowing with corpses. Three more bodies lay on the pavement beside the dumpster.'

Important, powerful; a cautionary tale about nationalism."

—*Kirkus Reviews*

"The story of Isak Gaši is at the same time horribly ordinary and incredibly extraordinary. His experience of having his everyday existence in Yugoslavia and Bosnia interrupted by war, being arrested, viciously beaten and becoming a refugee is all too ordinary and is a fate shared by hundreds of thousands of other people. Yet his story as an elite athlete and the manner in which he was with his wife's courageous intervention rescued from near certain death, and how he bravely went on to testify in some of the most important war crimes trials at the UN's International Criminal Tribunal in The Hague, makes his story extraordinarily compelling. As such, this book richly deserves to be read widely by both the general public and by those readers particularly interested in the collapse of Yugoslavia and the ensuing wars of the 1990s."

—Christian Axebo Nielsen, Associate Professor, University of Aarhus in Denmark, specializing in Eastern European studies.

"This powerful personal story of an extraordinary individual who survived imprisonment and torture during the war in Bosnia in the 1990s, and then became one of the most important prosecution witnesses against Serb war criminals for the International Criminal Tribunal for the former Yugoslavia, deserves to be widely read."

—Adam Moore, Assistant Professor of Geography, UCLA, and author of *Peacebuilding in Practice: Local experience in Two Bosnian Towns.*

"Eyewitness is captivating for a number of reasons. The story is well-told. It's history up close and personal. . .What's provocative and riveting, however, is the horrific struggle between good and evil that transcends Luka, Bosnia and Yugoslavia and mirrors what's inside us all."

—June Darling, Ph.D., author of *Mind-Bending Chats with Great Thinkers* and *Becoming Artists of Life.*

"A generation after the Bosnian War brought the horrors of ethnic cleansing to the world's attention, toxic forms of nationalism, race hatred, and fearmongering flourish again. Isak Gasi's unblinking, firsthand account of what happened in the early 1990s in his native Bosnia stands as a warning to what could happen in any nation today. That a society priding itself as a model of cosmopolitan harmony between Serbs, Croats, Muslims, and Jews and hosting the 1984 Winter Olympics as a showcase of positive pluralism would soon be engulfed in ethnic turmoil and bloodshed remains a sobering lesson that this courageous survivor keeps alive for the present. Gasi's compelling on-the-ground report of long-buried animosities erupting into irrational fury and ethnic cleansing is essential reading to understand similar problems that grip the world today. 'I see Yugoslavia's experience as a cautionary tale; it is my reason for telling this story,' he writes. 'What happened to us can happen elsewhere. Unless societies are vigilant, there is no such thing as 'Never again.'

A central message of this important book is that we must never forget, but we must also learn how to forgive. It is to Mr. Gasi's everlasting credit that after surviving torture, witnessing mass murder, and testifying about these crimes, he has sought reconciliation rather than revenge. After walking eye deep in hell and coming through to the other side, he has chosen to do everything possible to end the cycle of hate. Toward the end of his book, Gasi recounts a Cherokee story about the battle that takes place inside all of us between an Evil Wolf full of anger, envy, arrogance, resentment, false pride, and superiority, and a Good Wolf filled with joy, humility, kindness, empathy, generosity, and truth. When a child asks the storyteller, 'Which wolf wins?' he replies, 'The one you feed.' Isak Gasi's indispensible narrative is ultimately an inspiring account of survival, remembrance, and constructive forgiveness, of how one man walked through hell, came out the other side and learned to nourish the Good Wolf that lives in all of us."

—Michael C. Steiner, Professor Emeritus of American Studies, California State University, Fullerton

"*Eyewitness: My Journey to The Hague* is a work of courage, pure and simple. It is a heroic testament for our time of Isak Gaši's will to survive and to tell the truth about the genocide, crimes against humanity, and other war crimes committed against Bosnian Muslims and other non-Serbs in Bosnia and Herzegovina, 1992-1995.

In this book, Isak Gaši provides a riveting eyewitness account of his survival of imprisonment and torture in the infamous Luka prison camp in Brčko, in Bosnia and Herzegovina in 1992. After his release to Belgrade—where his wife and infant daughter had already sought refuge with an old friend and teammate from the Yugoslav national canoe and kayak team—he fled with his family to Macedonia, where he was hunted by the Serbian State Security apparatus. Ultimately, the family found asylum as refugees in Denmark.

What his torturers did not count on was the Isak Gaši would become a star witness for a number of the most prominent trials at the International Criminal Tribunal for the former Yugoslavia. His uncanny ability to remember and recount the details about his imprisonment, his own torture as well as the inhumane treatment and murder of his fellow inmates, was crucial for the success of the prosecutions. Prior to and during his incarceration, Gaši witnessed summary executions, and he was also part of a 'work detail' that was forced to cast the bodies of the murdered victims into the Sava River. Isak Gaši's expert testimony was able to establish 'that there was a similar pattern between the atrocities in Luka and those at Omarska and that it was part of a widespread, systematic campaign against Bosnia's non-Serb population.'

A former world-class athlete who competed internationally for Yugoslavia in the kayak, and who came from an extended multi-ethnic family, Isak Gaši was deeply troubled that ultranationalist Serbian politicians such as Slobodan Milošević, Radovan Karadžić and Momčilo Krajišnik, sought to destroy Yugoslavia as well the multi-ethnic Republic of Bosnia and Herzegovina through the creation of an ethnically homogeneous 'Greater Serbia. His anger in the face of the tragic atrocities committed in the name of Serbian ultranationalism was one of the factors that motivated him to testify in the trials.

It is indeed remarkable that Isak Gaši was an eyewitness to history as he managed to be present, on the scene, at a number of the ultranationalist and hateful speeches that caused Serb aggression to be launched against the non-Serbs in Bosnia. He was present, for example, at Milošević's infamous speech at Kosovo Polje, June 28, 1989, and also attended a speech by Radovan Karadžić in Brčko. He knew that their stories of Serb victimization and their demonization of Bosnian Muslims as 'Turks' portended disaster for the region.

On one occasion, while he was a prisoner in Luka, Isak Gaši was battered and kicked unconscious by several men. On another occasion, he was threatened at knifepoint with dismemberment. Somehow, he had the inner strength to remain calm so as not to incite additional punishment that would have been fatal. He remained calm in the hope that he would survive. And he remained calm in the hope that he would see again his wife Jasminka and his infant daughter, Adna. When he was finally released and reunited with his family, he realized he had a moral obligation to speak for those who could not speak, to speak for those who had been murdered, so as to bring the perpetrators to justice. He was inspired, no doubt, by the spirit of another witness, namely, Elie Wiesel, who wrote that "to forget the dead would be akin to killing them a second time." Isak Gaši would not let the victims be forgotten, and like many Bosnians of his generation, he kept his heart open to the hope that telling the truth about the war crimes would lead to justice. But Isak was one of the few who actually had the opportunity to give decisive testimony in the trials of Krajišnik, Karadžić, Milošević, Šešelj and Tadić at the ICTY. He had the courage to testify, even though one of the defendants, Vojislav Šešelj, attempted to intimidate him. It did not work.

Isak Gaši is honest about the psychological toll that resulted from his testimony. He shares that he suffered increased anxiety and that his nightmares returned. But his courage enabled him to return to The Hague and to continue to bear witness in successive trials. Now that same courage and that same heroic persistence have enabled him to re-tell his entire story so that we may also bear witness to the truth of the genocide and other war crimes committed in Bosnia 1992-1995."

—David Pettigrew, Ph.D., Professor of Philosophy, Southern Connecticut State University; member, steering committee, Yale University Genocide Studies Program

EYEWITNESS

MY JOURNEY TO THE HAGUE

EYEWITNESS
MY JOURNEY TO THE HAGUE

ISAK GAŠI & SHAUN KOOS

Brandylane
PUBLISHERS OF BOOKS SINCE 1985

ISBN: 978-1-947860-02-5

LCCN: 2018933445

Printed in the United States

Published by

Brandylane Publishers, Inc.

PUBLISHERS OF BOOKS / SINCE 1985

To Heidi, the brave.

TABLE OF CONTENTS

PREFACE

In the aftermath of the Second World War, the Swedish filmmaker Erwin Leiser produced the documentary *Mein Kampf*. At its conclusion he made the statement, "It must never happen again ... never again." Since then, world leaders have regularly quoted Leiser. The accepted wisdom was that Europe learned from the war and would not tolerate a repeat of crimes against its civilian populations.

War for territorial gain broke out in Bosnia in April 1992. It took international center stage for the next four years. The conflict was vicious, with thousands of civilian targets. Its course contradicted the sentiment "never again." It became the saga of a modern society splintering violently apart.

One of the war's civilian targets was Isak Gaši. He survived, seeking to make something positive from his wartime experience. His story chronicles the human heart—both how quickly our hearts can harden in response to propaganda and manufactured threat, as well as mankind's capacity for compassion and decency in the midst of upheaval and crisis. It is a story of good and evil, of families and friendships, of pursuing excellence, truth, and justice, and the importance of dignity and courage.

Twenty-four years later, in a world presently plagued by sectarian conflict and humanitarian crisis in countries like Myanmar, South Sudan, Iraq, Syria, Nigeria, Yemen, and Somalia, its lessons remain relevant.

ACKNOWLEDGEMENTS

A book emerges via a lapidary process, through rewrites using ever finer abrasives. My thanks to Glen Freese, PhD, Lee Hassig, Leroy Ledeboer, PhD, Adam Moore, PhD, David Pettigrew, PhD, Christian A. Nielsen, PhD, Brian Tibbets and Barb Tuggle for their expertise and feedback. Much credit also to Jane Zanol, Melody Kreimes, and Lorna Rose-Hahn for their incisive comments and encouragement. Gratitude as well to Isak and Jasminka Gaši for the meals, gallons of coffee, and late-night conversations that laid the foundation for this effort. Sincere appreciation to Robert Pruett and Brandylane Publishing for their outstanding support of this project.

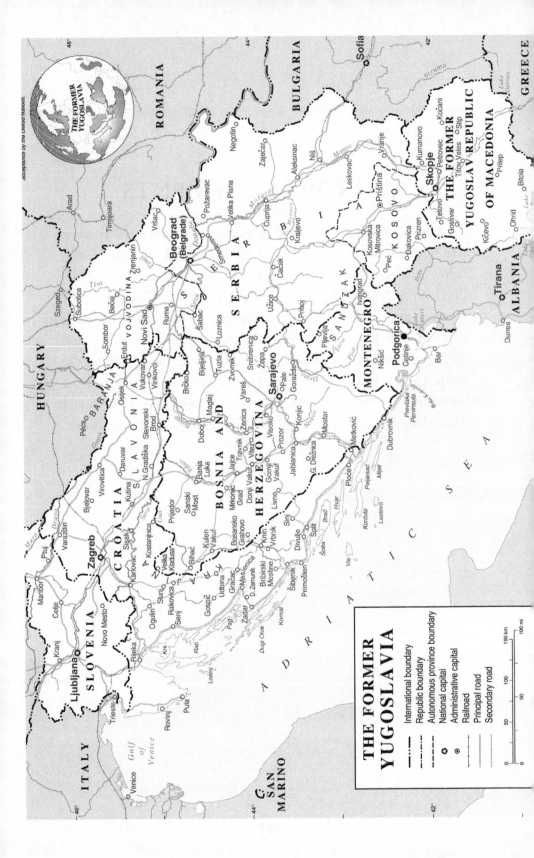

AUTHOR'S NOTES

On Pronunciation: Yugoslavs shared a common language, also known as Bosnian-Serbo-Croatish, or BSC. Bosnians use the Latin alphabet and include five additional letters. Š is pronounced sh like shake; Ž is pronounced zh like azure; Đ is pronounced dj like the soft g's in George; Č is pronounced ch as in church; and Ć is pronounced tj as in fortune. A guide to the pronunciation of main characters and locations is included in the appendix.

On History: Understanding my life experience, and what happened in Bosnia, requires some historical context. I have endeavored to provide that in the body of my story. For the interested reader, additional background, perspectives, and English language references are included in the appendix titled Historical Notes.

On Citizenship and Ethnicity: Serbian, Bosnian, Croatian, Macedonian, Montenegrin, and Slovenian indicate citizenship in a Yugoslav republic, and later, a post-Yugoslav state. Muslim, Croat, and Serb indicate an individual's ethnic identification. A Bosnian Serb is someone living in Bosnia, who identifies with Serb ethnicity and traditions influenced by the Orthodox branch of Christianity. A Bosnian Croat is a person living in Bosnia and identifying with Croat identity. That identity has historically been influenced by Catholic traditions. Similarly, a Bosnian Muslim is an individual living in Bosnia and identifying with Muslim ethnicity and traditions. Because ethnic affiliation in Yugoslavia need not indicate strict religious adherence or devotion, the Bosnian Muslim ethnic group is also frequently referred to as Bosniak.

1

BLACKBIRD IN THE DEAD OF NIGHT

June 1992

As I sat against the concrete wall, a blackbird landed on the ledge of a broken window. Backlit by the moon's glow, the bird peered inside, its shadow darkening the wall beside me. The bird's view was grim—more than two hundred men lying on a cement floor. Many of us were injured, some bleeding. Others had perished, their bodies stacked outside. There was no consistency to our clothing, no leadership or chain of command. Considering how few actually slept, the room's silence was unusual. The sensation was deathly quiet—a setting even Poe would have had difficulty imagining.

Having satisfied whatever curiosity its kind have in the ways of men, the bird flew away. I longed to do the same, recalling how freely I had once moved on the nearby river. To date no one had escaped from my place of confinement, the prison camp known as Luka.

Earlier that day I learned I was on a blacklist, scheduled for execution. There had been an arrest, but no charges, defense counsel, trial, or presumption of innocence. My accusers were unknown, invisible to me. Luka offered no avenues for appeal—complaining here invited your destruction.

We had been a city, and a country, with laws, individual rights, and social institutions. All that evaporated in a day, swept away by those who had been friends and neighbors. The change caught me blindside. In my naiveté, I had thought my country's complete rupture impossible.

At age thirty-five I neared the midpoint of a normal life's journey. With a wife and an infant daughter, I had much to live for. As I contemplated my life that night, its journey felt incomplete. There were events not yet experienced, things I wished to know. I wondered, *How do I survive this?*

2

MISSION COMPLETED

Twenty-one Months Earlier

When the pilot announced our descent toward Zagreb, I set aside the newspaper, glancing out the window at my native Yugoslavia. The fertile soils of Croatia's plains spread below, ripe with crops, promising a rich harvest. To my right, in the distance, lay our Slovenian republic, with its dark forests, pristine lakes, and alpine peaks. The countryside shone in the midmorning sun. I returned following a week in Copenhagen, Denmark, where I had represented Yugoslavia at the World Canoe and Kayak Championships.

While the trip had been productive, it always felt good to step down on home soil. Waiting for me in arrivals was my coach, Anto Čonda. A stocky, powerfully built man of mid-height, he stood patiently. Čonda had alert eyes and a hawklike nose. When he spied me, today's quarry, his gaze softened. He broke into a smile.

"Well, well. You are back and don't look the worse for wear. Eighth in the world—that's not bad. I talked with the Hungarian coaches. They said you were strong, even leading, pushing the pace. I wish I could have been there. How was it?"

"As you know, the marathon is long. I felt fine for the first thirty-two kilometers. When the Hungarian and Jepsen of Denmark raised the tempo at thirty-four kilometers, I couldn't match them. The last eight k's seemed to last forever. I was never so glad to see a finish line. In the Danish fog, even that was hard to make out."

"Well, good work nonetheless. Everyone at the boathouse is happy for you. The mayor is planning a community celebration next week. My car is parked nearby. Let's leave through that door."

Striding across the terminal, something seemed odd. I finally determined what it was. The large Yugoslav flag, prominently displayed a week before, had been taken down and replaced by the red and white checkerboard flag of Croatia.

— 3 —

COACH AND CONFIDANT

Čonda and I departed Zagreb, roughly following the Sava River's course south and east to our hometown of Brčko in Bosnia-Herzegovina (Bosnia). Like Slovenia and Croatia, Bosnia was a Yugoslav republic, one of six in total. The others were Serbia, Montenegro, and Macedonia. Brčko was a city with forty-five thousand residents, settled on the southern bank of the Sava—the river marking the border between Croatia and Bosnia.

An hour into our three-hour drive, as we approached the Croatian community of Jasenovac, I said, "I don't know if you noticed, but the Yugoslav flag was taken down back at the airport. During the flight I read the Zagreb and Ljubljana papers. They certainly present a different perspective than those from Sarajevo. There was a lot of complaining about the Yugoslav Federation, about how Milošević is trying to turn Yugoslavia into Serboslavia." I referred to Slobodan Milošević, president of the Serbian Republic and a member of Yugoslavia's collective presidency. "The articles talked about the raw deals that Slovenia and Croatia are getting."

"You know the old saying, 'Every horse thinks its pack is heavy.' These are unusual times. Driving into Zagreb, I had to detour the main square. The Croats were reinstalling the statue of their freedom fighter, Ban Jelačić."

"What do you think that means?"

"I suspect they'll push for independence now that the Communists are in retreat and other political parties are allowed. Of course, your friends will be following all that."

He referred to my organizing efforts on behalf of one of Bosnia's emerging political parties, the party of Democratic Action (known as the SDA in Bosnian). I was active politically, having studied politics at university. A delegate to the SDA's founding congress in Sarajevo in May, I now served on its executive committee in Brčko.

Until 1990, Yugoslavia had been a one-party state. Following the Second World War, our leader, Tito, declared the country a democracy that allowed only one political party, the League of Communists of Yugoslavia (SKJ in BSC). He maintained that multiple parties would chip away at the accord Yugoslavia needed.

In school, we were taught that Yugoslavia was a country of brotherhood and unity, an association of equal peoples and minorities. We were defended by the Yugoslav People's Army (JNA in Bosnian) and by each republic's Territorial Defense Force, both pledged to protect us against all enemies from without and within. We placed great faith in the JNA, one of the largest standing armies in Europe.

In January, the Communist party had called a constitutional congress. During that gathering, reform proposals from Croatia and Slovenia were rejected by Serbia's Milošević. In response, the Slovenes and Croats walked out. The congress collapsed, its failure ending one-party rule in Yugoslavia.

Within the republics, new parties formed and elections were scheduled. It was a heady, and potentially dangerous, time. While the Communist party was wounded, it was still powerful. The political situation was fluid.

I told Čonda, "We in the SDA think all the changes will present opportunity."

Less sanguine than I, as we passed Jasenovac, he said, "It was before your time, but remember what happened here," referring to the concentration camp established during Yugoslavia's Second World War occupation. The Nazis installed a group of Croat ultranationalists to govern Croatia and Bosnia. The puppet state was known as the Independent State of Croatia (NDH in BSC). Once in power, they went crazy, persecuting ethnic Serbs, Jews, and Gypsies. During the war years, more than three hundred thousand Serbs died in their camps.

He continued. "Your father lived through that time. You know from him that it was difficult, and very dangerous."

My father had been one of Tito's men, fighting to drive out the Nazis and helping to reestablish order after the war. To stabilize the country and achieve his goals, Tito had been relentless. After his death in 1980, Yugoslavia's politics grew increasingly unsettled.

Čonda turned to me, peering intently, before saying, "I know it interests you, but I don't see you as a long-term politician. You're too direct. You get frustrated by meandering talk and endless meetings. There are long knives in politics. You are surrounded by those who exist to talk and scheme. I wish you and your party the best in trying to take Yugoslavia forward, but be careful."

He was right about my dislike of long meetings and their blather.

"Ah, my old coach," I said to him. "You have always looked out for me. We have had many good times together. I owe you a lot."

As we drove on through the farm fields and wetlands on the Croatian side of the Sava, I thought back to my early encounters with Čonda. We first met twenty years earlier, when I was thirteen years old.

Mr. Trebinčević, the physical education instructor at our school, had told my best friend, Said Muminović, and me, "You two are strong and have good endurance. You could be good canoeists. I've mentioned you two to the coach of the canoe club. He is looking for a few new paddlers. If you are interested, talk to him. His name is Anto Čonda."

Said and I did, and were welcomed onto a team with eighty canoeists and kayakers. Ours was the sport of Olympic flatwater canoeing. We paddled long, slender, and very tippy boats designed solely for speed. Within weeks I thought, *I've found my sport.*

Four years later, when I was seventeen, Coach Čonda drove several of us to Mulhouse, France. We spent ten days living and training with the local canoe team before competing in an international regatta that the city hosted annually.

I had a tremendous time, bonding with the paddlers my age. Despite training twice daily, we had the energy of youth. As teams from Great Britain, Denmark, Austria, Germany, Switzerland, and elsewhere in France arrived for the competition, the number who went out each evening swelled. We were a congregation of healthy, confident, and fit young men and women curious about our counterparts from other nations. Excitement ran high. The race organizers hosted a dinner, plus opening ceremonies. I felt pride when my club was introduced. This would be my first significant international competition, my chance to confirm my club's high hopes.

Heading to bed that night, I was keyed-up, my level of nervous anticipation sky high. I tossed and turned, running the upcoming races over in my mind, sleeping little.

The following day, my qualifying heat in the five-hundred meters was one of the first races, so I was on the water in the early morning chill. Mulhouse is an industrial city of two hundred and fifty thousand. Its residents were just beginning to awaken as we approached the starting line. Perhaps not fully awake myself, I reacted poorly to the starter's pistol, trailing the leaders from the first stroke. At two hundred meters I was fourth, feeling sluggish and uncoordinated. My body finally adjusted to the task at hand. I had a fast final two hundred meters, winning the heat.

Afterward Čonda said, "Your start was terrible. There's no future getting caught napping at this level of competition. The others are too good. Next time, I know you'll warm up better. Your body is ready now. You should be fine for the semi-final."

I raced my semi-final at ten a.m., starting well. I came to the finish line together with the top junior paddler from Germany, finishing a close second. I was through to the final. That race was scheduled after the lunch break, at one thirty in the afternoon. As race time approached, the sun reflected warmly off the water of the Rhone-Rhine canal. The air was still, the water plate-glass smooth.

Sensing my nervousness, Čonda said, "Breathe deep. Slow down your pulse. Get as tranquil as the day. Stay relaxed but attentive until the gun sounds. Then explode."

As I paddled out toward the racecourse, I tried to heed his advice. I was about to compete against Europe's best juniors. To ease my internal tension, I told myself, *Perfect paddling conditions. Everything will go great.*

The nine boats in my final were called to the starting line. After the "Ready" command, the starter held us for several seconds, then fired his pistol. Everyone burst out. A second pistol shot sounded, signaling that someone had left early. A false start was charged to the entire field. The next boat to leave early would be disqualified. The restart helped me, discharging some of my nervousness. I felt more relaxed as we approached the starting line a second time.

At the pistol shot I got a strong start. Sneaking a peek to my right, I saw that I ranked fourth at fifty meters. Fourth is the "wooden medal" position, just off the podium and the real medals. I wanted to return home with something tangible. I told myself, *Pass someone,* something that proved easier resolved than done. The leading boats held their positions for the next three hundred meters. After the three hundred and fifty meter mark I slowly gained on the Dane beside me in lane four. By four hundred and twenty-five meters my boat had nosed ahead. We began to close on the two leaders, the German and a French paddler who had medaled at last year's world junior championships. The Dane beside me hung tough, remaining a contender.

With fifty meters to go I trailed the two lead boats by two meters, leading the Dane by less than one. Two meters before the finish line we leaned back to shoot our boats forward. A blanket could have spanned the gap between us. The officials needed several minutes to consult the finish-line photo. The announcer asked the crowd to applaud the exciting finish, then reported that the French paddler had finished first, with the German paddler and I tied for second. I would go home with silver.

I was elated, a feeling reinforced by seeing Čonda's grin register his approval.

That night, at competition's end, the organizers hosted a party. I had a great time with my fellow athletes. Full of hope regarding our futures, we exchanged addresses, vowing to meet at future world championships.

During the drive home, Čonda talked to me about peak experiences and the fact that there were higher and higher levels in the sport to aspire to.

"I was impressed this weekend. You can go far in this sport. But that path is long and difficult; no one makes it to the top without extraordinary commitment. Think about it. If that is your dream, I will do everything in my power to help you achieve it."

For my part, I was hooked and ready to undertake the quest. Two days later I went to his office to say, "I want to do it, to race and win at the Olympics. Will you show me the way?"

In the sixteen years since, I had paddled virtually every day, dedicating myself to the sport. Čonda had been my coach throughout. I am, by nature, outspoken. When I grew impatient with my progress as an athlete, challenging Čonda about it, he had a ready comeback—"When the athlete is ready, the coach will appear." I eventually comprehended that the responsibility for my performance was mine.

Along the way there had been triumphs and disappointments. In 1979, at age twenty-two, I was named to the national team. I remained a member of the team, representing Yugoslavia internationally, for the next eleven years. Racing for my country always provided great personal satisfaction.

As an athlete, I also knew that all good things must eventually end. I had told Čonda before I left for Copenhagen that the previous day's race would be my final international competition. Our travel together today offered an opportunity to acknowledge and reset our relationship.

Nearing the end of our drive, I said, "I want to thank-you. You have been a friend, and a great coach. You devoted an incredible number of hours to my development. I hope it was worth it."

As was his nature, Čonda simply smiled and nodded yes, sensing that I had more to say.

"Something has been bothering me, and for some time. When we started working together seriously, back after Mulhouse, I promised you an Olympic medal. I never achieved that. Mirko and Matija won multiple Olympic and world championships gold medals," I said, referring to two of my closest friends, who were also national teammates. "I beat them at times, but never on the biggest stage. I feel like I let you down."

"You shouldn't feel that way. We had our moments. Olympic success would have been great, but that wasn't our agreement. Here is what I think—your parents raised you too well. You have drive and did all the work that I asked. You wanted to win, and competed well. The difference between you, Mirko, and Matija is that you wanted to win and they *needed* to win. You have always been more content with life. You focused on paddling during training, then switched it off and enjoyed the rest of the day. At times, it hurt you with the selectors—they thought you had priorities other than canoeing."

I'd established that reputation with the canoe federation early on, turning down an opportunity to represent Yugoslavia at an international regatta in Romania in order to take my university entrance exams. To his credit, Čonda had supported my decision. Perhaps, in hindsight, I should have raced in Bucharest. I scored well enough on the exam to gain admittance to the school of engineering, but not well enough to qualify for the full scholarship I needed. My university schooling was delayed seven years, and by then was part-time, studying political science.

"If your outside and family life had been less balanced, perhaps I could have pulled more out of you. I never wished that. You had the university and your political and work interests; lately you and Jasminka have talked about starting a family. Go do all that. One day I hope to coach your kids. That would complete the circle. Don't worry, I've enjoyed this."

This was good to hear. Nevertheless, I still wished I'd accomplished more. I suppose most of us do.

The Jasminka my coach referenced was my wife of ten years. Her name is derivative of jasmine, the fragrant flower used in garlands and leis. She was well named. My wife was auburn haired and attractive, and at thirty-three still possessed of her youthful figure. She was smart, strong-willed, and opinionated—a firecracker. She was also fiercely devoted to me.

As Čonda and I drove through the Croatian town of Gunja, approaching the bridge over the Sava, I recalled a day six and a half years earlier when I had carried the Olympic torch over the bridge and into Brčko's downtown square. Its flame had been lit at the Temple of Hera in Greece, with the torch making its way to Sarajevo to open the 1984 Winter Olympic Games. I felt honored to be the first Bosnian to carry the Olympic flame into our republic. I saved the torch afterward. It symbolized my own Olympic quest.

We Yugoslavs felt pride hosting the Winter Games. The selection reflected how far our country had come since the Second World War. The Games showcased Bosnia's natural beauty. As is our custom, we proved to be gracious hosts. In the end, the sporting world was pleased by its experience here.

Driving over the bridge and entering Bosnia, I glanced to my left at a plaque placed to memorialize the Jewish citizens massacred at the bridge during the Nazi occupation. Every year, in the spring, Brčko students attended a memorial service for those Jewish citizens. The lesson taught—never again. Recalling all that, I thought, *That is surely an objective everyone aspires to.*

— 4 —
FIRST IMPRESSIONS OF SLOBODAN MILOŠEVIĆ

During my travels with the national team, I'd been struck by disparities between the standards of living in other Communist bloc countries and those the average Yugoslav enjoyed. We were much better off. With a population of twenty-three million and the added boost of trade with both the East and West, our economy had grown steadily. Compared to the other bloc countries, our economic model was decentralized; while most Yugoslav enterprises were state owned, they made provisions for local worker control.

I had an advanced technical degree in electrical power distribution, and worked for Brčko's public utility, Elektrodistribucija of Brčko (EDB). I had started working there in 1975 at age eighteen, leaving only once, for eighteen months of compulsory military service. In keeping with the Yugoslav ideal of worker participation, at EDB I served on the company's eleven-person executive committee, from 1984 to 1988. For two years I also sat on the governing board for EDB's parent, Tuzla Power, which sold electrical power throughout Central Europe.

In the late 1980s, the Yugoslav economy stagnated, and unemployment rose. It is difficult for a people to regress, even if they have started from a comparatively good place. As we expressed our displeasure with the downturn, cynical politicians looked for scapegoats, maintaining that the others within the Yugoslav federation were at fault. Their message, "Better to be shed of these others than banding together to overcome difficulties." Many of my countrymen turned to leaders offering these simplistic explanations and solutions.

Several of those leaders ended up playing an outsized role in my life, and I would impact theirs. Back then I was of no consequence to them. A mere spectator observing their rise, I sat in the cheap seats as they burst onto the world stage. Theirs was a political play that would transform into a tragedy.

I witnessed an early performance in 1985, while taking classes at the University of Belgrade. My course of study was "Marxism and the Yugoslav Social Order." One afternoon my academic advisor said, "Join me tonight. There's going to be a high-level discussion at Club 101. You will find it interesting. The academic society is debating Serbia's future."

I agreed enthusiastically, meeting him that evening outside the club. When we entered, an animated discussion was underway. It included academic luminaries like Dobrica Ćosić and Mihailo Marković. The principal points being made: ethnic Serbs in Croatia, Slovenia, and Kosovo had lost political status; Serb populations in those regions were vulnerable and could again be victims of genocide; Yugoslavia's 1974 constitutional reforms stripped Serbs of dominance and needed to be repealed. Listening intently, I thought, *The Greater Serbia movement, outlawed after the Second World War, is rising from the ashes. This doesn't sound good.*

A year later, those same academics coauthored the seventy-four-page *Memorandum of the Serbian Faculty of Arts and Sciences*. The memorandum tapped into long-suppressed sentiments, providing intellectual cover and rationale to politicians advocating old nationalisms and fear of the non-Serbs in the Yugoslav federation. Statements like the *Memorandum* had long mattered in Yugoslav politics—its publication became a turning point in the intellectual and political life of my country.

Two years later, on November 18, 1988, I drove to Belgrade with four of my EDB coworkers to attend a Meeting of Brotherhood and Unity. The main speaker was Slobodan Milošević, a rapidly rising star in Yugoslav politics. The meeting ground was a great open space in the New Belgrade area, near our federal buildings and at the confluence of the Danube and Sava rivers. On that overcast and chilly day, a million people had gathered. A giant Yugoslav flag had been erected behind the speakers' platform, while thousands of smaller versions waved from the crowd.

Of note, and somewhat alarming, were the many Četnik flags also being waved, as well as the thousands of crowd members wearing the old black Četnik pillbox hat with its skull and crossbones insignia. The Četniks were royalist guerilla units formed from the remnants of the Yugoslav army following the Nazi invasion in 1941. They had eventually reached an accommodation with the Germans and Italians during the war, forcibly opposing the Partisans, who fought to drive the Axis out of Yugoslavia. After the war, Tito banned the Četnik movement. It appeared they were being rehabilitated in Milošević's Serbia.

My friends and I stood in the midst of a huge Četnik delegation. As I studied their number, I thought, *This is going to be interesting*.

Milošević's address stirred the crowd. He talked about Serb grievances in Kosovo, as well as the need for constitutional reform that would enhance Serbia's authority within Yugoslavia. He claimed that Serbia had enemies both within Yugoslavia and without. He said it was now a time for struggle; that Serbs had beat the Turks and Germans before and could achieve victory again.

He was regularly interrupted by cheers. The response to what he said built and built; it became a deep rumble, like ocean waves collapsing against a shore. As I looked around at the delirium that he had whipped up among those near me, I thought the situation potentially dangerous—that if someone spoke out in dissent, they'd be torn apart by the crowd.

Milošević's speech had a rhythm and cadence, reaching something deep inside his audience—a drive that responded to ancient drumbeats and the heat of council fires. The story he told was universal. It had three acts—he talked of ancient glory, of a fall, and of a glorious redemption brought about by exercise of strength and true belief. The arc of his story borrowed from those told for millennia by the world's great religions.

He concluded his talk with a series of calls and responses. "Long live Yugoslavia! Long live Serbia! Long live Belgrade! Long live bravery! Long live our comrades in the struggle!" The responses thundered. He walked off the stage to "Slobo, Slobo, Slobo," chanted by one million less one.

While he spoke exceedingly well, to me there was something ominous and sinister to his theater. Knowing suicide ran in his family, I wondered, *Does that cast a shadow on his heart and empathies?*

I witnessed another command performance by him on June 28, 1989, in Kosovo. The occasion was the 600th anniversary of a great battle against the Ottoman Turks. The ceremony took place on the ancient battlefield. The battlefield monument, known as Gazimestan, was impressive. It was dwarfed, however, by the stage constructed for Milošević's speech. The crowd that day was massive; one million by most estimates. Most were ethnic Serbs— many coming from the far corners of the earth.

Looking back, I've asked myself, *Why was I there that day?* I wasn't a Serb, and Milošević wasn't the president of my republic. It may have been fate, but I'm sure my ego was also involved. I liked politics—the give and take of it, the competitiveness, and the potential for high impact. Promoting ideas and having influence appealed to me. Ever since my teen years, I had enjoyed, and grown accustomed to, the notoriety that came with being a successful athlete. Knowing that my athletic career was coming to an end, I must have wanted something to replace it. I'd had experience representing others at my work, so politics seemed a natural progression. With changes afoot in Yugoslavia, opportunities would arise. Milošević was considered a principal change maker in Yugoslavia. For some reason, I had a sense that our paths would one day cross.

Like a moth drawn to a flame, I wanted to see him in action again. That sun-drenched day in June was my opportunity. As we awaited his arrival, a newly commissioned work, *Saint Prince Lazar's Passion*, was performed. The company included two choirs, four soloists, an orchestra, and a narrator. I, and the rest of the great crowd, sat silent, transfixed by the performance.

On cue, Milošević descended from the heavens in a military helicopter. In response, the orchestra struck up Beethoven's *Funeral March*. Stimulated by his arrival, the crowd began chanting, "Slobo, Slobo, Slobo."

Serbia's leader paid his respects at the Gazimestan monument, then took a seat at the head of the crowd.

Following the national anthem, Milošević climbed the dais. His backdrop included a large stone Orthodox cross with four Cyrillic C's at the corners. The C's represented the Serb national motto *Samo sloga Srbina spasava*, "Only Unity Saves the Serbs." Dressed in a dark suit, with his dark hair graying at the temples, Milošević began his address. He spoke from notes, occasionally raising his finger for emphasis. The large crowd, his congregation, grew quiet. Milošević gave a nuanced oration, making subtle appeals to Serb nationalism and resentments, hearkening back to ancient and little-documented history, attributing the battlefield loss—and the resulting centuries of what he called slavery under the Ottoman Turks—to disunity and treachery within the Serb generalship, which in turn undermined the greatness and bravery displayed by Serb fighters.

As he stirred the audience regarding noble Serbian sacrifice in the dim recesses of Medieval history, I thought, *OK, but Bosnia's troops, sent by our king, were also there that day, fighting beside the Serbs and suffering just as severely. Why ignore that part of the story?*

Milošević then turned to predictions of the prosperity that awaited Serbia if its people demonstrated unity and solidarity of purpose. He proclaimed that Serbs had always defended Europe against Islam. He criticized Serbs for failing to believe in their greatness and for a propensity to compromise and accept less than they were entitled to. While talking about Yugoslavia and its component nations, he spoke also of Serbia becoming a great state in its own right. In the vision he painted for its future, he promised to make Serbia great again.

As I listened to his speech, I thought his delivery masterful, that he was almost like Hitler in his ability to sway an audience. Hearing him dramatize ancient myths—and speak of the superiority of one of our constituent nations—left me concerned for my country's future. I thought, *Yugoslav unity requires more compromise, rather than less. We need to damp down distinctions between our ethnic nations.*

The newly elected patriarch of the Serbian Orthodox Church, Pavle, joined Milošević in stirring the pot. He incorrectly claimed that Serbs originally settled Bosnia, and that our Muslim population was not native but of Ottoman Turk origin. He insinuated that Bosnia should be part of Serbia, and that Bosnia's Muslims belonged in Turkey.

This Serbian alliance between church and state, particularly when it concocted a myth of native inheritance and being a chosen people, sounded ominous to me. I wondered, *Could conflicts with Serbia become crusades?*

To promote crusading sentiments, the Orthodox Church had exhumed Prince Lazar's six-hundred-year-old bones, sending them on a yearlong tour throughout Serbia. Lazar lost his life during the Battle of Kosovo Field. According to the Serbian epic myth, the prophet Elijah, in the form of a gray falcon, offered Lazar the choice of victory at Kosovo Field, or eternal life, with Lazar choosing the latter. The Orthodox Church later elevated Lazar to sainthood, venerating him as a martyr. The Orthodox Church has used icons throughout its history—in accordance with that tradition, the Lazar exhibition represented strong imagery.

Lazar's bones were also brought into Bosnia for the first time, visiting cities along the Drina River. Bosnian Serbs flocked to see and touch them, bonding to brother Serbs in other republics. The display promoted a belief that the prince's spirit would soon rise, leading all Serbs to greatness.

Pavle also stirred his adherents against Croatia, writing that Croatian Serbs needed Serbia's protection from "Croatia's neo-fascist regime," likening Croatia's current leadership to the Ustaša ultranationalists who had committed genocide against Orthodox Serbs during the Second World War.

Left unmentioned in his history-telling were the Serbian atrocities against Bosnian Muslim populations during that war. That toll was also horrendous.

This twentieth-century history was the reason Tito had repressed nationalism and its tendency to regress to xenophobia. None of Yugoslavia's nations were without sin. To me, Pavle sounded like Cain talking about Abel, obscuring what we Yugoslavs had done to our brothers.

He and Milošević played a nationalism card, and trumpeted the supposed ethnic superiority of their people. This was artificial, Yugoslavia was a melting pot. Slavic tribes had been intermixing with the resident Greeks, Illyrians, and Romans since they arrived in the sixth century.

My country was not the interior of a remote island like New Guinea, but terrain reached by the great migratory waves of antiquity and the Early Middle Ages. The result was genetic pooling rather than isolation. We Yugoslavs were alike genetically, the product of many influences.

Bosnia itself was diverse. While Serbia had historically been majority Orthodox, and Croatia majority Catholic, Bosnia had its own unique Christian church during the Middle Ages. When the kingdoms of Serbia and Bosnia were eventually conquered by the Ottoman Turks during the fifteenth century, many Bosnians converted to the Muslim faith. The Ottomans provided strong social, political, and economic incentives for this. The historic multiethnic pattern continued to the present day, as ethnically mixed marriages were common in Yugoslav society. Jasminka and I were only one example.

During 1991, the government conducted a census. A census-taker visited our apartment, asking the usual questions about education, income, and marital status. When she got to ethnic identity I said, "We are Eskimo."

With me being the offspring of a union between an ethnic Albanian and a Bosnian Muslim, and Jasminka the child of a Croatian Catholic and a Bosnian Muslim, and with neither of us observing a strict religious tradition, our ethnicity was not straightforward. While my answer was partly in jest, it also reflected my concern that race and ethnicity, which shouldn't matter, had started to rear their ugly heads in my country. I believed that focus on these designations had the potential to tear my country apart. My answer was a gentle protest.

When the census-taker reacted, "Sir, this is serious," I responded, "I am serious, we are Eskimo."

Jasminka and I were surprised and pleased to hear a TV news report from Sarajevo several months later announcing the results of the census: "Bosnia has 44 percent Muslims, 31 percent Serbs, 17 percent Croats, 7 percent Yugoslavs. And guess what, we also have two Eskimos!"

The news report had a ripple effect. Several months later, after my paddling teammate Matija Ljubek was seriously injured in a car accident, Mirko and I drove to see him in a Zagreb hospital. The Croatian papers followed Ljubek's recovery. One wrote an article about three famous paddlers and friends reuniting. As Croatia and Serbia approached the brink of war, the writer noted that our visit provided evidence of "brotherhood between a Serb, a Croat, and an Eskimo."

---- 5 ----

BUDDING POLITICIANS

With multiparty parliamentary elections scheduled for November 1990, I diligently promoted the SDA party in my area. I also attended meetings and monitored developments in the other parties that had formed.

In the run-up to the election, I encountered another individual, the Bosnian Serb leader Radovan Karadžić, who would soon leap onto the world stage. In time, his life trajectory would also intersect with mine.

Karadžić came to Brčko to make a speech promoting his SDS party. During that address, he claimed that Serbs had been "forever in Brčko" and stressed that Brčko was vitally important to the future of Serbs and Greater Serbia. His address went deep into Serb epic mythology. He alleged that "Turk" atrocities had been directed at Brčko's Serbs centuries before, while warning of an ever-present danger from today's descendants of those "Turks." He vowed that through his political party, Bosnian Serbs would finally have the political strength to protect their interests.

I listened intently, coming away convinced that he meant business. My Serb brother-in-law—my sister Jagoda's husband—was one of his confidants. Both men were writers. I had never taken my brother-in-law, or Karadžić, all that seriously. While gifted with a keen imagination and the ability to convey it, my brother-in-law spent his time in bars with others in the local smart set. They expounded theories over coffee, plum brandy, and cigarettes. While he held forth, Jagoda provided for the family.

I knew that Karadžić was an academic who'd had difficulties breaking into Sarajevo's competitive intellectual scene. He had resented the snubs. A physician by training, he ran a private psychiatric practice, writing poetry on the side.

19

Listening to the tall, angular, silver-maned orator now, I came away with a higher opinion of his capacities. While he lacked Milošević's polish, psychiatric practice seemed to have provided him with insights into what motivated people individually and collectively. His address touched deep-seated emotions in the audience. Hearing it, I thought, *That was an effective call to action.*

Karadžić followed a script written in Belgrade. He took great interest in Brčko because it was a geographic umbilical cord linking Serbs together. My city was strategically important to the Greater Serbia concept and to the plans of Milošević and Karadžić. The Brčko region provided a narrow corridor, known as the Posavina, that linked areas in both Bosnia and Croatia that had high concentrations of ethnic Serbs. Without the link, large pockets of Serb population would be isolated from each other, and from Serbia. Controlling Brčko was essential to their aim of establishing an independent Serbian republic within Bosnia, then aligning it with Serbia.

I knew Karadžić was a dedicated roulette player and wondered, *Will he wager that there will be no international response? Will he gamble with all of our futures?*

Bosnia's ethnic distribution was highly intermixed, forming a tiger-skin pattern, with colors for each of the three principal nationalities scattered everywhere throughout the country. We were Bosnia, not Greater Croatia or Greater Serbia.

During this time, I also gave speeches. I enjoyed speaking and received good reviews. My stump speech was straightforward. I quoted from the section of the Bosnian constitution that assured that Bosnia would treat its Serb, Croat, and Bosniak populations equally, then talked about the tiger skin and the damage that would be done if it were not kept intact, and concluded with a quote from Tito's last interview. His request—"Just keep my Bosnia in peace."

When Bosnian President Alija Izetbegović came to Brčko for a rally, I was one of his warm-up speakers. Afterward he told me, "I liked what you said; so did the audience. I've heard good things about what you and your colleagues are accomplishing here. Keep it going."

In the November elections, the Communist party polled highest, with twenty-seven percent in Brčko. My party, the SDA, came in a close second with twenty-six percent. Locally, we sat in a kingmaker position. We opted to form a coalition, and to share power, with the Croatian Democratic Union (HDZ) and the Serbian Democratic party (SDS), rather than with the Communists.

At the republic level the same coalition took 202 of the 240 seats in the Bosnian Parliament. The Yugoslav constitution allowed a republic to secede with a two-thirds affirmative vote in a referendum. Following the elections, separatist sentiment began to percolate in Bosnia, while it surged in Croatia and Slovenia.

Croatia's President Franjo Tuđman wanted Croatia recognized internationally as an independent nation. He also led a Greater Croatia movement that desired to annex the Herzegovina region in Bosnia-Herzegovina. Annexing Bosnian territory was a personal fixation. To accomplish that goal, he sought the cooperation of Serbia's Milošević.

As Yugoslavia threatened to come apart, Milošević and Tuđman schemed how best to carve Bosnia up. In March of 1991, they met secretly in the northwest Serbian town of Karadordevo, discussing how they would divide and incorporate a dismembered Bosnia into their respective republics. Left unresolved between them was the status of the unhappy ethnic Serb population inside Croatia. Croatia desired its current borders plus a significant piece of Bosnia. Milošević wanted Serbian, Croatian, and Bosnian borders redrawn to allow all ethnic Serbs to live together in a Greater Serbia. His map included much of Bosnia and a meaningful portion of Croatia. For him, western expansion was Serbia's manifest destiny.

While Tuđman and Milošević agreed on Bosnia, they were at loggerheads over Croatia.

Tensions ran high. They increased on June 25, 1991, when both Slovenia and Croatia declared that they had left Yugoslavia to become independent states.

The JNA soon got involved, teaming with Serbian irregular forces to take and hold Croatian territory. The combined forces achieved significant early victories, most notably in Vukovar, a city on Croatia's border with Serbia. Vukovar fell following a three-month bombardment. When the city fell, a massacre of the non-Serb civilian population occurred. Survivors fled, seeking refuge.

In Croatia, rape, torture, murder, and terror were used by both combatants as instruments of war, designed to cause a mass exodus of their opponent's population. An innocent-sounding term, "ethnic cleansing," was used to describe the tactics. The phrase brought to mind a purification rite, implying that those departing—or murdered—had somehow been unclean and undesirable.

In Bosnia, Serb leaders threatened the same methods should Bosnia attempt to secede from Yugoslavia.

As the JNA mobilized to do battle in Croatia, I had a bird's eye view. We lived in a third-floor apartment at the southwest corner of our building. Our balcony overlooked the garrison for the Brčko region, just fifty meters away. The garrison housed the JNA's 395th Brigade. Including its active reserve, the 395th was a force with thirty-four hundred soldiers. I had once been a member myself.

As war raged in Croatia during the summer and fall of 1991, Brčko functioned as an important JNA staging area. The railway and highway through town saw continual military traffic. Gazelle helicopters frequently landed and took off from the barracks. From my balcony I often observed anti-aircraft fire in the night sky, while at the boathouse we occasionally heard artillery fire from the front lines of the Croatian War. Those lines approached within ten kilometers of Brčko.

In September 1991, the United Nations imposed an arms embargo on Yugoslavia. The embargo's purpose was to prevent the level of violence in Croatia from escalating further. Within the SDA, we discussed the fact that the arms embargo would have profound implications for Bosnia, should we secede. We had few weapons, and knew we would experience great difficulty buying more.

Once war broke out between Serbia and Croatia, we realized that the potential for war in Bosnia had increased exponentially. Geographically, we sat between the two combatants. We would be drawn into their crossfire, especially since both Croatia and Serbia had designs on our territory.

While politicians on all sides vied for power and territory, life for regular citizens proceeded with everyday events and milestones. Jasminka and I realized an important one at this time. On September 26, 1991, our daughter Adna (Bosnian for Eden) was born. That day Jasminka told me, "This is the greatest event of our lifetimes."

Adna's birth brought me back to earth, down from my political orbit. I began to realize the depth of my hopes and dreams for her, and for our relationship. I suppose all new parents are like this. Gazing at my newborn, I knew she would not disappoint. The onus was on me to be the father she deserved.

A few days later, my younger sister, Ramiza, also gave birth, making these joyous times within our extended family.

Jasminka took a one-year maternity leave. Her life revolved around Adna. Yugoslavia's politics were far removed from her considerations. For my part, I tried to be helpful and supportive. For me, fatherhood was a new, and challenging, discipline to master. I think Jasminka, and my mother, eventually gave me passing grades.

To celebrate Adna's christening and our good fortune, my friends Matija Ljubek, Mirko Nišović, and their wives traveled to Brčko. In keeping with tradition, they placed gold coins on Adna's head as their best wishes for a long and happy life.

Neighbors and relatives lavished attention on our newcomer, throwing baby showers that resulted in what Jasminka called "an embarrassment of gifts." The experience affirmed we were part of a community.

How many times I have since wished, *If only things could have stayed that way.*

— 6 —

MOUNTING TENSIONS

With Adna's arrival, Jasminka and I wanted a larger automobile. I took a bus to Belgrade to order a new Fiat. On my return trip, a Serb paramilitary group stopped the bus, ordering all Muslim passengers to step outside. When we had disembarked, a soldier decked out like Rambo told the bus driver to open the luggage compartment.

He then told us, "Unload your luggage. Line up here with your bags in front of you." We did so.

"Now empty the contents of your bags onto the ground." Everyone complied, except me. I didn't like being ordered around by an unofficial soldier.

"Hey, I said empty your bag."

"Do it yourself. You don't have authority over me."

As the paramilitary and I circled each other, the bus driver yelled, "Give in to him! They might shoot us!"

This prompted a second paramilitary to intervene. "We are not here to rob you people. We are checking for weapons. Bus driver, you empty his bag."

The bus driver did as instructed. When the bag came up clean, the second paramilitary said to me, "Man, I don't understand you. You have a lot of hard bark on you. One day it is going to cause you trouble."

Three weeks later, Jasminka and I traveled to Belgrade to trade in our old Fiat and return with the new car. Driving home, a group of Serbian paramilitaries stepped out of the woods just past the town of Morović, Serbia. They motioned us to stop, then asked for our IDs and destination. When these checked out, they waved us on.

Several kilometers later the roadway emerged from oak woods and entered Croatia. In the distance, I saw a group of Croatian soldiers blocking the road with their rifles at the ready. I stopped the car thirty meters away, saying, "Jasminka, follow my lead." We got out, raised our hands, and lay facedown on the pavement. A minute later a pair of boots appeared. A soldier nudged me in the back with his automatic weapon.

"What are you doing?"

"Being safe."

"Let's see your ID. Have you seen any Serb soldiers nearby?"

"I was stopped by a Serb patrol three kilometers back."

"How large a group?"

"I saw four, but there may have been more in the woods."

"All right. You can go. I see you have a new car. If you want to keep it, I'd suggest you drive only in Bosnia. This is no longer a place to be driving new cars."

By this time, I was becoming disillusioned with the SDA. I had originally been persuaded that it would be a party for all those within Bosnia who favored tolerance and coexistence. While the party initially talked about democracy and openness, it had become insular. Bosnians who had been Communist party members were considered suspect and were overlooked in the SDA power structure. There was also increased pressure to become a practicing Muslim. I was repeatedly asked, "Why didn't we see you at the mosque?"

I thought these changes undercut the party's appeal and effectiveness, with the party overlooking talent and competence in favor of ideological purity. The issue compounded when our leader, Izetbegović, proposed having Bosnia join the Organization of Islamic States. His proposal raised eyebrows in Bosnia and elsewhere in Europe.

Each of Bosnia's three ruling parties had become exclusive to an ethnic group. Their power-sharing coalition began to corrode, experiencing mounting disagreement and distrust. The outbreak of war in Croatia during the summer of 1991 severely aggravated tensions, both in Brčko and at Bosnia's parliamentary level.

While the SDA (Bosnian Muslim party) and HDZ (Bosnian Croat party) headed in the direction of holding a referendum for

Bosnian independence, Karadžić and the SDS strenuously opposed the proposal. The SDS wanted Bosnia to remain in a diminished Yugoslavia that would look to Serbia for leadership. Bosnia's ethnic Muslims and Croats needed only to look to Serbia's Kosovo province and the second-class treatment of Kosovo's Muslim population to envision how minority status in a Serb dominated Yugoslavia would play out.

As sentiment for a referendum grew, Karadžić continued his saber rattling. On October 12, 1991, he threatened a bloodbath in which Bosnia's Muslims would "disappear from the face of the earth."

Earlier in 1991, Izetbegović had directed Bosnia to comply with a national directive to disband our Territorial Defense Force. I argued against the directive, convinced that complying would leave Bosnia defenseless. The Territorial Defense answered to the Republic and was not under direct JNA control. They could function as an opposing force to the paramilitaries, and even to the JNA.

At SDA meetings, I grew impatient with our leadership. I thought they were indecisive, regularly changing their minds regarding our future course. I found such vacillations maddening.

For his part, Izetbegović worried that building up a Bosnian army would be labeled provocative by Serbia. He maintained that his choices were extremely difficult, that choosing between Serbia's Milošević and Croatia's Tuđman was a choice between either "leukemia or a brain tumor." He perceived both to be wolves, waiting for an opportune moment to strike Bosnia.

Izetbegović and Karadžić had a back and forth in the press. Karadžić said, "The Muslims cannot defend themselves if there is war," to which Izetbegović responded, "The Muslims will defend themselves with great determination and will survive. They will not disappear as Karadžić has said; they cannot disappear."

At this time, Vojislav Šešelj, the head of Serbia's Radical party, visited Brčko. Šešelj controlled a large paramilitary force known as the Četniks, who took the name and styled themselves as successors to the Serb nationalist movement from the Second World War. Šešelj was an ardent Serbian ultranationalist comfortable with violence. He had engaged in fistfights within Serbia's parliament, and once beat up a political opponent following a televised debate. He prescribed deportation for Bosnia's Muslim citizens, saying we should go back to Turkey.

Though I could not know it then, Šešelj and I would also one day meet face to face, fiercely opposing each other.

Accompanying Šešelj during this visit were the leaders of two other paramilitary groups, Dragan Vasiljković (Captain Dragan) of the Red Berets and Željko Ražnatović (Arkan) of the Serb Volunteer Guard (also known as Arkan's Tigers). Captain Dragan would one day play a vital role in my life.

He was a soldier of fortune with dual Australian and Yugoslav citizenship. Ražnatović was an officer in Yugoslavia's state security apparatus who was on Interpol's most-wanted list. All three men led forces that had featured prominently in the conquest of Vukovar, Croatia. They visited Brčko to make plans for taking my city, in the event Bosnia declared independence.

The SDA had no reaction to their visit. Our leader Izetbegović believed that the international community would come to Bosnia's defense if Bosnia followed a legitimate path to independence. Others of us were less certain about the West's willingness to intervene.

Frustrated by the SDA's vacillations, I left the party in November 1991. The Brčko and Tuzla newspapers reported my resignation, as did local television news. In the months that followed, political developments came fast and furious. They affected all of us, setting our future course, and scattering us to the winds.

In January 1992, an internationally brokered ceasefire was declared in Croatia. At the time of the ceasefire, Serbs controlled twenty-five percent of Croatian territory. Ten thousand lives had been lost. It was reported that five hundred thousand ethnic Croats and two hundred and fifty thousand ethnic Serbs had been displaced. The Croatian situation would stalemate for the next three years, with intermittent fighting and ongoing movement of refugees.

An unfortunate consequence of the Croatian ceasefire was the fact that it allowed the JNA and Serbian paramilitary forces to disengage and move southward, to focus on Bosnia.

With this repositioning, Karadžić and his SDS party felt confident enough to declare an independent Serb republic within Bosnia. The declaration claimed sixty percent of Bosnian territory, including the Brčko corridor. This was a political declaration—one not yet supported by facts on the ground. More than a million Bosnian Croats and Bosnian Muslims lived in the areas Karadžić claimed. In conjunction with the declaration, the SDS pulled out of Bosnia's Parliament.

In January 1992, I observed Serbian irregulars, the Red Berets, training Brčko Serbs at the barracks. The Red Berets were police units funded by Serbia's interior ministry. Under the command of Captain Dragan, they trained a force of seventy special operatives to some unknown purpose.

My work required traveling throughout the Brčko area to install and repair equipment. I regularly visited nearby villages. The villages outside Brčko were typically mono-ethnic. On several occasions, I saw JNA trucks arrive in Serb villages, their drivers unloading cases of automatic rifles, then setting up a table and chairs. At an appointed time, a line of male villagers would form, and rifles and bullets were distributed and recorded. On one occasion a soldier offered me a rifle, thinking I was a resident. I declined. I never saw the JNA distribute weapons in Muslim and Croat villages.

I shared my observations regarding the activity at the JNA barracks—as well as the arming of Serb villagers—with SDA leadership. By March the enlisted men stationed at the army barracks had moved to new quarters in a Serb village twenty kilometers from Brčko. Their activities could no longer be observed from my balcony. Several dozen officers plus revolving groups of paramilitaries remained at the barracks.

In early February, President Izetbegović, with the encouragement of the European Union, called for a Bosnian referendum on independence. In response, the Bosnian Serb party scheduled a rally in Brčko, which I attended. One of the party's leaders, Momčilo Krajišnik, spoke, as did a number of Serbian academics. Several had been professors when I attended the University of Belgrade. During the Tito years they had provided his programs with intellectual support. I saw they were now flexible in their thinking, forsaking Titoism for Serb nationalism. They played to the energy and pulse of the rally crowd, seeking its approval. As with Milošević at Kosovo Field, this scene provided me another glimpse into the seductions of personal ambition within a mass movement.

In calling for a Serb communion, the academics reminded their audience of the wars that Serbia had waged throughout its history, applauding them as sacrifices in the cause of freedom. Following up, Krajišnik assured the crowd that Serbia could be counted on to aid Bosnian Serbs in a Bosnian conflict. The intense atmosphere of the rally left me deeply troubled. I thought, *I just witnessed the birth of a hungry, and angry, nation, and Krajišnik is its midwife.*

In time, he and I would also meet, and battle.

During the run-up to the referendum, a Sarajevo TV reporter interviewed me, asking my position. In his broadcast I said, "I favor independence now that other republics have seceded, and ours is now a handicapped Yugoslavia. I hope for an independent state that welcomes and tolerates all ethnicities." That public statement later came back to haunt me.

The referendum took place in late February, passing with ninety-nine percent of voters favoring independence. Approximately two-thirds of eligible voters participated. The Bosnian Serb party boycotted the referendum, obstructing voting in the areas it had designated Serb Autonomous Areas (SAOs in Bosnian).

President Izetbegović announced Bosnia's independence from Yugoslavia on March 3. Bosnia received formal recognition from the U.S. and the European Union on April 5. The European Union rejected Karadžić's application to have his self-proclaimed Republika Srpska recognized as an independent nation. The EU also denied

Milošević's request that Serbia's and Bosnia's borders be redrawn to reflect ethnic concentrations, ruling that Bosnia's existing borders constituted the new international borders.

Refugees from the Croatian War had been moving through Brčko for almost a year. In early April 1992, a caravan of more than one hundred buses arrived. The passengers were Croats fleeing ethnic cleansing in Serb-controlled areas of Croatia. They had been provided safe passage through Brčko en route to a Croat-controlled area, laying over in Brčko for a day.

Jasminka learned that a baby had been delivered on one of the buses. She asked me to bring several boxes of food to the passengers, while she put together a large bundle of Adna's baby clothing and supplies for the newborn. When we arrived at the bus station, the physical and emotional condition of the refugees shocked her.

"Isak, these people seem so lost, so abandoned. If it happened in Croatia, could it happen here?"

"It's difficult to say. The Croats and Serbs have unfinished business from the Second World War. That's what their war is about. We in Brčko have always gotten along. Hopefully we can stay peaceful here, finding a middle ground until this all blows over."

As we drove home, she said, "That was shocking. I knew what happened in Croatia was bad, but their stories were something I never imagined. They are desperate, traumatized. So many refugees have drifted through Brčko. I didn't recognize what they were going through, the amount they suffered. Do we get caught up in the day-to-day and not see, or are we afraid to look because of what it will mean—the decisions it will require? I feel like I find enough that is normal every day that I assume the problems will work themselves out. I've been so focused on Adna. I know I don't want to leave. Why is it so hard to see the future, to know what we should do?"

"You're asking hard questions, Jasminka. I wish I had answers. We've never been through anything like this. We'll have to see what comes and respond."

That month, reports of ethnic violence occurring elsewhere in Bosnia filtered into Brčko. The reports conflicted, depending on which ethnic group's media outlets reported. I had sources within the SDA. I knew the situation had turned bad for Bosnian Croats and Muslims in some areas of Bosnia. Despite unease and tension, things weren't truly bad yet in Brčko. I held out hope. While aware that hope was not a plan, I had not yet formulated one.

My workplace sat adjacent to the army's equipment and heavy-weapons depot. In early April I watched the JNA move its artillery from the depot to a Serb village outside Brčko. As a former JNA soldier, I told myself, *The army is professional. They won't take sides in a Bosnian conflict.*

I took encouragement from the fact that police patrols and checkpoints in Brčko, which had increased dramatically in recent months, remained multiethnic and seemed intent on maintaining peace and order.

The community discussed establishing a council for the national defense of Brčko. Its proponents envisioned a volunteer militia force drawn from all nationalities and coordinated through the local JNA garrison. They envisioned a defense force with sufficient firepower to quell any radical or terrorist threat erupting in the Brčko region. I saw promise in the proposal, attending the initial organizing meeting. The meeting fell apart when several local Croat and Muslim leaders walked out, disgusted by what they saw as a Serb-dominated power play. I stayed, but it soon became obvious that the idea was going nowhere.

Walking downtown in mid-April, I encountered the local Catholic priest. We did not know one another, so I introduced myself, then said, "I am not Catholic but have moral questions. I'd like to know your thinking. Could we talk together some time?"

"Yes. Certainly. I am free at one this afternoon. Stop by the church then. The day is nice. We can sit outside in the garden."

When I arrived that afternoon, he greeted me cordially. Looking at me expectantly, he asked, "What is on your mind?"

"Earlier I mentioned that I have moral questions. With all the tension that has been building in Brčko, and with reports of violence occurring elsewhere in Bosnia, I'm wondering whether and when a person is justified in taking up arms. While I believe the JNA will stay impartial and put down unlawful activities, what if they don't?"

The priest was a skilled listener. We discussed the moral and practical aspects of the issues I raised. His position was, "One man does not have the right to take the life of another."

He also said, "I hope, and will continue to pray, that you are right about the JNA."

We parted warmly. We would see each other in different circumstances six weeks later.

On April 20th, my mother—as well as my sisters Jagoda and Ramiza along with their children—moved across the Sava to a village in Croatia. My brother Ramiz's wife, Suada, and their two children accompanied them. They left out of safety concerns. I encouraged Jasminka to join them. Her response was an emphatic, "Adna and I are not going."

By this time, several of my former colleagues on the SDA's executive committee had also left the community.

My brothers and I talked about leaving. I advised against doing so. My younger brother Mirsad challenged me on this. He and I were close growing up. We had maintained a strong bond as adults. Our personalities meshed well. We could both be irreverent and headstrong. Mirsad was blond and good-looking. He had been a clever boy and a gifted student. He was the Gaši many thought would go far. After graduating from high school, he attended the University of Belgrade on scholarship. He enrolled in political science and was on a path toward law school. However, after a year he returned home saying, "It isn't for me. I can't see myself as a lawyer, poring over books and briefs all day. I'd go crazy. I've got to have more freedom and action."

With his student deferment gone, Mirsad fulfilled his compulsory military service, training in artillery. After his discharge, he became a heating and air-conditioning technician in Brčko. He remained single and fun-loving as an adult. I often wondered if there were also elements of recklessness and fearlessness in his nature. However, in this case he was the one being cautious and sensible.

I told him, "We need to stay and stand our ground."

Mirsad gave in. We all decided to remain in Brčko, standing together.

7

THE DEMANDS FOR APARTHEID

On the afternoon of April 27, I attended a meeting of the Brčko Municipal Assembly. One of the assemblymen, Đorđe Ristanić, the leader of the local Bosnian Serb party, was on the agenda. I had heard rumors that he would present demands to divide the city. There was a strong turnout for the meeting, including a television crew and a half-dozen or so print journalists.

I knew Ristanić. We attended the same grammar and high schools, sharing several classes. Back then he was not a standout. He'd been a slow thinker who required time to process things. I knew he worked as a technician for the large textile firm, Interplet, and had stayed active in the JNA reserves.

Đorđe was early on the agenda. He looked good, dressing for the meeting in his military uniform. His tightly curled brown hair was trimmed, his full lips set resolutely. His blue eyes, with their characteristic bags beneath them, peered at the audience. They did not betray anxiety. He appeared to be a man on a mission, confident that he knew something most of us did not.

His delivery was forceful and direct, the message simple: "The Bosnian Serbs want to be part of Yugoslavia. We will not be deterred." His demand to the Assembly was territory—Brčko was to be divided into three sections for each ethnic group. He produced a detailed map. Serbs were to control the lion's share, including the city's economic centers. He stated, "The division must take place within six days, by May third. If not, there will be war. We require an answer."

Ristanić had the entire room's attention. This was it, or at least the start of it—what citizens had worried and speculated about for months. Ristanić had laid some cards on the table, and called. The reaction to his demand was muted. There were no theatrics—people knew this was real, a danger time. The assembled media were wide-eyed and engrossed, more participants in an unfolding drama than observers and chroniclers.

Mayor Ramić—our tall, thin, mechanical engineer—soft-pedaled, saying, "I take your proposal seriously. Give me a day to consult others and to give the proposal the consideration it deserves."

News of the Ristanić proposal spread through the city. By the time the meeting adjourned and we disgorged from the meeting hall onto the pedestrian mall, the proposal was being talked about everywhere. Fear showed on many faces. The overly practical focused on the details, arguing about whether the proposal could actually work.

That evening I walked down to the boathouse, then hiked along the riverbank. The river was where I went to think. As was common in the spring, a fresh northerly breeze blew down the Sava. I wore a coat against its chill.

I thought about the river, and its secrets. The Sava is Yugoslavia's largest river. Almost one thousand kilometers in length, it is the Danube's largest tributary, draining to the Black Sea. For centuries, the Sava and Brčko formed the border between the Ottoman and the Habsburg empires. That geographic position made Brčko a crossroads—a place where trade and the exchange of ideas occurred—and a place where invading armies either set off from or arrived. Brčko had literally resided on the fault lines between Christianity and Islam, and between East and West in the Roman Empire. These waters, and the bridge that spanned them, knew conflict and accommodation. Walking downstream from the boathouse, I crossed railroad tracks. The tracks linked the national rail system to the coal mines outside Tuzla, sixty kilometers away. The spur to Tuzla was known as the "Youth Railway." It began as a public-works project following the Second World War. Built primarily by high-school students working summers, the line took almost twenty years to complete. Its achievement represented the patriotic, almost utopian, spirit that existed in Yugoslavia following the war.

Later in that evening's distracted wandering, I hiked up onto the deck of the bridge that connected Brčko to Croatia. It too had significant history.

During the Second World War, my father fought with the Partisans. His force liberated Belgrade, and later pushed the Nazis out of Brčko and Bosnia. Covering their retreat, the Nazis mined this bridge. In their haste, they miscalculated. The bridge blew before all German troops had crossed. Many ended up buried in the river.

There those unfortunate soldiers joined Brčko's Jewish population. That population arrived in Bosnia in 1492. Bosnia had a long tradition of religious tolerance, and was one of the Ottoman lands that welcomed Jews expelled from Portugal and Spain during the Inquisition.

Four hundred and fifty years later, on the eve of the Second World War, Bosnia had a Jewish population of fourteen thousand. In Brčko there were one hundred and fifty Jewish souls, with their synagogue prominent in the central downtown area.

The situation for Jews in Yugoslavia changed disastrously in 1941 with the Nazi occupation. Following their incursion, all of Bosnia was placed under the control of a Nazi puppet regime (the NDH) established in Croatia. The NDH rounded up Brčko's entire Jewish community on December 10, 1941, bound them with wire and marched them to this bridge. They were beaten with hammers, then tossed into the river to drown.

An additional 236 Jewish refugees from Germany, Austria, and Czechoslovakia sheltered in Brčko prior to the Nazi invasion. Six days after the massacre of Brčko's resident Jewish population, the refugees were transported to the Brčko gymnasium for "registration." They too were bound by NDH personnel and driven to the bridge, where they suffered the same fate. The Jewish synagogue was then destroyed, and eventually replaced by the downtown police station.

The NDH established eight concentration camps in Croatia. The most notorious was Jasenovac, located two hundred kilometers upstream of Brčko at the confluence of the Sava and Ulna Rivers. The majority of its victims were ethnic Serbs, but Jews, Gypsies, and Partisan sympathizers also suffered severely.

In Bosnia, the NDH assembled Jews in Sarajevo before transporting them by train to the camps. The train from Sarajevo to Jasenovac traveled through Brčko, where it refueled. Alert to the train's arrival, sympathetic townspeople brought food and water down to the train tracks for those locked in the cattle cars. My mother was one of those sympathetic people. On one occasion, she and her cousin baked a dozen loaves of bread, baking metal files into two of the loaves. Soldiers from the local garrison guarded the train, checking foodstuffs before allowing them to be passed up to the train cars. Bread loaves were broken in half. Those baked by my mother and her cousin made it through. The next day a report reached Brčko that the locks on two cars of the Jasenovac-bound train had been compromised, allowing passengers to escape into the Croatian countryside. In reprisal, the NDH shot the sergeant responsible for the Brčko guard detail. He was my mother's second cousin.

As I stood on the bridge deck, I considered the good and evil that had occurred here. The bridge towered over a stretch of river I had paddled daily; for me it had been a place of good memories. As I considered what my family should do, I knew that not deciding would itself be a decision.

I had seen many countries, been to places as distant as Seoul, but felt deeply rooted in Brčko. Recalling Ristanić saying we had until May 3, I thought, *We still have six days.*

Sixty feet below me the Sava River flowed, pushed by the melting snows of Bosnia's high mountains, coursing toward Belgrade. In Belgrade a torrent of a different sort had waited until spring to unleash. I wondered, *Can it be held in check?*

When I returned home, Jasminka told me she had received a call from a school friend living thirty kilometers from Brčko. "Snežana says the army has taken positions around her village. They are surrounded. No one knows what will happen next. I told her we have the extra room, to come now if it looks dangerous."

We did not hear more from her. That night two explosions rocked Brčko's Catholic Church. A passing car threw grenades into the church courtyard. The blasts blew out windows, damaging the church's exterior.

On the radio the next morning a reporter asked, "Is nothing sacred?"

— 8 —

INNOCENTS LOST

Later that morning Mayor Ramić met with a group of Bosniak intellectuals. They decided to accept Ristanić's proposal, "in principle, for the sake of peace." This was communicated. A meeting to hammer out the details was scheduled for May 1.

The following day, April 29, Ristanić received directions from Bosnian Serb leader Radovan Karadžić to establish a war presidency in Brčko. Though we did not know it yet, Karadžić had cried "Havoc," and was about to let slip his dogs of war. Telephone calls were placed to Brčko's Serbian population, telling them that Muslims and Croats in the community had drawn up lists with the names and addresses of Serbian men to be killed and Serbian women to be raped. These reports were total fabrications, intended to create fear and inflame support for violent action. As Hitler had demonstrated fifty years before, big lies, repeated often, can have big impact.

On the evening of April 29, the bells of Orthodox churches in Brčko tolled three times. This was a special, and secret, signal. Serb families opened their windows, letting in the fresh spring air. That night, small squares identifying the ethnic identity of the occupants were placed on homes and apartments in the city.

While the rest of us slept, Greater Serbia marched on Brčko.

I slumbered beside my wife. We awoke suddenly, startled by a loud noise. It was dark. I checked the clock—4:50 a.m. Adna, only nine months old, began to cry. Jasminka comforted her, while I got up to investigate. Opening the bedroom door, I felt the unexpected chill of outside air. Switching on a light, I said, "Jasminka, stay back. The picture window has shattered. I can't tell how. Let me clean it up."

I put on shoes, then stepped across the broken glass. It crunched beneath my tread. As I swept it up, a loud boom rumbled through the city, shaking our apartment building. Now doubly concerned, I turned on the radio, hoping for news. Hearing none, I recognized voices in the hallway, where several of my neighbors had gathered. Stepping out to talk with them, we soon proceeded down to the second-floor landing, joining a dozen or so others. All in various states of undress, we were a motley congregation. If the situation had been different, the scene would have been comical—surprising your neighbors when they are sleepy, seeing them as they lived behind closed doors. Windows on one side of our building had blown in. It was the side facing northeast, toward the downtown area. Several windows had survived. I said to my downstairs neighbor, "You were lucky to have had yours open."

We agreed that the cause of the disturbance was not local or from the nearby barracks. It seemed to have occurred some distance away. None of us could pinpoint its source.

"It came from the direction of the river. It sounded like an explosion. I think the windows broke from a shock wave," said one.

"Maybe one of the JNA's ammunition depots was sabotaged," said another. Lacking anything concrete, and given the tension that had built within Brčko in recent months, we were hesitant to conjecture or say much.

Our first-floor neighbor and good friend, Mira Lazić, was there. A woman in her sixties, Mira cared her for ailing Serb husband and ninety-year-old mother. She had raised her own family, and had subsequently adopted Adna, Jasminka, and me. Mira was exceedingly sharp and well-connected. She told me, "I'm heading downtown at first light to see what I can find out. I'll check with my brother-in-law, the police captain. Surely he knows what is going on. You have your work Isak. I'll check in on Jasminka during the day. I'll let her know what I learn, and we can talk later."

With Mira on the case, I decided to return to my family, wishing my neighbors a good day.

At six thirty a.m. I left for work. My company's executive director met me and my coworkers at the gate, saying, "Something big has happened. We are still waiting for official word. I want you all to return home and await instructions."

Shortly after I arrived back home, Mira came to our door. The diminutive sixty-eight-year-old was breathless, flushed from either exertion or concern. I invited her in.

"I need to sit down." We went into the kitchen. At the table, Mira took off her oversized glasses, dropped her head, and smoothed her short-cropped hair before starting in.

"The railway bridge and the bridge to Gunja have been blown up. Sections of both are lying in the river. Many pedestrians are dead. The estimate is more than one hundred. There are so many heads and legs strewn about downtown. It is awful—gruesome, horrifying—worse than a warzone. The city center is in total disarray. No one knows who set the charges. There are many conflicting rumors.

"This is what I know from my brother-in-law. The gate controlling pedestrian traffic was opened just before the explosion. That is why so many people were involved. Many were workers coming home for the May First holiday. Others were refugees from Prijedor. Something bad happened there two days ago."

I tried to recall what I had heard about Prijedor, a city of one hundred and ten thousand, some two hundred kilometers from Brčko. Bosnian Muslims made up half the city's population. The reports had been disturbing.

The city's decline started two months before with a propaganda campaign that produced a stream of vicious rumors. These rumors included allegations that the city's Muslim population planned an armed takeover to which ethnic Serbs must proactively respond. There were bizarre accusations that Prijedor's Muslim physicians had somehow intervened in the pregnancies of Serb women to produce only female offspring, were castrating Serb boys, and had deliberately given their Serb patients the wrong medicines.

A local Serb paramilitary group, the Wolves of Vučjak, took over the region's TV transmitter, changing its broadcast from Bosnia's TV Sarajevo to Serbia's TV Belgrade. The city's radio stations began referring to Prijedor's Muslims as mujahedeen and Islamic extremists intent on driving out Christians. The radio said these extremists would resort to rape and murder.

Judging from what Mira said about people fleeing, the incendiary talk must have changed to threats or violent action.

She continued, "My brother-in-law told me that our Bosnian border police were overpowered at four thirty this morning. Soldiers in black masks arrived in unmarked military vehicles, disarmed the police, and forced them into the vehicles. They then pushed a car out onto the bridge. It was packed with explosives. They also set timers on the explosives that were placed on the bridge months ago. They drove away before the bridge blew. That was the explosion we all felt. He couldn't say what is next. The police are waiting for instructions. Everything is very upset and disorganized."

Hoping for news, we turned on the radio. It broadcast that the two bridges had been destroyed, that the perpetrators were not yet known, and that the JNA was investigating. The mayor promised to update the populace later in the day.

I called my two brothers over to my place. Only Mirsad could come. At nine a.m. we left the apartment, walking toward downtown and the Gunja Bridge. Several hundred meters before the bridge, we saw two corpses on the sidewalk. One was partially covered by a piece of plywood. The bodies lay in a small park on the pedestrian mall, directly across from the police station. They were naked, their clothes torn off by the explosion.

Just then, three policemen emerged from the station. They appeared lost. No one had secured the downtown area.

Seventy-five meters farther on, in front of the Posavina Hotel, I saw the legs of a child, a boy, perhaps six years old. His lower torso had been separated from the rest of the body. Pausing to contemplate the tragedy, an awful feeling overtook me. It went past any defense I had. I couldn't make sense of what I was seeing. Time seemed to slow. For a period of time, I couldn't think, hear, or speak.

I finally said, "This terrible image is going to stay with me forever. How can it have happened?" As I asked this, I thought about Adna and the devastation Jasminka and I would experience at her loss. I wondered, *Where are the child's parents? Did they suffer the same fate?*

Seeing these victims rocked me. The scene was so foreign and out of place in the Brčko I knew. It felt surreal. The strange, numb feeling lingered. When Mirsad finally turned away, I followed him saying, "I need to get Jasminka and Adna someplace safe today. I hope Jasminka will agree to leave."

"Yes. We need to think about where and how. We no longer have the bridge to Croatia."

As we talked, an army personnel carrier with ten soldiers arrived at the nearby bridge. We walked closer to learn what was going on and saw that a fifty-meter span of the bridge's steel structure lay twisted in the river. Having worked with explosives during my JNA service, I understood the precise and concentrated work done by those who had blown the bridge. I told Mirsad, "Look at how that section sheared and fell. The break is so clean. Whoever did this knew what they were doing."

Soldiers from the personnel carrier took charge, ordering local police to clear the site. During the next fifteen minutes, additional army transports arrived. Troops began to fan out around the downtown area. At ten a.m. we left, walking back to my apartment. Soldiers were stationed every one hundred meters. Once home, I called my father to tell him what we'd seen. I asked his ideas for getting Jasminka and Adna to a safer place.

When Jasminka got wind of that conversation, she challenged me, asking, "Why do I have to go?"

After that, from our balcony, I heard shooting. It came from a Bosniak part of town. "That is the reason," I said. "I can't protect you and Adna."

Just then, a downstairs neighbor, Danilo, came up to our apartment with his wife, Vera, and with Mira. Vera had been a school friend of Jasminka's. They remained close.

Vera said, "You must take Adna and leave Brčko. Danilo will drive you. As a Serb he'll be able to cross the checkpoints. You must go. I know for certain that war has started in Brčko."

Mira concurred, saying, "Vera is right. You need to leave for Adna's sake. Don't worry, we will look after things here for you."

I let Jasminka absorb this, then said, "That sounds like a good plan. We are most grateful. Please give us a moment to consider where it would be best to take them."

I could count on my friends Mirko Nišović and Matija Ljubek to shelter my family. With war festering in Croatia, finding a safe passage to Ljubek's home in northern Croatia would be difficult. Mirko's home in Belgrade, Serbia, seemed the better option.

I called Mirko. We talked about a rendezvous point, settling on Bijeljina, a town fifty-five kilometers away on the Drina River, the border between Serbia and Bosnia. Reports had trickled into Brčko that Bijeljina had been taken over by Serb paramilitaries. I hoped that Danilo and Mirko, both Serbs, would be allowed to enter and leave. We decided to meet at the Hotel Kren in downtown Bijeljina. Mirko said he would depart immediately. His trip normally took less than two hours.

Jasminka packed what she and Adna needed for a two-week stay, saying, "By then those in charge will have sorted things out and restored order." I could see she was intent on returning to Brčko.

We left at noon with Danilo driving. The road to Bijeljina passed through a self-designated Serb Autonomous Area. Serb authorities had established checkpoints entering and leaving the SAO. Long lines of vehicles backed up behind them; many were Brčko Serbs leaving the city. After an extended wait at each, Danilo flashed his Serb ID, and we were waved on. Twenty kilometers from Brčko, we encountered a long line of JNA vehicles. The convoy of tanks, armored personnel carriers, artillery pieces, and troop carriers extended for more than two kilometers. The convoy had pulled to the side of the road and parked. It faced the opposite direction, toward Brčko. The JNA's mobilization could be perceived several ways. I convinced myself what I hoped was true, that the JNA protected all Yugoslavs and had mobilized to promote order and separate belligerents.

After another checkpoint and wait before Bijeljina, we pulled in at three p.m. A typical forty-five-minute journey had taken three hours.

The city center was eerily quiet. Serbian flags flew everywhere. Arriving at the hotel, we entered an indoor scene bustling with soldiers. Concerned when we could not find Mirko in the lobby or the coffee shop, I phoned his wife. She said, "Mirko left three hours ago. I haven't heard from him since."

We found a sofa in the lobby and settled in. As we waited, a booming voice from behind asked, "Isak, what are you doing here?"

I turned to see a bearded paramilitary dressed in a camouflage uniform with the insignia of Arkan's Tigers, a Serbian paramilitary unit, on his sleeve. It was Stevan Pešut, a kayaker from Vukovar in Croatia who had been on the national team with Mirko and me.

I greeted Stevan, then said, "We are here waiting for Mirko. He will take Jasminka and Adna to Belgrade."

"Aren't you going as well?"

"No, I'm heading back home."

"Are you stupid? I was here in Bijeljina, and also in Vukovar and Zvornik when they were taken. I advise you to go with Mirko to Belgrade. Brčko is next. There is going to be big trouble there."

Taken aback I said, "I hear what you are saying and will consider it. It's appreciated. Good to see you again. I wish the circumstances were different."

"Think about what I said."

The hotel lobby pulsed with energy; soldiers hurried in and out. Jasminka and I felt out of place, observing a Bosnian Serb event we weren't part of or welcome at. To make things worse, Stevan hectored me twice more about the dangers in Brčko, saying I must go to Belgrade.

To our relief, Mirko finally walked in. A powerful six-footer with a body like Hercules, he looked uncharacteristically stressed and ashen-faced.

"I was stopped before the border to let a JNA convoy pass. Then I got lost following signs to cross the Drina. They must have been for the convoy. I was in the middle of a military mobilization. It was hell getting out of it. By then I was on back roads and dead ends. It cost me two hours. I almost ran out of gas."

"We're just relieved you made it. Stevan Pešut is here somewhere. He is with Arkan's men. He told me to go with you to Belgrade."

"Judging from what I saw driving here, he is right. The JNA and the paramilitaries were together."

I needed to make a decision. I had rarely been a follower, typically making my own decisions. As a younger brother, I chafed when Ramiz offered elder brother advice—what I called "lessons." I stayed true to form here. Against the advice of my friends, I decided to return to Brčko.

My reasons were complicated. I did not want to be the Gaši male who cut and ran at the first sign of trouble. I felt an obligation to my father, brothers, and nephews back in Brčko. To this point in my life I had been able to persevere through whatever difficulties I had encountered. I thought that the disruption directed at Brčko would be short-lived, and that by being there I could assist in making things right. I also had my work. I didn't want to jeopardize my job—or look like a coward to my peers. In Belgrade, I would be a distant bystander. Brčko was my home—deep down I wanted to understand what my home was about to experience.

I told Mirko, "I'm returning to Brčko with Danilo. I can't run out on my family and Jasminka's parents."

After a couple of strenuous attempts to change my mind, he said, "I think it's a mistake, but do what you have to. Jasminka, we need to get on the road or we may never escape this place. I'll get the car while you say goodbye to your man."

We followed Mirko outside. Our leave-taking was short and direct. I felt that Jasminka supported my decision. She said, "I will see you in a couple of weeks, if not sooner. Check on my parents, and whatever you do, stay safe." I kissed my wife and daughter, thanked Mirko, and they set off.

Much later I learned that when Jasminka and Adna left for Serbia, they joined an exodus of nearly two hundred and eighty-six thousand refugees from Bosnia, most of whom had gone to Croatia. According to a reliable source, "By the beginning of June this figure had risen to three-quarters of a million, and to 1.1 million by mid-July. By the end of the year, almost two million Bosnians—nearly half of the population—had lost their homes."

Danilo and I headed back to Brčko. My travel companion was not a big talker, so there was little conversation during our drive. I was lost in thought. Now physically separated from my family, I considered the many obstacles to rejoining them. When the car passed the area where the JNA convoy had been parked, it was gone. I thought, *All that military might has disappeared, but where, and to what purpose?*

An internal voice, the one that warns us to back away from the precipice, sounded its alarm. I wondered, *Is this the start of something terrible? Should I have gone with Mirko?* I recalled the Bosnian author Ivo Andrić's ruminations on the "meaning of a few hours of forgetfulness in an evil hour and a dangerous place." Written about a different period in our history, I wondered, *Am I being forgetful at an evil time? Should I ask Danilo to turn around and drive me back to Bijeljina?*

I decided to let the situation play out as it would. Staring into an abyss, I decided to enter. Such was the power of my wishful thinking.

Danilo and I arrived in Brčko just before eight p.m. Soldiers manned security posts along the streets. All seemed quiet. I hoped that this was a good omen. Arriving at our apartment building, I thanked Danilo then headed upstairs. My apartment was dark and silent; it felt lonely. During the eight years we had owned it, I had never spent a night there without Jasminka.

Once inside, I phoned Belgrade. Jasminka told me the trip had gone fine, aside from the fact that Mirko had again gotten turned around on the road out of Bijeljina. She said, "I couldn't believe all the JNA equipment moving into Bosnia. There is also a lot of material leaving Bosnia. Is Brčko being looted? On the highway to Belgrade we saw dozens of cars with Brčko registrations on carriers. There were even vehicles taken from my work. I'm really worried about my parents."

Hanging up the phone, I was anxious to check on our families in Brčko, yet already ached for Jasminka and Adna. I was also grateful for Serb friends in Brčko and Belgrade who had dropped everything to help my wife and child.

Exhausted, I dozed off on the living room sofa. I had a dream. In it I worked as a border guard on the Croatian side of the Sava River Bridge. My commander instructed me, "Check on those refugees camping below. Make sure they are okay, and aren't burning the woods down." I hiked down a path to the levee and bottomlands beneath our post. Half a dozen campfires blazed. Adults and teens huddled around the fires, conversing in low tones. Bands of young children scurried between these congregations, playing excitedly. One of the children noticed my uniform, broke off from his play, and ran up to me. A boy of about six, he was dressed in black jeans, a blue winter jacket with a red stripe, and black Puma sport shoes. He was handsome, and looked well cared for. He was inquisitive—a talker blessed with youthful enthusiasm: "That's a real gun, isn't it? Did you ever shoot it? I like your radio! Can I hear you talk into it? My dad was in the army. He had a gun, but they took it. I'm going with my mom and brother to my cousin's. We rode on a truck and a bus to get here. My dad stayed back. He is protecting our shop."

We walked through the encampment. The boy introduced me to his mother. An attractive woman in her thirties, she held a toddler. She looked exhausted, but also seemed amused by her precocious son. Parting from them, I said, "Have a good evening and safe travels tomorrow."

The night passed uneventfully. At four a.m. a crowd formed. We, and the Bosnians on the other side of the bridge, were scheduled to open the gates and allow pedestrian traffic at 5. The bridge had been disabled to vehicle traffic months before, when the war in Croatia broke out. That morning my captain and I received multiple requests to open the gates early. With the flood of refugees from Prijedor, the crowd had swelled to one hundred and fifty by four thirty-five a.m. The captain called the Bosnian border station several times, but got no answer. He then said, "Since they are not at their post, I don't see a reason to wait. These people are cold and anxious to get going. Go ahead and raise the gate." I did so. It was four forty-five a.m. The decision was popular with those waiting. I spied the boy and his mother as they walked past. She smiled and the boy, still in his black jeans, coat, and sneakers, gave me a big wave. I returned his wave and thought, *I wonder what a boy like that becomes when he grows up? I'd like to see that.* The crowd passed, slowly fading into the distance. Theirs was a 900-meter hike to the Brčko side. Many carried luggage and walked leisurely, talking with their fellow travelers. Their voices carried along the silent riverbank. The lights of Brčko pulsed in the distance. The first intimations of a rising sun were evident on the hilltops. It would be a cool, clear day.

Several hundred meters downstream a group of fifteen commandos hid beside the river. They had overpowered the police manning the Bosnian border station thirty minutes earlier, forcing them into military vehicles and driving them away. They then set timers on the charges that had been placed on the steel bridge structure months before. They also pushed a car fifty meters out onto the bridge. The car, a Russian Lada, contained explosives. At 4:50 a.m., one of the commandos noticed the crowd of pedestrians crossing the bridge from the Croatian side. He alerted his commander, who responded, "We're proceeding as planned."

I awakened then, crestfallen. In my dream, I had raised the gate. Why hadn't I seen what was coming—for the boy, for my family, for Bosnia?

I knew then I'd made a terrible mistake returning to Brčko. I now realized that "It," the malign threat that our community had feared, and so often spoken of, but never named, had finally arrived.

— 9 —

BARBARIANS STORM THE CITY GATE

At eight a.m. the next morning I called my father, who told me, "Stay home. Don't come to my neighborhood. There are too many soldiers on the streets. It isn't safe here."

Later that day I listened as Mayor Mustafa Ramić addressed us via a special television broadcast from the Hotel Posavina. Captain Petrović of the local JNA garrison stood beside him. Ramić said that martial law had been imposed, that he had turned temporary control of the city to the JNA, and that a commission had been established to determine responsibility for the demolition of the two bridges. He implored, "Please stay home, disregard rumors, and remain calm. The army and police will protect the public."

Days later we discovered that Mayor Ramić's next action was to leave Brčko. After his address, I drove my car to the home of Jasminka's parents, where it could be garaged. Phone service in their neighborhood had been cut off. They were greatly relieved to learn that Jasminka and Adna were safe in Belgrade. After lunch with them, I walked back to my apartment. Along the route, additional checkpoints were being set up. That night I sat on my balcony listening to distant small arms fire as tracers raced across the skyline.

Concerned about their well-being, I checked on Jasminka's parents early the next morning. They were anxious about the deteriorating situation, but at that point remained secure in their home. Returning to my own apartment, I crossed a pedestrian bridge over the River Brka. The Brka is a tributary of the Sava. The bridge spanned seventy-five meters. As I reached the other side, the barrel of an automatic rifle appeared over the bridge abutment, pointing at my chest. Startled, I pulled up. I'd had the same reaction years before, when I'd stumbled upon a *poskok*, a horn-nosed poisonous snake, while hiking in the mountains. I stood stock still then, and did again.

The soldier wielding the rifle ordered me to lie face down. After I complied, he demanded, "Where is your ID?"

"In my back pocket."

A second soldier said, "It's okay. I know him. He is Isak Gaši. Isak, you need to head home immediately. Don't delay. Things are about to start happening here."

As I arose to leave, a group of three pedestrians approached the bridge. Soldiers stopped and searched them. One pedestrian carried a pistol. A soldier disarmed him, told him to kneel, and struck him in the face with the butt of a rifle.

I was free to go, and hurried home. Having a rifle pointed at me brought home the new reality. The situation was dangerous, and deadly serious.

I was not yet aware that fifteen hundred paramilitaries from Serbia and Karadžić's Republika Srpska had arrived in Brčko, unopposed by the JNA. Their assignment was to ethnically cleanse the city. Doing so would ensure that Brčko did not have a resident population of Croats and Muslims intent on protecting their lives, liberty, and property.

After I arrived back at my apartment, Mira came by. She had heard reports of grim fighting elsewhere in town. Learning about my encounter at the bridge, she said, "It's not safe. You should stay home and stop moving around so much."

Back in my apartment, I responded to a knock at my door at about seven p.m. Waiting outside were two military policemen. My gut clenched. I wondered, *Are they here to arrest me?*

"Are you Isak Gaši?"

"I am."

"Our records show that you possess a pistol. Where is it?"

I had been given a target pistol at a regional sports award ceremony several years before. I had only fired the high-quality firearm on a couple of occasions.

"It's in its case in my back room."

"We are here to confiscate it. Show us where it's located. You will receive a receipt. Hang onto it."

After I handed the pistol over, the police wrote me a receipt and departed. Relieved by the limited purpose of their visit, I breathed far easier once they were gone.

The next morning, two JNA warplanes flew overhead as I stood on the street in front of my apartment building. They flew low, from the southeast, at an altitude of one hundred meters. Fifteen seconds later, a series of explosions reverberated from the direction the planes had headed. The population of that neighborhood was ninety percent Croat and Muslim. Moments later, the planes flew back.

That evening I called my father and learned that Serbian Guard paramilitaries under the command of a Major Mauzer controlled territory all the way to the Brka River. He said, "A Serbian flag is flying from the minaret of the White Mosque. The paramilitaries say they are going to 'liberate' the city by driving out all of us."

He had heard that the home of Jasminka's parents was empty, but knew nothing more. When I later relayed that news to Jasminka over the phone, she cried out in alarm, pressing me for information. All I could tell her was that they had vanished, that people were leaving, when they could, and that I'd try to find out more about their whereabouts.

That night I learned that Serb forces had pushed past the Brka and taken control of her parents' Bosniak neighborhood. The fighting there had reportedly been fierce. I couldn't tell her that.

Months later, I heard the story. When Serb forces began their approach, Jasminka's family sheltered with fifty others in the basement of an apartment building. They received reports that paramilitaries were dropping grenades and shooting RPGs into the basements of large buildings. Deciding to make a run for safety, they shot out streetlights, gathered half a dozen vehicles, and waited until past midnight. Driving as a convoy through Bosniak neighborhoods with their lights turned off, they reached a checkpoint controlled by Bosniak fighters. After spending several days in an outlying village, Jasminka's family found transport to the bridge at Slavonski Brod and Croatia, eventually making it to a refugee camp on an island in the Adriatic.

The day of their departure, Brčko's chief of police, Stjepan Filopović, a Croat, was forced out and replaced by a member of the SDS's war presidency, Dragan Veselić. Veselić told Croat and Muslim members of the police force that their services were no longer needed. Confiscating their weapons, he informed them they would be targets if they remained in the community. Several members of the force were arrested and transported to the JNA barracks. There they joined hundreds of others who were being processed before being taken away by bus. I watched the processing from my apartment, unsure of its purpose.

By this time, the Brčko hospital had been taken over by Major Mauzer's paramilitaries. Following the bridge bombing, the hospital had been filled with the regular sick and with bridge casualties. Needing beds, Mauzer ordered the discharge of non-Serb patients.

Jasminka called that night, saying that she intended to return to Brčko with Adna, taking the bus from Belgrade. That prospect had me terror-stricken. When I tried to dissuade her, she was adamant about coming. "I don't like it here in Belgrade. I've got to find out what has happened to my family. I have to find them."

"Jasminka, it is not safe. Brčko is not what you think. People are dying. I can't protect you. Don't do it."

Reluctantly, she agreed to stay.

Two days later, on May 5, the radio contradicted rumors of continued fierce fighting, reporting that order in the city had been restored. The report went on to say, "The downtown market has received new shipments and will be open tomorrow with a good selection of products." The announcer encouraged citizens to come out of hiding and return to the city center.

That day was my birthday. Although skeptical about the announcement, I thought, *If true, what a birthday gift.*

That evening Mira invited me to dinner. Afterward she said, "I need to resupply. Will you go with me to the market tomorrow?"

The next morning, Mira and I had coffee together before heading downtown at eleven a.m. The city was very quiet, hunkered down— few civilians were out. The market was near the police station. Approaching it, we passed several policemen.

The market was open air, located in a large courtyard. The walls of stout buildings built in the Austro-Hungarian style surrounded it on all sides. Only one entrance was open, off of the pedestrian mall, Braće Ćuskića Street. The gate to the market's rear entrance was closed and locked. Entering, we saw a few stalls open and approximately fifty people milling around.

After shopping for five minutes, we heard shots ring out from the direction of Braće Ćuskića Street. They sounded close. A general panic arose. The crowd scurried about pell-mell. Some tried hiding behind market stalls, while others scaled a fence behind some restrooms.

"We need to hide," urged Mira. I looked about for a hiding place but found none.

"Mira! Mira! Mira!" cried a voice from a nearby building.

We looked up and saw a woman on the building's second floor landing motioning to us. We ran through an entry that opened into a courtyard behind the building, spotting an open staircase. Sprinting toward it, we climbed the stairs. On the second floor, Mira's friend stood at the door to her apartment, waving to us. Once safely inside, we found the curtains drawn and the lighting dim. The woman was highly agitated.

"It is crazy for you to come downtown! Don't you know they are killing people here?"

She directed us into her living room. The room overlooked Braće Ćuskića Street. It looked across the street to Stari Grad, the old town, which housed the arts-and-crafts market. The municipal police station was located on an adjacent corner, seventy meters away.

Five minutes later more shots rang out from the street below. Mira and I went to the picture window, pulling back a corner of the curtain to get a view of the street. We saw a group of six people in civilian clothes being lined up. The civilians faced the wall of a building. Behind them stood six paramilitaries, black balaclavas covering their heads and faces. The armed men stood less than twenty meters away from us, their backs to our window.

Their commander screamed, "Motherfuckers, I'm going to kill thirty of you for every one of mine!"

He finished his announcement with "bre," an exclamation and threat intensifier unique to the Serbian dialect. Seconds later he ordered his men to fire. The six civilians collapsed to the ground. Mira gasped. Thunderstruck, I could not move.

"Bring me more," yelled the commander.

The soldiers headed toward Brčko's atomic bomb shelter, where a large group of civilians were congregated, held hostage. Minutes later the paramilitaries returned, leading four men dressed in civilian clothes. One of the civilians looked like one of Jasminka's relatives. The soldiers marched the four men in front of a different building, then told them to turn and face the wall. They were then executed, just like the first group.

The violence stunned me. I didn't know what to make of the madness, the berserk behavior. While I had seen serious fistfights in the army, I had never seen someone killed. The victims looked helpless, like sheep meekly heading to slaughter. The murders seemed to happen in slow motion, almost like a car accident developing. Then everything rushed into focus, with the grave damage done. Dropping the curtain, I pulled back from the window, returning to the sofa, shaken. Mira had been shocked into silence.

Her friend exclaimed, "You see! This has been happening for the past three days. It's a nightmare I can't escape. The killings haunt me. I don't sleep at night. The only thing between that wickedness and me is my front door. I fear someone will knock and come for me."

A short time later another great commotion arose from the street. I went to the window, and saw two men in police uniforms shoot three men in succession. Witnessing this act by the local police caused an awful feeling of despair to well up within me. These were members of a force that I respected—one I had once thought of joining. The physical and emotional impact of their violence was overwhelming. My head spun. It felt as if something inside was about to burst. I began shaking, uncontrollably.

Mira's friend ushered us into her kitchen where she brewed an herbal tea. We spent the rest of the day there. When we heard shots or noise from the street, no one went to the window. I'd already descended through the gates of hell, to the realms of violence and murder. I couldn't bear anymore evil that day. My mind drifted off. I had the same sensation of numbness I experienced when coming upon the broken child three days before. It felt like an awful dream.

For a long time, I stared blankly at the wall. Later, something deep inside kicked in. I was again able to think.

Time passed slowly. Berserkers roaming outside, and no refuge with the police, meant there was no escape. We tried to imagine a safe passage back to our apartment building. Mira eventually hit on a plan.

With martial law in place, curfew that evening occurred at 8:00. At seven, Mira placed a call to a friend who operated an ambulance. It could travel the city streets unencumbered. The vehicle pulled up on a side street at seven forty-five p.m. Hanging back in the shadows, we made a run for it. When we climbed into the back, the driver, a Serb, recognized me and demanded of Mira, "What is he doing here?"

"He's a friend and it's a long story."

I later discovered that Jasminka's second cousin was murdered below us on Braće Ćuskića Street.

— 10 —

INTERNED AT WORK

I stayed home the next day, venturing out only to visit Mira on the first floor for some provisions.

Earlier in the week, JNA cars with loudspeakers had driven through my neighborhood announcing, "Citizens, if you are concerned for your safety, come to the army barracks. The army will be arranging transportation to safe areas for the next three days."

From my balcony, I had seen long lines of civilians at the barracks, going through some sort of registration process. Bus traffic to the barracks was constant. I saw civilians load onto the buses before being driven away.

Many of the houses in the development across the street from my apartment building now sat empty, the residents taking the JNA up on their offer. Mid-morning on May 7, three large JNA trucks parked on my street. Paramilitary soldiers jumped down. They proceeded into the houses, emptying them of valuables. Once the trucks were loaded, they drove off.

Brčko was being looted.

The next day, I felt trapped in the apartment and wanted fresh air. My third-story balcony was exposed and not an option, due to reported sniper fire. That afternoon I walked downstairs to visit Mira.

"Good afternoon, Isak. You're just in time for coffee. You look like you could use some. It's nice outside. Let's sit there."

Mira's patio was on the opposite side of our building and protected from sharpshooting. It was a warm, cloudless day. Out of doors at last, I experienced the sensation of the late afternoon sun on my skin. After the violence and menace of the past week, it felt reassuring—conjuring up memories of vacations on Croatia's Adriatic coast. Basking in the sun's warmth, I started to relax and, despite the coffee, grew drowsy.

After ten minutes, Mira brought up what we had seen on Braće Ćuskića Street.

"I can't stop thinking about what happened downtown. That was awful. I don't understand it. Something evil is at work. I hear the talk, and it's not good. There is real danger for you here, Isak. You shouldn't go out. Even your apartment is not safe. You should move in with us until things change. Whatever you do, I want you to promise that you'll stay off the streets."

"Okay, you are right; I don't know what happened that day with the police. They used to be people you could count on. Now it's as if there are no laws. Do they just follow orders, and question nothing? What allows them to murder people in the street?"

The conversation seemed to summon its subject, and Mira's counsel soon proved prophetic. A Serb policeman, Slobodan Mitrić, drove up. He lived across the street from Mira. Noticing us, he walked over. I wondered, *What now?*

"Gaši, I didn't know you were still in Brčko. We don't need you here doing nothing. There are problems with the power grid. You are needed at Elektro Brčko."

The following morning I received a call from work: "A car will be by to pick you up in an hour."

When I arrived, my executive director told me, "We are all on a war labor assignment. You will need to be on site and available for work around the clock. You electricians are bunking in the technical goods warehouse. We will drive you back to your apartment later today—get a sleeping bag and whatever clothing you need."

After being confined to my apartment with nothing to do, I felt some release by the chance to work and to move around. I had always enjoyed camaraderie with my coworkers, and an element of that remained. I did not discuss the present situation in Brčko with my Serb counterparts. There was nothing to be gained, with perhaps everything to lose. I also suppressed my instinct to call things as I saw them. I was in survival mode, trying to figure a way out of a great predicament.

The fighting had downed power lines in many places, which meant much work for us. We worked fifteen hours a day. Traveling to calls, we were stopped at checkpoints. After the first week, Director Ristić took me aside. We had always gotten along well. He said, "I'm going to keep you here working in the warehouse as much as I can. With a name like Gaši, it is not safe for you out there. When we are shorthanded, I will have to send you out. When you do go out, make sure you have all your documentation and carry this letter from me. Perhaps it will help."

I knew what Director Ristić referred to.

Our family name, Gaši, was unusual in Brčko. It was not Yugoslav, but Albanian. In Serbia, significant animosity existed between Serbs and the Albanians who were the overwhelming majority population in the Serbian province of Kosovo. The Albanian population in Kosovo desired political autonomy and independent status as a seventh Yugoslav republic, while Serbs saw Kosovo as the birthplace of the Serb nation and of the Serbian Orthodox church.

In Kosovo, tensions between ethnic Serbs and ethnic Albanians regularly threatened to boil over into violence.

Only a couple of dozen Albanians resided in Brčko, so we were a true minority. In the Yugoslav language, the proper word for Albanians is "Albanci." Serbs had a derogatory name for us—"Šiptar." Like "nigger" in English, it was a hostile term. When I was a boy, I occasionally heard the taunt, "Gaši is a Šiptar name." These were fighting words and I felt obligated to defend our family name. Those were my first encounters with prejudice. I didn't like it.

When alone now with my Bosniak colleagues, our tendency toward gallows humor would elicit the occasional joke regarding our situation—followed by belly laughs—and I could feel the tension lift for a minute. At times I would get lost in the work, in the old routines, and forget what Brčko had become. Then some new event would arise, jolting me back to reality.

The heavy weaponry returned to the JNA depot next door. Artillery fire from the depot went on day and night. I wondered who and what was being shelled. Driving around town on work detail, I saw heavy damage in areas where Muslim and Croat populations were dominant.

On May 14, I received a work assignment near my parents' home. One of my Serb coworkers allowed me to visit my father, driving me to his home. As I stepped out of the car, he opened the trunk, offering me several cartons of cigarettes.

I walked in to find my father, my brothers, Ramiz and Mirsad, and Jagoda's son, Jasmin, gathered around the kitchen table. We had lost contact when I was interned at work.

"Hey! Look who just walked through the door! We've been worried about you, man. It has been a week and no word from you. You've got a tool belt on, so they must have you working. What are you seeing out there?"

Our reunion was short and poignant, lasting fifteen minutes. I gave my father my month's wages and the cigarettes. I asked, "What do you think happens next?"

Shrugging his shoulders, he said, "I don't know. They are holding us here, not letting us leave. They must be preparing us for something.

Who'd have thought the JNA would allow this? Letting in these bastard paramilitaries from Serbia. They must have planned this for months, and kept quiet about it. I don't know what to tell you, Isak; keep your head down, and maybe we'll survive this."

The uncertainty of our situation had us all subdued. While it was reassuring to be among my kin, this was the first time that I'd ever seen my father cast about for a solution. He had always been a rock, someone incredibly tough and resilient. He had seen the full gamut during the Second World War. If he thought this situation desperate, it must be.

Outside, with Ramiz, I learned that the police had been to the house three days before. Their records indicated my father possessed a pistol. When he could not produce the firearm, they badgered and beat him. He was sixty-seven years old. Ramiz said, "We couldn't stop it, even after Mirsad told them that he had lost the pistol many years ago. Mirsad asked them to beat him instead. Watching Dad get hurt and humiliated that way was terrible."

The next day, back at EDB, I had an encounter with Major Mauzer, the commander of the Serbian Guard paramilitaries. Mauzer was a nom de guerre, taken from the arms manufacturer of the same name. The major was Ljubiša Savić of Bijeljina. He had descended on Brčko heading a six-hundred-man paramilitary force. In sacking Bijeljina in early April, he encountered little resistance. It was rumored that during the takeover he had allowed his men to execute local Albanians.

Mauzer's experience so far in Brčko had been different, encountering spirited opposition and house-to-house fighting. He pulled up to my workplace in a jeep, accompanied by a policeman and two Panther paramilitaries. He headed to director Ristić's office. When he and Ristić emerged, the director asked all EDB workers to gather for a meeting.

When we had assembled, Mauzer told us to form two lines, Serbs in one line and Muslims and Croats in the other. The line of Serbs included six men; ten men formed my line. Mauzer then addressed us. He was a stocky, muscular man in his mid-thirties. He was dressed unusually for a military man, in a camouflage uniform but wearing Adidas sneakers rather than military boots. He wore a radio headset around his neck. Nothing covered his head. As he talked, he waved a pistol around for emphasis. He was extremely upset.

The major started down our Bosniak and Croat line, asking each man his name. He threatened each of us individually, accusing us of various crimes. A Serb had stayed in our line. When he gave his name Mauzer said, "You are a Serb, what are you doing with the balijas?"

"Well, they are my colleagues."

"When your father or brother is killed, it will be the likes of these that killed them." As he said this, the veins in his neck bulged and his pistol arced about wildly.

When Mauzer asked me my name, I answered "Isak" only. I was certain that giving my full name, and identifying my Albanian heritage, would be risky. I was relieved that my father had given me a Christian name (Isak is the Bosnian version of Isaac). Thinking I was Catholic, Mauzer called me a "dirty, stinking Ustaša."

When he finished this roll call, Mauzer addressed us collectively, saying, "Power went down at the hospital. One of you electricians must have sabotaged it. When the power was out, two of my soldiers died on the operating table. If it happens again, I know where you are and will kill you all."

Turning to director Ristić and pushing a pistol up under his chin, Mauzer said, "I'm going to teach you a lesson. How can you let these Muslims and Croats influence you? You are the Serb and in charge!" My director's face turned red then white. His eyes flared wide. He stared straight ahead, unmoving. Having obtained the reaction he sought, Mauzer turned away.

He followed up with a diatribe about the rapid military inroads the Serbs had achieved, announcing, "We Serbs will soon be in control of all of Bosnia. From then on we all know who is going to be running this country."

With that pronouncement, he departed. Two of his Panther soldiers and a policeman, Mišo Čijević, set up shop in an office. They called the men from my group in individually for questioning. They asked whether we possessed weapons, telling us the work site would be searched. We were asked to sign a loyalty oath.

During my interrogation Čijević asked, "Gaši, will you support, and are you prepared to serve, the new Serb authority in Brčko?"

I knew the safe answer, but instead told the truth: "If I had known the regime would be like this, I would already be a thousand kilometers away."

My response prompted Čijević to rise, grab his weapon, and strike me in the chest with the butt of the rifle.

"Gaši, I want you to know we looked for you last night at your apartment. Now we know where you are. We will finish our business with you later."

As he announced this, one of the soldiers played with a shotgun, racking, ejecting, and re-racking a twelve-gauge shell. The action was for my benefit. It further provoked me. I could feel my pulse hammer as I awaited an attack. Thankfully, none came. I was dismissed. Walking away, I thought, *They have made a judgment on me, and a harsh sentence is coming.*

——||——
THE MASS GRAVE

The day Mauzer visited my workplace, a roundup occurred in my father's neighborhood. The four men at my father's house were arrested and driven in a troop transport to Luka. Luka was located on the Sava River, three hundred meters downstream of the Gunja Bridge. It was the largest port facility in Bosnia. The extensive warehouse center there had been converted to a prison. My father later told me what transpired.

Ramiz was the first in my family interrogated. While Ramiz was away, the policeman in charge approached my father saying, "Old man, why are you here? You must be very dangerous to be arrested." My father knew the policeman by reputation but had never met him before.

He saw that the policeman's pants were spattered with blood. As a World War II fighter who later served in military intelligence, he understood the dangerous games being played.

"I thought I could establish a rapport with him. Men with jobs like his need to take a break. They get worked up during a violent interrogation. His question was my opening. He could make decisions. I pulled out a pack of Parliaments and asked if we could smoke together. We walked off and had a leisurely smoke."

During that interlude, Ramiz returned to the warehouse, saw only my brother and nephew, and grew gravely concerned. Mirsad tried to reassure him. Several minutes later my father and the police captain reappeared. The captain pronounced my father a "good man," and told the four of them, "You are free to go."

Being freed from Luka did not mean an offer of a lift home or a document ensuring safe passage. They were men of the type the paramilitaries hunted, and they had a three-kilometer trek to get home.

I continued working for the next two weeks. My guard remained high, but as the days passed and the police did not follow up on the threat to arrest me, I began to hope that something had changed.

The war had a profound impact on Brčko's animals. On repair runs we repeatedly encountered animals that had lost their bearings. Once we saw six sheep clustered tightly together, moving in a zigzag fashion across the landscape. When they spotted our crew, they made a beeline toward us, seeming to ask us for help and shelter.

We frequently ran into dogs and horses in similar circumstances. They looked to us for answers. Finding none they seemed to accuse: "You domesticated us to your purposes, yet now you're killing each other and have abandoned us. Is your kind deranged?"

Working in a conflict zone was dangerous. The hazards were driven home on several occasions. On May 16, two of us were sent to repair downed lines near the Brčko hospital. On the way, we were stopped at a checkpoint in front of the Hotel Galeb. Paramilitaries lounged in chairs on the sidewalk in front of the hotel.

Looking past them, into the hotel parking lot, I saw a dumpster. It was filled to overflowing with corpses. Three more bodies lay on the pavement beside the dumpster. I couldn't believe what I was seeing. Afraid of drawing the soldiers' attention, I looked away, sickened and mortified.

When we arrived at the hospital, a soldier serving as a sentry pointed us toward the repair area. He accompanied us through the waist-high grass to a transmission vault. Electrical lines connecting the hospital to several outpatient-clinic buildings were down, lying in an open field. A housing complex stood one hundred and fifty meters away. Houses in the complex had sustained damage; several of their roofs had burned away. This was the neighborhood where Jasminka's parents lived. I again wondered, *Did they get out? Are they safe?*

As we set to work powering down the lines, six shots rang out in rapid succession. I felt the bullets whiz by. We hit the ground, burrowing into the tall grass. After fifteen minutes the soldier asked, "Why don't you try again?" My coworker stood up, which raised more gunfire. We gave up on the repair, crawling out of the danger zone.

That evening, back at EDB, I was told, "Your wife is on the phone in the office." I felt mixed emotions walking to take the call. Jasminka had called two other times. While anxious to know how she and Adna were faring, I didn't want extra attention from my Serb coworkers. I figured some were spies and that calls were monitored. My end of the conversation was easily overhead by others in the office. Previous calls from Jasminka had been minefields. She asked questions I could only cryptically respond to.

That night Jasminka announced, "I've bought bus tickets for Adna and me. We are coming tomorrow. I've got to find my parents."

I knew she would follow through with this, despite our earlier agreement. I felt sick to my stomach, filled with a pervasive dread. Up to now, I had the consolation that my wife and child were safe, and would survive. Jasminka's intention would change all that.

I told her, "Don't do it."

I said this softly, so as not to draw attention, but there was urgency, frustration and anger in my voice.

"I'm coming. Nothing is going to stop me."

I'd been attracted to Jasminka for her spunk and fire. Now those qualities were a dire threat to all three of us.

To save her, and Adna, I started digging my own grave in front of my Serb coworkers.

"Jasminka, if you come here, this is what you will find. You no longer have an apartment, you no longer have a car, you no longer have possessions, you no longer have parents, or a sister, to console you. This is a place of death and destruction. Our friends are being killed and thrown into dumpsters. You will be killed. Adna will be killed. If you bring Adna here, you are not fit to be her mother. If you come, you will no longer have a husband. Stay in Belgrade. Never speak of coming here again."

She did not come. Thank God.

Two days later I was assigned to a work crew that included my technical director and two other electricians. We were sent to a large substation located in an open area, about one hundred meters from a Muslim neighborhood. When we arrived, two policemen were on-site. They waited behind the substation, perhaps using the building as a shield. We drove up and got out. The door to the substation was around the corner, exposed to the neighborhood. A drainage ditch surrounded the building. The entry to the building had a bridge that spanned the ditch.

One of the police said, "We haven't seen anything. I think it is safe to enter the building." He escorted us to the entry, standing beside the technical director as he unlocked the door. As the director worked the lock, shots sounded. Both the director and the policeman were hit. My coworkers and I dove into the drainage ditch. The policeman lay flat on his back, about two meters from me. He'd been shot in the chest and was dying. One of my coworkers suffered a heart attack from the stress and strain. We tried to help him and the technical director, dragging them down the ditch and around the corner. An ambulance arrived ten minutes later. Both of my coworkers survived.

The policeman died where he lay. His father, also a policeman, had received a report of the shooting on his radio and raced to the scene. He became enraged when he learned of his son's death. "Who here is Muslim? I will avenge my son."

To save our skins we kept silent. Witnessing a man die beside me, then seeing the grief and bloodlust passions aroused in his kin, was frightening. I felt trapped, that my time was running out.

For days, I had seen a white, refrigerated Bimeks truck drive to and from the large, open field across the street from EDB headquarters. The truck made two deliveries daily—one in the morning and another in the late afternoon. Bimeks owned the slaughterhouse in Brčko. Its trucks transported products to retail butcher shops. I recognized the driver—a technician who worked at the police station.

On May 23, another electrician and I received an assignment to replace isolators on the power poles across the street from the EDB facility. The poles carried high-voltage lines. The isolators were located on the poles, twenty-five meters above the ground. I climbed up. While I was on the pole, the Bimeks truck drove past and into the field. The truck stopped beside a gigantic hole being worked by a bulldozer, one hundred and fifty meters from my position. The view from twenty-five meters up was very clear. I saw a crew of JNA soldiers unload thirty bodies from the truck. All of the bodies wore civilian clothes. The soldiers tossed the bodies into the hole, then the bulldozer pushed dirt onto them. I now understood what had been going on for days in the field.

The site was a mass grave, located two hundred meters from where I slept. The thought made me shudder. The day's work assignment had been an ascent to another hell. After climbing down, I did not mention what I had seen to my Serb coworker.

I had two Muslim coworkers who had previously been detained at Luka prison camp and then released. When alone with me they shared some of their experience. One was Osman Stranjac, who had been incarcerated during the first week of May. He told me he saw eighty people murdered on one day. The eighty represented about one third of those imprisoned. The victims had been taken from the general population of detainees and marched into an adjoining room. There they were lined up against a wall before being shot at close range. The men next door could hear this happening. As Osman told the story, the memory remained profoundly unsettling. He stopped several times to compose himself, to wipe away tears. After the killing, guards assigned him to a work detail that carried the bodies—all eighty of them—out of the warehouse to load onto JNA trucks. When the twelve men finished their work, they were ordered to line up. A paramilitary walked down the line, dispatching every third person with a pistol. The eight men left standing were told to say nothing or face the same fate. They were then allowed to return to the warehouse.

Another coworker with a troubling story was Midhat Zelenjaković. Before coming to EDB he had been a professional volleyball player. I knew Midhat well. He told me about an evil character at Luka. The individual's name was Goran Jelisić. He had run roughshod over prisoners during Midhat's incarceration. Jelisić called himself the "Serb Adolph." Midhat described the treatment that a local Croat, Stjepan Glavočević, received from Jelisić. On May 9, Jelisić took Stjepan out of the warehouse for questioning. When they returned forty minutes later, Stjepan bled profusely from facial wounds. His nose had been cut deeply, and half of his right ear was carved off. Jelisić and another guard paraded Stjepan around the warehouse to upset the other inmates. Jelisić held a pistol, pulling Stjepan by his shirt collar. He told his audience, "This is the reason you are here at

Luka. This man is a Catholic Ustaša who has been killing innocent Serb civilians. I want to know what his punishment will be."

The prisoners made no response. "I think it will be death," said Jelisić.

He began to beat Stjepan, who blurted out, "I am begging you people, please say 'death.' I want to die. I don't want to live." Jelisić released his hold on Stjepan's neck and offered up his pistol to the prisoners. When he had no takers, Jelisić turned and shot his captive twice in the back of the head.

Midhat said, "We all sat stunned—assaulted by the echoing discharge, the smell of burned gunpowder, and the brutality."

At nine a.m. the next day, May 26, a red van pulled up at the EDB gatehouse. Two policemen stepped out and went into the director's office. I was summoned moments later. I knew the two policemen—Pantelić and Knezević. Director Ristić told me that they had come to arrest me. Pantelić told me to put my hands behind my back, then tightened a cable tie around my wrists.

The director asked him, "What can I say when people ask about Isak?"

"You can say that he was taken by Serb police for questioning."

When the director asked "Where? Why?" he was told, "Keep your mouth shut and stop asking questions."

I was escorted outside, put into the back of the van, and driven away.

12

ARREST AND INCARCERATION

I entered the police station with my two captors. Seven officers milled around the front desk. I was booked, escorted down a hallway to the right and locked in a room—number thirteen.

The room was unlit; my eyes took a moment to adjust. I found a wooden bench and sat down. The bench had no back but sat flush against an angled wall, allowing an occupant to recline against the wall and rest. Light coming from under the door allowed me to make out the shapes of two others. We introduced ourselves. One of the men, Slavo Božić, lit a cigarette. A local Serb troublemaker, his face flickered weirdly in the match light. The second man was a Bosniak, Nedžad Dizdarević, from my father's neighborhood. He said, "I was arrested at my house at three a.m. yesterday. I've been here for the past thirty hours."

Five minutes later a key turned in the lock. A policeman called for Nedžad to come out. I could see he was dressed in bloodstained pajamas and looked battered. After the door closed, Slavko asked, "Why are you here?"

I figured that he was a plant trying to obtain information. "I was picked up at work. I'm not sure why. Frankly I'm surprised you are here, since you are a Serb."

"No, no. It doesn't matter. I was picked up at random. They must have thought I was up to no good."

After thirty minutes the door to the room opened again. Petar Zarić, a local Serb, stood in the doorway. Petar was a karate athlete and coach who had apparently volunteered for police duties following Brčko's takeover. We were acquainted; our relationship had always been cordial.

As he said, "You are to come with me, Gaši," his tone indicated a changed relationship. Petar was in power and I would be doing his bidding. Another man dressed in camouflage stood behind him. Petar told the man to cut my cable tie. He then handed me back my ID book. Hoping I'd be returned to work, I asked, "What is next?"

When Petar replied, "I'm taking you to Luka," I immediately felt numb, going weak in my knees. My mind flashed to the Luka stories of my coworkers. An intense sense of dread overcame me. I asked myself, *Is this truly happening?*

I did not have long to collect myself. I was told to climb into the bed of a pickup truck, then driven less than a kilometer to Luka. The truck stopped at the facility's front gate, which was manned by two men. I recognized one as a Brčko policeman. As I jumped down from the truck, the policeman said, "Follow me." We walked toward several low prefab buildings that housed the administrative offices of the warehouse operation. As we approached the buildings, a second policeman from Brčko's force, Branko Pudić, intercepted us.

Pudić began berating me. "We finally have you. You have been delivering weapons to Muslim fighters in Brčko and helping to fortify their barricades. People have seen you do that. We know that you have been working with terrorists. You are working for the Green Berets, for Islamović and Jasikolić!"

Caught off guard by the absurd accusations, I said, "I don't know what you are talking about. I have never met those men nor even heard of them."

In reaction, he drew his service revolver, using it to push me from behind. Seconds later, the revolver come down sharply on the back of my head, causing intense pain. I reeled unsteadily, my strength draining away. Pudić pushed me into the building, toward an open doorway. I stumbled into a room with a table. Four men sat on three sides of the table. They faced me, staring. Their gaze felt incredibly stern. I attempted to collect myself, to assess the new situation, sensing that what unfolded in the next minutes would be deadly serious. I thought, *Get focused, stay calm. If you show fear, they will want to know what you have done to be afraid.* Deep down, and right below the surface, I was profoundly afraid.

Of the four seated at the desk, two were dressed in paramilitary camouflage and two in the olive drab of the JNA. I started things off by saying "Good day." A paramilitary seated on the right side of the table arose angrily. His camouflage uniform bore the large double-eagle insignia worn by Četnik fighters during the Second World War. It was now worn by fighters aligned with the Serb Radical party. When he stood, he was very bow-legged. A bandage covered his forehead. In his right hand, he clutched a heavy brass fitting used to connect firehoses. He said, "Motherfucker, can you greet us in the Serb way?"

I said yes, then gave a greeting that ends "with God's help my brothers."

The paramilitary, who I later learned was called Ivan Repić, responded, "Oh good, you know that one. The same to you, and fuck you."

I estimated that he was ready for action and extraordinarily dangerous. He ordered me to sit down on a bench that faced the desk and the other three men.

"Where were you in 1982?" demanded the second paramilitary.

The question momentarily threw me, but then I remembered violence had erupted between Serbs and Kosovo Albanians in 1982. Kosovars had rioted, demanding independence from Serbia. The query related to my Albanian heritage and presumed allegiances.

"I have always lived in Brčko. I have never had dealings in Kosovo, in 1982 or in any other year."

The next man to speak was Miodag Nadić. He was a former paddler, twenty-six or twenty-seven years old. We knew each other. Based on my earlier experience with Petar, I let him establish our current relationship. He was a graduate of the naval academy and an active duty officer who had seen duty in the Croatian War. He greeted me, telling the others, "What he has said is true. He is from Brčko and a well-known athlete that I know personally. In my experience, he has been a person of good character. I don't think there is reason to treat him harshly."

His words calmed the situation. A second lieutenant sat beside him, writing down notes as Nadić questioned me about my activities since April 30. I told them I had been working for EDB. When asked about my wife I said, "Jasminka is staying with friends in Belgrade." After he finished questioning me, he instructed Pudić, "Take him to the warehouse and leave him there unharmed."

Pudić walked me across the street to an entrance on the left end of the warehouse. It opened to a large room—thirty-by-fifty meters. The room was empty except for a chair located near its center.

Pudić said, "Sit on the chair and don't move."

Doing so, I absorbed my surroundings. The smell was overpowering—the foul odor of a dead animal that had decayed in the woods. The room's walls were pocked with hundreds of bullet holes and blood spatters, the floor strewn with pieces of human skull and discarded, bloody clothing. I thought, *This must be the killing room that Osman described.*

Still unsteady from the policeman's assault and my interrogation, my thoughts careened. *Why are they taking so long? Why was I left alone? Am I going to be shot?*

After forty minutes, Pudić returned, directing me toward a door that opened into a second warehouse space, a room as large as the first. The scene was misery incarnate. The room contained a couple hundred dirty and downtrodden men. I recognized most of them. They came from Brčko; almost all were Muslim with a dozen or so Croats and two Albanians. All wore civilian clothes. Some were in pajamas. Many of the men were cut and badly bruised. Most lay prostrate on pieces of cardboard lined up along the perimeter walls. The room reeked—like barnyard animals. A couple of the men acknowledged my arrival with a glance or a quick nod, but I heard no greetings, even from those I knew well.

Pudić said, "Find a place to sit." Scanning the room and seeking fresher air, I found an open spot near a garage door to the outside. Although the door was padlocked, it had openings that would allow air to enter and an opportunity to look out. I sat down next to a large oil stain with my back to the wall, contemplating my new surroundings. No one approached me. My fellow inhabitants appeared to be alone on isolated cardboard islands. I thought, *I'm going to need all my faculties to survive such a godforsaken place.*

After fifteen minutes, the one woman incarcerated in the warehouse came up to me. I knew her as the impoverished soul who sold flowers and religious tracts and who cleaned the White Mosque. Her name was Zinca. She was imprisoned with her sixteen-year-old son. She knelt next to me and whispered, "I have cardboard for you.

It will protect you from the floor. I will pray that Allah looks out for you." I thanked her.

Two hours later, Repić, the paramilitary who wanted to be greeted in the Serb way, entered the warehouse accompanied by two guards in JNA uniform. As Repić stood in profile, I saw that his hair was pulled back in a ponytail. He scanned the room, then shouted, "Where is that Šiptar who arrived today?" Three of us of Albanian descent looked at each other, unsure who should stand up. When no one did, Repić said, "I want the sports athlete." I stepped forward.

"Step closer," he said, concealing his right hand behind his back. I sensed danger, feeling my body respond. My heart rate and respiration increased. My mouth felt dry, like it was filled with cotton. My muscles tensed.

When I was within his striking distance, Repić displayed the weapon he had been hiding. It was the same brass fitting he brandished during my interrogation. It looked like it weighed six or seven pounds and could do real damage. When I tried to back away, one of the guards hit me hard in the back with the butt of a rifle. Realizing there was no avenue for retreat, I prepared for a frontal assault. Angered, I wanted to lash out and fight Repić. Knowing resistance would be futile—a death warrant—I resigned myself to taking a beating.

"What is your nationality?"

"I am Yugoslav."

"Where is your Yugoslavia now?" responded Repić, taking a swing at my head with the brass fitting. I ducked. The blow came down hard on my shoulder. I staggered but remained upright.

"The guy is strong. You'll have to hit him again," said one of the soldiers.

Repić swung; I ducked, taking another blow on the shoulder that knocked me to the floor. When I was down, all three men set upon me with their boots, kicking me repeatedly in the head and abdomen. I tried to cover up, but was eventually kicked unconscious.

When I came to, I was lifted to my knees from behind. Repić faced me, drawing his pistol. He forced it into my mouth. After more berating that thundered in my ears, he paused, then pulled the trigger of the pistol. I heard a click.

"Well, it looks like you were lucky this time. Next time I will have a bullet for you."

After that I saw Repić's mouth move, but could not hear what he was saying. He must have told the men to let me loose. I fell to the floor, remaining there for a long time. I could feel that significant damage had been done. I wondered if it would be permanent, and if that even mattered. I eventually regained enough strength to crawl across the room to my cardboard. No one offered assistance. This made the beating even worse. I felt utterly alone.

Later, as I lay on my mat, I sensed someone nearby. It was Zinca. She pressed her forehead to mine and softly murmured, "I am with you. You are going to be okay."

She began to pray for me. For the next thirty minutes, I felt as if I received my mother's care. It was comforting, something I desperately needed. Even as my physical being flirted with shock or worse, I realized I was in the presence of someone with extraordinary compassion and courage. To me she was, and remains, Mother Bosnia. And this was a woman who toiled at the bottom of Brčko society. She was barely noticed by the rest of us. I later had reason to think, *The prophets were right—the meek are the best among us.*

— 13 —

BLACKLISTED

That night, after it grew dark and the guards had left, several others visited me. I was told, "We avoided you earlier because you are on the blacklist. People on the list get killed. Fraternizing with someone on the list is dangerous."

I racked my brain to think of what I had done to be marked— and whether there was a way to get off the list without completely compromising my principles. If I survived, I wanted to be able to live with myself.

That night I could not sleep. The air temperature had dropped. The concrete floor was cold. My cardboard provided a little insulation, but we had no blankets. My head and body ached intensely. Music blared from the offices across the street. I heard a woman's screams. I lay there shivering, wondering, *Did the guards use the music to drown her cries out?*

The next morning, I arose feeling terrible. My ears rang. I had a deep pain on the top of my head. I had no recollection of taking a blow there, guessing that it happened when I was unconscious.

Late in the morning a local Serb in a police uniform entered the warehouse. He walked with a distinctive limp. I knew him—Konstantin Simonović, a twenty-three-year-old high-school dropout who worked as a house painter. His mother ran a brothel. Konstantin was well known around town, often called by his nicknames Kosta and Kole. I perceived him as a person who wanted to impress, someone who could be easily manipulated. I had never seen him in a police uniform. I thought, *The attack on Brčko has given him the chance to be someone important.*

Kosta introduced himself. "My name is Konstantin Simonović. I am the deputy commander of the Luka Investigating Prison. You are here being investigated. I will often be present during your interrogations. It is in your interest to give me names and to tell me the truth."

He then proceeded to go through a roll call, a procedure he followed every day.

Later that morning Kosta returned, calling for me. We left the warehouse together, walking across the street to an interrogation room. As we entered the room, I recognized Petar Kaurinović, a police inspector. Also present were Zoran Kondić, a crime tech on the Brčko police force, and Petar Zarić, the man who had driven me to Luka the day before.

Kaurinović was in charge. A tall, thin man in his mid-forties, he was prematurely gray and looked older. He started in saying, "Isak, I am surprised you are here. You know, your father and brothers were here before you."

The statement threw me off guard. I must have shown my concern. I had not seen my family members at Luka and feared for their safety.

"No reason to be alarmed. I made certain that they were taken care of," said the inspector. "They were released. You needn't worry about them."

"I am very grateful to hear that. Thank you."

"Isak, do you possess any weapons?"

"I do not."

"But we know you have a pistol."

"I had a pistol, but it is no longer in my possession. I turned it over to military police when they asked for it several weeks ago."

"If that is true, do you have a receipt?"

I produced the document from my pocket. The inspector scanned it, then said, "It is important that you have this. It could save your life in the future."

He posed other questions: "Do you know others with weapons? Do you know anyone who has fired on Serbs?"

I sensed that naming others might curry favor, but answered, "No."

He then changed direction asking, "Do you know Muslim extremists or anyone fighting with the Muslim Green Berets?"

"I don't know anyone like that."

"If that is the case, are you a member of the SDA, and did you vote in the referendum?"

"I was a member of the SDA, and I did vote in the referendum."

"Did you vote in favor of independence?"

"I did."

"That was a big mistake. We saw you on TV, supporting independence. That could cost you your life. None of the men here have said they voted for independence. You are the only one. You are either stupid for admitting it, or the bravest one we have here."

"If voting for what you believe is now a death crime in Yugoslavia, then so be it."

The inspector made note of my defiance, jotting something down in his notebook. As when I didn't sign the loyalty oath, I knew I had given the wrong answer, but I couldn't lie about myself. This was my identity—who I was. I didn't want to apologize for that.

Perhaps showing some resistance mattered, making the inspector think I had reasons to feel that way. He may have wondered, *Does someone important support him?* At any rate, he again changed tactic, asking, "Have you been ill-treated during your time here?"

The question was a trap. Complaining at Luka was one of the worst things a prisoner could do. While the rules to survival were unwritten, we prisoners quickly intuited them. I answered, "No."

Looking puzzled, the inspector asked, "If that's so, why do have bruises and cuts covering your face and head?"

"I don't know about that; it must be from sleeping on the concrete floor."

"I see. Well, tell me if anyone mistreats you. We know you and who you are. We would like to help you."

"Well, if you want to help me, then please help me leave this place."

"Isak, I have no more questions for now. You are free to return to the warehouse. I will check to see if we can shorten your stay here. I can't make any promises."

Dismissed, I returned to the warehouse. It was mealtime.

We were fed twice daily. The food was bread and tea in the morning and a large loaf of bread with two ladles of stew in the afternoon. The loaves were broken into quarters and shared among four, as was the stew. We shared a single set of utensils.

Late that night I sat quietly, with my back to the concrete wall. A blackbird landed on the ledge of a broken overhead window. Peering inside the building, it surveyed the scene.

Having satisfied its curiosity, the bird soon flew away. I longed to do the same. I had once moved so freely on the nearby river. The bird's flight made me recall the thousands of hours I'd spent paddling this stretch of the Sava.

The river's serious fishermen and I were well acquainted. As I'd return from a three-hour training session, they'd hoist their catches, extolling their skill and good fortune. I'd give a thumbs-up and yell, "I'm looking forward to one of your famous fish dinners!"

Many of my hours on the Sava were exceptional. Mornings were quiet and peaceful, with mists hovering over the surrounding farm fields before giving way to the warming sun. On the water I felt close to and attuned with nature. I experienced the changing seasons, appreciating how the river's scent varied with them. The fresh, sweet air of spring eventually gave way to the weighty, rich aroma of summer's ripening earth. The fields grew lush and the air languid. I could anticipate the time when the local honeysuckle, wild garlic, and thyme would bloom, releasing their perfume, and the days when white storks would fly overhead at the end of their five-thousand-mile migration from South Africa. Paddling downstream on those mornings and turning the final bend above Brčko, I would capture an image of my town glinting in the sunlight, knowing what others meant when they wrote about shining cities on a hill.

Other seasons presented different challenges. I worked outdoors, and winters in Brčko were harsh. Climbing power poles in subzero temperatures was no treat; getting my spiked stirrups to penetrate the slick, frozen poles required the use of a hammer. On windy days, the work while exposed on the pole was truly bone chilling. Training after workdays like these was a test of will and desire. I knew that great paddlers were made during the winter months. For the world's best, there was no offseason. By December my club mates had gone into hibernation, the cold and the piercing wind driving them indoors. From then on, I was a solitary figure on the water. On calm winter days, my canoe and the occasional passing barge made the only waves on the Sava. Several winters the river froze over, forcing me to exchange my canoe for a set of cross-country skis. Always comfortable near the Sava, I took long ski tours along the levee on the Croatian side. Unlike on the water, the skis left a record in the snow of my passing.

Those living nearby, whose picture windows faced the river, knew my patterns as well as the fishermen. Sitting by their hot stoves on a biting cold day, they'd see me paddle past and later say, "I saw you out there today. It's minus ten, man! Are you crazy, or just obsessed? How can you enjoy such a cold and lonely sport?"

What I would have given that night at Luka to be alone in my canoe again, preferably with a sixty-second head start.

While most of us were held in this large warehouse room, several dozen men and women were also interned in the one-story office buildings across the street. Those buildings housed the interrogation rooms along with the facility's only restrooms. Using the restrooms required permission from our guards. Using them could be dangerous; it was an area of ambush. One never knew which guards were on duty there, or their emotional state. Nevertheless, it offered privacy, something non-existent in the warehouse, where twenty-liter buckets served as toilets.

Alone with my thoughts that night, I meditated. It was a disciplined reverie. As an athlete, I'd used visualizations to prepare for performance. I fell back on this old skill for self-preservation and perhaps sanity, contemplating individuals and images I held dear. The memories instilled an element of hope and fighting spirit in me. I let them wash through. The images returned in vivid detail; even the simple events in daily life—having coffee on our veranda or gathering around my mother's table—were now precious to me. I hoped my remembrances would somehow escape the murk and desolation of Luka and reach those I loved. I wanted them to know my inner devotions.

I considered my wife Jasminka and our ten good years together. She'd been proud of me, and happy with her work, friendships, and family relationships. Our relationship deepened with the arrival of Adna. Being a father had already provided me immeasurable satisfaction.

Today's news of the blacklist, combined with my experience during the past five weeks, made me question, *Will I ever see them again?*

14

NO ESCAPE

The next day, my third at Luka, brought a new challenge. Our food was heavily salted and the doors to the warehouse were locked. Trips to the restroom and the water fountains were prohibited. Our jailers were messing with us, letting us know how vulnerable and inconsequential we were.

The following morning, when the warehouse was unlocked, every one of us queued up for the chance to visit the restrooms and to relieve our thirst. I have never appreciated water—life's essence—as much as I did that morning.

I had selected my sleeping space because of its proximity to the sliding door with its openings. They provided a very limited view, primarily sky, to the world outside Luka. Since my imprisonment, the weather had been good, the sky blue and relatively cloud-free. When the breeze was right, from the southeast, the vents allowed fresh air in. At those times I sat close, drinking in the freshness, clearing Luka's pollution and corruption from my lungs. I imagined that the breeze started in Bosnia's high mountains, and had been filtered by mountain snows and forests. When the fresh air came, my hopes rose. Its arrival meant there was something decent and pure out there, occasionally making its way to us, letting us know of its continued existence.

A couple of hours later, as we fell into line for breakfast, a man gave me a nudge, then introduced himself. He said, "I'm the father of the boy you rescued from the Brka River."

I tried to recall that day. I'd been walking to the boathouse from the downtown area. Approaching the Brka, I saw several pedestrians on the bridge in a panic, pointing down toward the river. Running toward them I spied a boy trapped in an eddy coming off a bridge support. It was springtime and the river flowed hard with winter runoff. The boy bobbed in the swirling waters, twenty meters from shore, his neck elongated, stretching for height. I hopped the bridge parapet, and slid down the bank. Jumping into the river upstream of the boy, I had to fight its hydraulics to reach the eddy. As I approached the boy, our eyes met. He was wide-eyed. He reached out toward me, speechless, then dipped below the water surface, out of sight. I felt panic, *Am I going to lose him?* Something brushed my pant leg. Reaching down, I felt an arm, pulling it to the surface. When the boy emerged, he began clawing at me—powerfully—seeking support. I thought, *This won't work.* Turning the boy and enveloping him from behind, I said, "Calm down. I've got you. It's going to be all right. Grab onto my shoulders, and I'll swim us to shore." He complied. When we approached the riverbank, someone reached down, pulling us from the water.

After several minutes, the boy recovered. A woman said, "I know his family. I can take him home."

I asked, "Are you good to go?" He nodded yes.

"Good. The next time we swim together, let's wait until the water is warmer!" We parted smiling.

Until his father mentioned it, I hadn't thought about the event for years.

I now thought, *We are all drowning here. The world doesn't know. There is no one on the riverbank to help.*

The man said, "My son is now grown. He has given me two grandchildren."

"That sounds like a blessing. I hope we are both soon back with our families."

Later that day, in the early afternoon, I received permission to use the restroom. Inside that building I encountered two women. I knew one well. Her name was Ružica—the girlfriend of one of my friends.

"How are you doing, Isak?"

Knowing that my face was puffed, bloody, and bruised, I responded, "As you can see. I'm sorry to see you here, Ružica. Where are you sleeping?"

"Here in the offices."

"I wish I could talk more. The guards only give us three minutes. I've been gone too long from the warehouse and had better get back. I hope you remain safe."

She touched my shoulder.

Two hours later she entered the warehouse, scanning the room, accompanied by a soldier. Seeing me, she walked over.

"Come with me, Isak. Don't be afraid."

She introduced me to the Serb soldier, saying, "He is my friend. He wants you to clean his rifle."

"Yes, I can do that."

When we entered the office area, the soldier directed me toward a bench, giving me an unloaded rifle with some cleaning patches and gun solvent. The soldier took a seat in an adjoining room. Disassembling the rifle and scanning the barrel, I saw it was dirty. I wondered, *Was it used here—against prisoners?*

Ružica said, "Let me get coffee."

When she returned with two cups, we fell into guarded conversation.

When sure that no one could overhear, I asked, "Are you being treated decently?"

"Well ... I please them."

"Are there other women here in your situation?"

"The number varies, sometimes as many as a dozen, currently eight. We have several Catholic nuns now."

I asked about her boyfriend, learning he had left Brčko to fight in the resistance. When I finished with the rifle, I told her, "It has been good to talk with a friend. I hope we find some way out of this mess. You will be in my thoughts."

As I lay awake that night, I assessed the warehouse, considering escape. The sills of the windows on the wall opposite my sleeping area were eleven feet above the floor. The windows were gone; their glass had blown out with the bridge explosions. Several pipes draining the roof ran down the interior walls. Climbing up a pipe, I could reach a window. The window openings were large—a man could crouch on the sill. I was confident I could lower myself down the outside wall and absorb the four-foot fall. From there it was fifty meters across railroad tracks to the riverbank. I had heard that two guards were stationed outside. In the dark, I thought there was a fighting chance of reaching the river. Once in the water, with its current, the cover of darkness, and my ability to swim underwater, I thought my chances of success would improve.

Hearing that I was on a blacklist and a priority target stimulated me to make an attempt. One consideration held me back: I had convinced my father and brothers to stay in Brčko. Should I escape, the authorities would look for me at my parent's home. Knowing nothing of my whereabouts, my relatives would be tortured and perhaps killed. In that aftermath there would be no real life or freedom. I decided to stay put and find out what Luka had in store for me.

13

MEN WITH NO EYES

The next morning, someone new entered the warehouse. Dressed in a police uniform and Ray-Bans, he carried a police baton on one hip and a pistol on the other. A black balaclava was folded into a hat atop his head. As he strolled through the warehouse, prisoners backed away in fear. I thought, *This guy is bad news.* His appearance and demeanor reminded me of the "man with no eyes" in the movie

Cool Hand Luke. He scanned the room. Spotting me to his right, he walked over.

"How are you doing, neighbor?"

Not sure who addressed me, I asked, "Is it you, Ranko?"

The man lifted his shades so I could see his brown eyes. It was Ranko Češić, who lived in an apartment at the other end of my building. He and his younger brother lived with their mother. A six-footer with broad shoulders and an oval face, Ranko was seven years younger than me. Our relationship had been cordial but perfunctory—hello-neighbor-how-is-it-going interactions. I knew that he had been a juvenile delinquent and had a reputation as the sort who would attack the weak and avoid the strong.

Ranko got down to business asking, "Isak, how has it been going for you here?"

"Good so far."

"Well, unfortunately, I have received many complaints from the people who worked with you at Elektrodistribucija. They say you are a troublemaker, someone who doesn't like Serbs. Is that true, do you have something against Serbs?"

"No. Absolutely not."

"But they heard you talking to your wife. Saying harsh things."

"Ranko, she wanted to come back—with the baby. I told her not to. I can assure you, I didn't do anything, and don't think that way."

He nodded slightly. "Since we are neighbors, and I haven't seen you cause trouble, I'll let it go this time." He then left me to start in with another prisoner.

The next day Ranko entered the warehouse to assemble a prisoner work detail—about a dozen men altogether—for the police station. He said, "You've got a lot of muscle. You go too."

At the station, I and two others received an assignment to clean the third floor. Climbing the stairs to our assignment, we found broken glass everywhere. After twenty minutes, we heard a commotion in the front of the building and looked out an open window to see what was going on. I saw a police officer shoot a civilian in the chest. This prompted a second civilian to turn and run away. That man was shot in the leg. After he went down, the policeman dispatched him with a bullet to the back of the head. From my vantage point, I could look across the pedestrian mall to the apartment where Mira and I found refuge on May 6. Today's event summoned that experience. I again overlooked a killing field.

Several minutes later, angry voices resounded from the back of the building. Crossing the room and looking down through a large window, I could see that two men cleaning the parking lot had been cornered, pinned against the lot's iron gate. The trapped men were then shot. The shooter's voice erupted in triumph. Viewing this savagery, I felt treed, fearing what would happen next. Terrorized, one of the men with me soiled his pants. Minutes later we heard someone downstairs bellow, "Where are the other Turks? I'm going to kill them all."

We were in a panic, looking about desperately for a hiding place or an escape route, finding none. Just then a local Serb policeman named Boro Kaurinović appeared. Saying nothing, he motioned us toward an adjacent office, unlocking the door, then locking it behind us. We found a closet, entered it, and closed the door, hoping to be forgotten. We waited, jammed together in the dark. It was hot and hard to breathe. It felt like a casket. I took slow breaths to calm myself. Time passed slowly. After thirty minutes, we heard the office door unlock. We listened silently, uncertain who was there. It was Boro.

"Come out. There is a truck downstairs for you. It will take you back to Luka."

We stepped out and returned to the prison. Boro had saved us.

Back at Luka the guards ran the spectrum: some were decent, while others were sadistic. That night six of the latter burst into the warehouse at one a.m., carrying long flashlights. They struck us with the lights while yelling, "All prisoners get up. You are going to sing Serb songs. You will sing to Serb glory. Sing them loudly, as loud as you can."

We sang for forty minutes. Those deemed not singing loud enough were beaten. I could not tell who beat me, as the light shone brightly in my face. I didn't get hurt too badly and felt lucky. I had sung with fervor.

After our tormentors departed, I remained wide awake. Wakefulness had been my normal state since arriving at Luka. While I figured that I occasionally nodded off, I had no recollection of real sleep. I felt continually anxious, fearful, and on guard. There was great tension in my mind and body. The days and nights ran together. Luka was a busy place that kept long and irregular hours. A steady stream of prisoners left the warehouse for interrogations, returning worse for wear. Prisoners were released and replaced by new arrivals. Each day produced new and unanticipated forms of brutality. In me, the bizarre events and dangers had combined to create a deep, foreboding sense of stress and uncertainty. The effect was intentional; it was also universal. I could see worry and despair writ large on the faces of my fellow inmates. Watching one prisoner kneel and flog himself for hours with his belt, I knew that some of us had already been badly broken.

During the times when I was being beaten or directly threatened, I felt almost out of my body, with a second stream of experience occurring. In my mind's eye, things happened and events unfolded, but I was also an outside observer, assessing what occurred while trying to evaluate my actions and responses. I used to experience something similar when competing. I could place myself outside the boat, observe what was occurring, and make adjustments. I was seldom overwhelmed when competing. What occurred now was different. I was having difficulty coping with all that was happening. It was so sinister. I felt that I must step outside it and get some distance, a different perspective, if I was going to survive.

Today's events increased that feeling. After seeing the murders at the police station, and experiencing my own fear, I was greatly discouraged. I could not understand why this obscenity was happening.

——— 16 ———

THEATRICS FOR THE DAMNED

The next morning, standing in the queue for the restroom, I overheard a news report on the guards' FM radio. The news was from Belgrade. It announced that the United States had proposed United Nations sanctions against Serbia for its role in promoting the Bosnian War. While the report denounced the United States, for me it struck a chord. I thought, *The United States is the one country with the power to bring the war to an end. Sanctions mean they are starting to get involved.*

My stomach had been bothering me. I regularly doubled over with cramps and diarrhea. En route to the latrine, I was stopped by Kosta, who asked, "Isak, are you having stomach problems?"

"Yes."

"I think there may be a medicine that will help you."

Two hours later I was called to Kosta's office. He sat at his desk. At six-foot-two, he was a tall but not physically imposing man who favored his left leg with a limp. Kosta had a large head, attractive appearance, and dark hair. His blue eyes did not have the addled, likely drug-induced, look evident in the gazes of his colleagues, Ranko Češić and Goran Jelisić.

"Isak, sit down. Since your stomach is bothering you, I've got a proposition for you. For as many names of Muslim extremists that you give me, I will give you the same number of pills to help your stomach."

I didn't like the proposition, but weighed the importance of seeming to be cooperative. I decided I should.

"That sounds fair." As I said this I thought, *Now I have to come up with a list of people beyond Kosta's reach.*

To satisfy Kosta, I wrote down the names of soccer players that played outside the country, along with the names of SDA executive committee members who had already left for Croatia. When I finished the list, Kosta asked me to sign it. In exchange for the list I received eight pills. After several hours, I could feel that the medicine helped.

Later that day I witnessed Kosta's half-sister Monika in action. Prisoners referred to her as the "female monster." She was an attractive young woman, perhaps seventeen or eighteen years old. She looked too young and innocent to be a monster. Her mother, the brothel keeper, had established a temporary brothel for paramilitary soldiers at the nearby Westphalia Café. In reality, it was a rape camp. The Muslim and Croat women incarcerated there were subjected to the unspeakable.

Monika entered the warehouse in midafternoon. She was accompanied by Kosta and Goran Jelisić. The twenty-four-year-old Jelisić was the killer I had heard about from my coworkers at EDB. He and Monika were reportedly lovers.

Monika strode around the warehouse, clutching something in each hand. In her left she held a large, glass Coke bottle; her right gripped a pistol. The bottle was half filled with what was reported to be a foul-smelling liquid. Prisoners said it smelled like muriatic acid.

Monika searched for Admir Didić. Admir slept on the wall opposite me. A boy of eighteen, he had been captured while working as a courier for the Bosniak resistance. He had been at Luka for two weeks. Admir was beaten more than any other prisoner, several times daily. His face was now virtually unrecognizable. He had lost half a dozen teeth. He kept them in a kerchief in his pants pocket. When Monika walked over to him, Admir seemed dazed and unaware of her presence.

"Didić, are you thirsty?"

I did not hear Admir's response. Monika grew agitated, pouring the contents of the Coke bottle on Admir's head, which was covered with open sores. He cried out in pain. His cries seemed to enrage her. She raised the Coke bottle before smashing it down on his head, shattering the bottle. Admir crumpled, unconscious.

Ćasim Suocović, a Brčko postman, and his teenage son occupied the bed spaces next to Admir. Both had slunk back in their spaces during the attack. Monika took note of this. When finished with Admir, she stepped toward them. She pulled up her skirt in front of Ćasim, exposing herself as she declared, "I know you Muslims like these things."

The postman averted his gaze, prompting Monika to drive the pistol down on his head. His son cried out in protest. The activity seemed to stimulate Jelisić, who put on his own show. "Fuck all you balijas. I've killed ninety-eight people. I want to kill ninety-eight more." He stomped about, kicking prisoners and menacing them with his firearm.

Seeing that things threatened to get out of hand, Kosta tried to calm Jelisić down. He had a positive effect, as the trio departed shortly thereafter. The incident made me wonder, *Did they sit in Kosta's office planning this depraved theater? How much more of this can I witness before I snap?*

17

ONE ON ONE WITH JELISIĆ

Several hours after Monika's unnerving performance, I encountered Osman Vatić in the restroom. Osman was one of Brčko's leading citizens, a lawyer considered among the best in northern Bosnia. He was being held in the administrative offices. I knew him well from the SDA. A wealthy man, he had made a contribution of fifty thousand deutsche marks to the Brčko branch of the party.

When a law student in Sarajevo, Osman stumbled attempting to board a moving train. Both of his lower legs were crushed. They had to be amputated below the knee. Fitted with prosthetic legs, Osman got around on crutches. A gifted athlete, he turned to marathon swimming after his injury, becoming national champion.

I knew him to be a virile, barrel-chested man. Now, badly bruised, he appeared broken and diminished. He hobbled toward me on his crutches asking, "Do you know me?"

"Yes, of course Osman."

"Two weeks ago, when your father was here, the guards asked if he knew me. He said he didn't."

I thought, *That sounds like the Bible and Peter denying he knew Jesus*, before saying, "I think we are on a blacklist. People are afraid to acknowledge us." Osman nodded in agreement. As we parted he said, "I hope we someday see each other on the outside."

That night I congregated with a half-dozen others along the wall closest to the river. We conversed in whispers. Men opened up a bit on moonless nights, when the guards had gone and the speaker could not be seen. The afternoon's events troubled people. Several needed to express themselves.

A person could learn a lot during these gatherings. A large stain darkened the floor beside my sleeping space. I assumed it was an old oil spill. This night I learned about the spill, which occurred two days before my arrival. On that day prisoners were told, "No walking for twenty-four hours." They were to confine themselves to their spaces and remain absolutely quiet. Late that afternoon one of the prisoners broke down. He got up and starting pacing around. During his march he yelled out, "Fuck them. I am going to walk."

Moments later a guard burst into the room carrying an AK-47. The walker had sat down. The guard went from inmate to inmate pointing his rifle at each and demanding, "Did you walk?"

He came to a frightened old man who said, "I didn't walk, but he did," pointing at the defiant one. The guard strode toward the walker asking, "Is that true?" He waited for a response. Receiving none, he shot the man from a distance of ten feet, then said, "Didn't I tell you Muslim bastards there would be no walking today? Let's see which one of you decides to walk after this."

I now understood the dark spot on the floor was no oil stain at all. After hearing the fate of the man who previously occupied my resting place, I again felt the hopelessness intrude. It started in my gut and drifted upward. The feeling had grown stronger with each return. It was now quite powerful. I told myself, *Don't give in to it*, but the battle was getting difficult. My confidence about being freed from Luka, never high, was at low ebb.

The next day started out uneventfully, a warm, calm day in June. Walking to the latrine early that morning, something felt odd. I tried to put my finger on it, deciding it was the eerie quiet. Normally on a beautiful summer day one would hear birds chirping and sounds of the city awakening. Those sounds were now absent, as if hushed by a perilous power. In the alternate reality in which I now lived, the background noise and comforting hum of the universe seemed to have vanished.

The morning proceeded without incident, although I thought I heard some people being dropped off outside the warehouse. About two in the afternoon I heard shouts coming from the office area. "Come on! Move! Get outside!"

I peered out through the vent in the sliding door. It provided a narrow window on the outside world, but a good vantage of the building directly opposite me. I saw four civilians walk out of the office building. My neighbor, Ranko Češić, prodded them forward. I also saw two policemen leaning against the office wall, observing. Ranko walked up to the civilians. They stood in the roadway six meters from me. He shot two of the men in the back with a Scorpion automatic pistol. The two men fell lifeless, followed ten seconds later by the two others. In all I heard six shots fired. I had witnessed my neighbor kill, and in cold blood. For years, a killer in waiting had lived five doors down in my apartment building. Once again, this was something I would not have believed possible. The violence prompted a commotion in the warehouse. It quickly died away, replaced by the smell and silence of fear. I remained highly agitated. That flame slowly receded, replaced by the dull numbness. As it came on, my mind drifted. I did not hear things or remember what happened next. The daze came of its own accord. I no longer tried to control it.

My trance was interrupted as dusk descended. Kosta came into the warehouse, calling for me. I wondered, *What does he want me for?* I got my answer as we exited the building.

"Motherfucker, why did you play smartass here? The names you gave me were worthless."

I tried to mollify him saying, "Those were the only people I knew. I don't know their whereabouts."

When we entered Kosta's office, the lights were off and it was difficult to see into the room's corners. Kosta said, "Sit in that chair and do as you are told," pointing to a chair in the middle of the office. He then instructed a guard to handcuff my wrists to the bottom rung of the chair. Looking up from the hunched forward position, I felt completely defenseless. This made me angry. I could feel a rage gathering. Now hyperaware, I saw someone standing in the shadows, his back turned to me. He appeared to be staring out the window. As the individual turned, I recognized him. It was Goran Jelisić. Jelisić stood six feet tall. He had jet black hair and a nose that crooked to the right and caused his left eye to droop slightly. His thin lips curled into a mean-looking mouth. His build was slight and his hands small; he weighed perhaps a hundred and fifty pounds. He wore a cast on his right forearm. I had heard it protected an injury inflicted by a prisoner. The prisoner, enraged rather than cowed by Jelisić's mistreatment, had grabbed one of the instruments of torture, a hammer, and gotten in two blows before being shot dead.

Jelisić had a deranged stare. I decided that it would be dangerous to look at him directly or otherwise challenge him. He was reportedly a person who killed for the sheer pleasure of it. Rumors circulated that during the takeover of his hometown of Bijeljina he received instructions to "kill as many Muslims as possible."

From the desktop, he picked up an enormous Bowie knife in a scabbard. He pulled out the sixteen-inch knife blade, examining it. The blade had a thick spine. It looked stout enough to hack and tear.

"I originally planned to finish you with a bullet, but I have changed my mind. I intend to slice you up instead."

My thoughts raced to the story my coworker Midhat had told of the time that Jelisić had cut and terrorized Stjepan Glavočević so badly that he begged for a death sentence.

Throughout my incarceration, I had told myself that if I knew I was about to be slaughtered, I didn't want to go out meekly, like a sheep. Confronted now by Jelisić, and strapped down defenseless, I had no choice. I fought down a seething anger. I knew I must not show my thoughts.

Watching Češić, Repić, and Jelisić in the warehouse, I had been struck by their displays of aggression. They moved about stiffly, like silverback gorillas on a rampage. All three jailers seemed to lose themselves in their fury. This evening, however, Jelisić acted calm and calculating. He seemed more threatening this way.

"You think you are so smart. I have heard many stories about your arrogance. We are going to see how arrogant you are now."

I told myself not to disagree, protest, or challenge him. I could only wait it out. I could feel my heart racing and sweat pouring out. I could accept a bullet, but the thought of being dismembered alive was terrifying. I could neither fight nor flee. Straining against my bonds would only have encouraged Jelisić. I sat silently.

He bore in. "I'm going to start with your arms. Later I will take off your legs. Yes, we are going to butcher you." He walked toward me, then circled me once. Facing me again, three times he said, "You are a smartass, aren't you?" Each time he stuck me in the left shoulder. Each stick drew blood. The jabs hurt, but didn't yet feel crippling. I could only wait for what came next.

"Those tested my blade. It is very sharp, isn't it? I could cut your throat, but that would be too quick. I want you to suffer. Maybe I should start with your legs first, then your arms. Which is it? Legs or arms?"

My thoughts raced to Jasminka and my parents; I now knew what mattered most at my core.

Jelisić paused for a minute, twirling the big blade. He turned his back to me and said to Kosta, "I want to cut him deeply. Now. Can I?"

Kosta did not immediately respond. The delay was agonizing.

Finally, he said, "Let's wait. He is well known and someone important may want to protect him. We will wait a few more days. If no one orders his release, he will be yours. You will have your chance soon."

Kosta then turned to me. "The next time I call you for an interview, give me real names. You were lucky this time. Next time I will pay you back." He then ordered the guard to unlock the handcuffs and told me, "Leave, and keep your mouth shut."

The guard led me back to the warehouse. Once there, I lay down. Having just experienced Jelisić face-to-face, I knew Midhat's report of his cruelty was true. Lying there, I felt the shield of my adrenaline slowly drain away. As it did, a feeling of helplessness and hopelessness descended. Deflated, I stared blankly at the wall.

Later that night, when the guards were gone, my friend Meho approached saying, "Let's talk." We walked to the far wall. Two others joined us. Meho asked, "What happened when Kosta took you? You came back white in the face." I told them that Jelisić wanted to use his knife. One of the others said, "The word is that Jelisić loves to kill us Muslims, but the Croats even more. He went up to Vukovar and got involved in the war there. The Croats captured him. That bend in his nose is from where they broke it. Later they bound his legs and kept dropping him upside down into a well. He almost drowned. This is all payback. He got a taste for killing in Bijeljina and found out he liked it. When he gets the okay, none of us stands a chance. For your sake let's hope somebody wants you freed."

After the group broke up and we retired to our spaces, I felt somewhat better. There was some comfort in shared misery and their interest in my well-being. A couple of times during my imprisonment I had pondered prayer. Praying was something I had witnessed the times I'd been inside a mosque or a church with friends, but not something I had ever tried. Today's events told me that I would not be leaving Luka without help. They threatened to extinguish all hope and I wondered if prayer might help hold me up. That night I prayed for deliverance, both for myself and the other prisoners. Uncertain about whether to pray to a supreme being or instead to a change in the spirit of Bosnia's people, I did both. Perhaps it helped; for the first time since I landed in Luka I awoke the next morning knowing that I had actually slept.

18

SHAME

I felt subdued the next day. A JNA major dressed in camouflage, Vojkan Djurković, visited the prison that morning. He wanted to address us.

"All of you, gather around. For those of you who are new, I am the commander of Luka camp." Turning to two brothers who had been in the camp since the early days, he said, "You remember how things once were. It was madness. I restored order and saved people like you two. I am not a war criminal. I saved as many of you as possible. The interrogations now are different. Organized. It is going to be safer here from now on. It will not be what it used to be." He asked the brothers to attest to his statement, which they did.

About an hour after his departure, six paramilitaries swooped in. They began kicking us and hitting us with shovels. We covered up the best we could.

Later that day our guards brought us coffee and cigarettes. Games like this—the misdirection, the beatings and berating, the bad food and water, the radio that blasted Serbian music for hours on end, being deprived of the ability to clean oneself—all seemed intended to break our psyches.

That evening, the door to the warehouse was unlocked and pushed to the side. A car drove slowly inside. Its tires rolled by six feet from me. Jelisić and Češić walked beside the car, which came to a stop in the middle of the warehouse.

"Everybody up! Face me!" Češić commanded.

He walked to the front of the car, then announced, "We know you Muslims like to see naked women. We have a treat for you. Here is our present to you."

He pointed to the car, where a young Muslim woman had been duct-taped to the hood. I knew the woman—she was a nurse from Brčko. She had been stripped of her clothes. The two jailers continued the cruel charade, telling the driver to slowly drive the car through the room. During the slow promenade, the woman suffered in silence. As the car drove by, we inmates averted our eyes in shame. That was the point—to make us ashamed, to show we were impotent and unwilling to risk all to protect her. I think we were all conscience stricken.

Inside I raged. So much for the promises of Major Djurković and last night's prayers—the spirits of Jelisić and Češić were unmoved. There had been no reason to make the woman suffer like that. Whatever biochemistry causes memories to endure, I felt the scene sear into my marrow. The inability to act—my complete lack of power—fueled my anger and frustration.

19

A RIVER'S SECRETS

Early in the evening on June 5, I received permission to visit the restroom. Still bothered by intestinal distress, I had lost weight during my ten days of imprisonment. My pants hung loosely. My belt was tightened two notches to hold them up. Once inside the facility, I sensed someone lurking outside. Listening intently, I discerned a man's breathing. Concerned, I made no sound, hoping to outwait my pursuer. After several minutes he whispered, "I need to talk with you. Don't worry, I'm not here to harm you."

I stepped out, facing an officer from the Yugoslav People's Army. The second lieutenant, an ethnic Serb, had been present during my initial interrogation. He looked to be in his mid-twenties. He appeared to be someone with self-control, a normal person. During my interrogation, he had taken notes. I had a sense then that he had not been against me, unlike the two paramilitaries.

Now the man's eyes showed concern.

"It is important I speak with you. You are on a termination list and scheduled to be killed in three days. For you to survive, someone important from outside Brčko must intercede on your behalf. For God's sake man, I listened to your interrogation. I heard where your wife is. Is there a phone number in Belgrade where she is staying?"

Processing the message, I reached into my shirt pocket. It held a business card from my friend Mirko Nišović. After his Olympic success, Mirko had opened a riverside restaurant in Zemun, a suburban area on the outskirts of Belgrade, Serbia. The card was for his restaurant, and included a phone number. I passed it to the second lieutenant.

"My wife is staying with this man, Mirko Nišović. You may know of him. He is the Olympic champion."

"Yes, I have heard of Nišović. I'd like to keep the card so that I can call him."

"Yes, do. Thank you for taking an interest in me. Please ask Mirko to let my wife know that I am thinking of her."

Late that night, as I lay awake, I considered the fact that my life depended on a tattered card and a possibly sympathetic JNA soldier. I was now on death row, counting down the hours, desperate for a reprieve.

The next day, my attention was momentarily diverted by more of Luka's theater of the absurd. Two of the prisoners had been labeled "Muslim snipers" by the guards. The two men had lived near one another in the village of Kolabara. One man, nicknamed Jovo, was intellectually disabled; the other, named Blek, was also easily confused. When accused of being a sniper, Jovo would agree. Guards beat the two men regularly.

Jovo was a favorite target of Goran Jelisić, and in very bad shape. He normally had difficulty walking. With the beatings, his amble was now grotesque. His condition was further complicated by a compound fracture of his right arm that had gone untreated. His nose was split open to the bone—maggots had infiltrated the wound.

Jovo slept ten feet from me. He liked to smoke, and regularly asked me to get cigarettes for him from other prisoners. I did so. Interacting with him, I could only wonder about the reasons able-bodied men pick on poor souls, treating them so savagely.

Word had traveled to the federal police in Serbia that two Muslim snipers had been captured in Brčko. At ten in the morning a blue Volkswagen Golf drove into the warehouse. The car doors featured the Serbian coat of arms and read "Ministry of Internal Affairs." Three men emerged from the car. One was a major in the JNA; the other two were policemen. Kosta entered the warehouse, introduced himself to the three men, and asked the reason for their visit.

"We are here for the Muslim snipers," said the major.

Registering surprise, Kosta pointed them in the direction of Jovo and Blek. When approached, Jovo tried to tell the major that he was a sniper, but couldn't pronounce the word correctly. The officer stared at him, incredulous. He turned toward Kosta, upbraiding him: "This is ridiculous. If all Muslim snipers were like this one, I would not have lost a single man in this war. This man needs medical help. Make sure he gets it."

With that, the men from the ministries departed. That afternoon a physician arrived to treat Jovo, Blek, and several others. For the first time, guards delivered fresh water to the warehouse. We no longer had to travel to the restroom to slake our thirst.

That afternoon I was assigned to a work detail along with three others. We went outside with three guards, marching to the back of the warehouse. Continuing down toward the river, we crossed railroad tracks that had several railcars parked on them. We followed a gravel path. Beside it were twenty or so bodies piled on top of each other. The sight took me aback. I felt the strange numbness return. The corpses were all in civilian clothes. They seemed odd, their bodies and heads misshapen. I asked myself, *Are they real?*

Despite my daze, I noticed a strapping blond dressed in jeans and a distinctive yellow paddling shirt. The shirt was marked with a bullet hole in the center of the back near the shoulders, and a large bloodstain. Though I could not see the man's face, I felt a shock like an electric current course through me, then pure nausea.

My friend Elvedin was big and blond and wore a shirt like that. He also had a pregnant wife, a two-year-old son, and everything to live for. I thought, *Don't look again. Don't make sure. Knowing will be too painful.*

Interrupting my thoughts, a guard ordered, "Pair up, take a body, toss it into the river. Continue until all the bodies are gone." We had no choice. They had guns on us.

As I started the grim task, I remained in the dreamlike state. My head spun. When a partner and I picked up a body, it seemed different, as if it were oval and flattened. It felt like lead weight as we struggled down the path to the river's edge. After we threw it into the water, it sank. The second body did not. It rolled over. I thought I saw the man's eyes move, peering at me, into my soul. That took me somewhere very remote, an interior place I'd never been. I felt like I was drowning and wondered, *Will I come back up? Is there a life after something like this?*

While we performed our dreadful duty, the guards pulled back behind the railroad cars. The reason was soon apparent. Rifle shots rang out from the Croatian side of the river, the bullets ricocheting off the railroad cars. We were caught in the open. I knew we were easy targets and thought, *Stay low. Whoever is shooting from the Croatian side must be aiming over our heads.*

To make the situation worse, we could hear the guards arguing about whether to shoot us. One pointed his rifle at me, ordering, "Go back to the river!" I heard his rifle cock.

Just then another guard said, "Stop talking bullshit. Leave them alone." He won the day. We were allowed to retreat and to return to the warehouse. As we entered we were warned, "You had better keep quiet about what you did and what you saw."

That night I thought about the bodies, recalling an incident from my youth. A stretch of the river was closed when I was ten. There was little rainfall that summer, and the river level dropped so much that a sandbar emerged in the middle of the river. Several of my friends had swum out to the sand island, discovering several large bones there. The police and a dive team were called in to investigate. They eventually found the remains of several dozen bodies, including skulls with helmets attached. These were German soldiers who had died during their army's retreat from Bosnia near the end of the Second World War. The Sava River Bridge had been mined to cover the retreat, and these soldiers did not make it across in time. Their remains migrated with the river bottom, propelled by the Sava's eternal current. More than two decades later they had moved downstream two kilometers. Also found were the bones of unknown victims from that era, thought to be remnants of Brčko's Jewish population.

I went down to the river with my father to watch the police at work. I returned several times on my own to observe. After a week, the group watching along the riverbank included German families. These people made an impression. They seemed desperate to learn about long lost family members, and still grieved, even after the passage of twenty years.

It would now be Bosnia's fate to grieve. I wondered, *Will the bones of those we just buried turn up on a sandbar twenty years from now?* I felt anger that the river and Brčko's people were being violated, and by individuals attempting to hide evidence of their crimes.

I also thought about my friend Elvedin, hoping that he was not one of the war's victims. A memory told me otherwise. Several years before, two men had jumped him down by the boathouse. Club members who came upon the scene later told me the story. The assailants had Elvedin down, but had not bargained on his great strength. He threw them off and beat them into submission. One witness told me, "He fought like a lion. You should have seen it, Isak. He was so strong. It would have taken four men to subdue him."

One of Elvedin's attackers that day was Ranko Češić. He now ran amok at Luka.

20

RELEASE

June 7, 11:30 a.m.

Hearing car tires on the roadway, I watched a Mitsubishi Pajero jeep drive up to the offices. Two Red Beret paramilitaries got out and entered the office building. One Red Beret was not familiar to me. The other had been to Luka before and had a reputation for torturing. After ten minutes, the two Red Berets emerged, accompanied by Kosta. The three men entered the warehouse.

The unfamiliar soldier announced, "I'm here for Isak Gaši. Please come forward."

I stood up, cautiously.

"Isak, don't be afraid. You can relax. We are friends. Colleagues. It's okay," said Kosta.

As I walked toward the trio, the whole room listened.

"Isak, please step closer. I am Rade Božić," said the Red Beret soldier.

I shook Božić's hand, noting the captain's insignia on his paramilitary uniform. He also wore the white belt of a JNA military policeman. From his bearing and clothing, I could tell he was a professional soldier.

"I am pleased to meet you and convey greetings from your wife."

"My wife? Have you been in Belgrade? Did you see her?"

"Unfortunately, no, but some friends were with her. They instructed me to personally pass along her greetings to you."

I thanked him, but remained thoroughly perplexed. Did the Red Berets' presence represent an opening, a glimmer that might be parlayed into my release, or did the reference to Jasminka mean that she and Adna were in danger?

"Captain, we can go to my office where you two can get better acquainted over coffee," said Kosta.

"Yes, that's a good idea. I'd like that."

I followed the party out of the warehouse and across the roadway. At his office, the two Red Berets and I took the available chairs while Kosta stepped out. Božić started in saying, "I have heard good reports about you."

He faced and addressed me, while his associate sat off to the side. As he spoke, I tried to size him up. He did the same with me. Božić looked fit, in fighting trim. His face was symmetrical and well-proportioned. Creases surrounded his almond-shaped eyes. His eyes looked luminous, like those of a snake. As they focused on me, the skin between his eyebrows formed a triangle.

"The reports are accurate, but nevertheless, I am here."

"Tell me about yourself and your life here in Brčko."

I gave him a summary, concluding, "I experienced a good life here. A normal life."

Seeing me from the hallway, two half-drunk soldiers barged into the office demanding to know what was going on. I could tell that Božić was someone significant by the way the men backed away once they realized the Red Beret, rather than Kosta, occupied the office.

For the next twenty minutes Božić posed general background questions regarding my work, schooling, and military experience. He was a skilled and opaque questioner, giving away nothing regarding the reasons for his visit. I was forthright but careful with my responses.

Finally, demonstrating that he had some background information, Rade asked about my canoeing and whether I had friends in Belgrade. I told him about Mirko and our years of training and racing together. I also said, "There are other friends there from my university days."

The promised coffee was delayed. I grew nervous about being away from the warehouse for so long, knowing the other prisoners would have suspicions that some in their number were being implicated.

"It has been good to talk with you, captain. Since I'm not that keen for coffee this morning, is it permissible for me to return to the warehouse?"

"Yes, that's fine. You seem a good man. Perhaps we'll have reason for a coffee some other day."

"I'd appreciate that."

As I got up to depart, Božić asked, "Is there anything I can do for you?"

"I'd like to leave Luka. If we are friends and colleagues as Kosta said, can we do that?"

"I will check into whether that is possible."

I thanked him. We shook hands.

When I returned to the warehouse, a dozen prisoners huddled around, asking if the Red Beret was a sports friend. One suggested that the reference to Jasminka was significant. Several others concurred, predicting that I would be freed. Five minutes later the jeep drove off.

I didn't know what to make of the visit. I'd been tested, but for what? With the jeep and its occupants gone, I wondered, *Did I pass, or fail?* At that juncture, it was the question of my lifetime.

At two in the afternoon the vehicle returned with Rade Božić and a different Red Beret. Kosta stepped out of the office building to meet them, and, after a brief conversation, entered the warehouse saying, "Isak, come forward."

He then declared, "Isak, the time has come for you to paddle again for Yugoslavia." He handed me my ID along with a document with the camp commander seal that said that I had been detained and subsequently released. As we walked outside to where Rade

Božić waited, I fought down a swelling sense of exhilaration, telling myself, *You aren't in the clear yet.*

"Do you have any possessions to gather?" asked Božić.

"No, but if it's permissible, I would like to tell the men inside goodbye." The soldier's face registered surprise, but he gave his approval.

I went back inside. For the next five minutes, I exchanged goodbyes with my comrades. They expressed happiness for me. Many came with requests, asking me to remember them to their families. These were profoundly affecting, becoming another one of my indelible Luka memories. As much as I detested the place and was grateful for the chance to leave, I also felt bonded to these men. I walked away hearing, "Best wishes" and "May Allah be with you, Isak."

Outside, Rade asked for directions to my apartment.

"You can drive to the JNA barracks. Mine is the apartment building next door." I felt both enlivened and confused. While confident we were leaving, I didn't know where to or why. Leaving could mean many things, not all positive. My guard remained up.

Arriving at the apartment building, Rade said, "Go inside and pack for a long trip. We are going to follow you inside, not because we don't trust you, but so there are no problems with other tenants." One tenant, my friend Mira, was very pleased to see me. She flashed two thumbs up.

In the apartment I threw my passport and several changes of clothing into two gym bags. I felt filthy, but only had time for a quick wash. The face that stared back from the mirror was gaunt and haggard.

When I exited the apartment building, Mira rushed up extending a satchel. "So good to see you, Isak. This is for you. It has Jasminka's jewelry plus whatever money I could find in your apartment." Mira had gone into the apartment after my arrest to save what she could before looters arrived. "I'll call Jasminka and let her know you have been here."

Back in the jeep I asked, "Can we stop at Elektrodistribucija for a minute? I'd like to see my director and tell him goodbye." Rade agreed. I had an additional motive. I wanted my work colleagues to know that I rode with Rade in the event something happened.

At my workplace, I spoke briefly with director Ristić and a half-dozen of my coworkers. It was a connection restored, their smiles and well wishes something I would treasure. For some of us, it was our last time together.

From them I heard, "Isak, great to see you!"

"You were trim enough already. No need to have gone on a diet!"

"I saw your father and brothers last week. They're good."

As we departed, Rade said, "You have good and loyal friends back there." He then turned the jeep to the right and drove down the road that led to the mass grave. The route immediately concerned me, as the grave would be an easy place for an execution. The vehicle reached the site, but then continued on.

My relief evaporated five hundred meters later when the jeep turned into Brčko's customs zone. The customs zone, a fenced-in free-trade depot for imported goods, was located on the city's outskirts. The facility had been converted to a military encampment. I would be out of place here and wondered, *What's next?*

Sensing my unease, Rade said, "I need to check in here. This is my base, a place for all the soldiers who are not local." I could see soldiers in the uniforms of various paramilitary groups: White Eagles, Panthers, Četniks, Red Berets, and Arkan's Tigers, as well as those from the regular JNA, the Serbian Secret Service, and the JNA's Special Forces.

Rade parked the jeep in front of the customs building before stepping inside to place a call. I surveyed the base and saw that beyond a military encampment, the facility was also being used to bundle and ship a small mountain of durable goods and household possessions. The booty looked like war spoils. I suspected that the paramilitaries had been looting Brčko to enrich someone. While the soldiers' unit decals proclaimed wolves, panthers, eagles, and tigers, the animal image that flashed through my mind was the hyena. Looking back at the Pajero, I saw the luxury vehicle had Prijedor plates. It was definitely not military issue.

Rade returned several minutes later saying, "There are difficulties that require us to stay here tonight."

I felt my gut churn. I was behind enemy lines and didn't belong. My presence would inspire questions. I had no basis to trust Rade, yet knew that he was the only person here who might look out for me. The reasons for his involvement with me remained a mystery. I doubted he could shield me for long.

As we parked and unloaded for an overnight stay, a truck arrived and parked seventy meters away. A group of paramilitaries walked to the truck, huddling around. Two body bags were hoisted from the truck bed. The soldiers seemed upset. It appeared the dead were comrades. Several of the soldiers looked about—the look I'd seen at the substation when the policeman died. I felt sick with apprehension.

I said to Rade, "They may kill me here. Maybe you should take me back to Luka."

Rade did not answer. He appeared to be lost in thought. His silence seemed interminable.

Moments later, a soldier from the guardhouse hailed Rade. He took a call there. I stood outside—an isolated island in a Serbian sea.

From the guardhouse, Rade made a sign. He walked over and said, "Things are better. We are clear to leave now. We'll be heading to Belgrade. We'll be taking you to your wife."

I thought *Yes!* before saying "That's good. Excellent."

Rade dismissed the other Red Beret, and we drove off in the jeep. With the mystery of our destination revealed, I felt relief and an impatience to be reunited with my family. We were on the road to Bijeljina that I had traveled with Jasminka six weeks before. As we approached a checkpoint, Rade was recognized and waved through. Ten kilometers later he veered off the highway, taking a back road toward Ugljevik Township. Since this was not the road to Belgrade, I grew concerned, asking, "Is this our route?"

"Don't worry. I've got a job to do in Ugljevik."

Other than that, Rade had said nothing. To break the silence I asked, "How old are you, sir?"

"I am twenty-seven."

A few moments later he asked, "Isak, do you know the person responsible for your release?"

"I have no idea."

"Captain Dragan. Do you know who he is?"

"Yes, I do. He has been written about often in the papers."

"Well, the big boss himself ordered your release. He is waiting in Zvornik, and will accompany us to Belgrade. He's heard good things about you and wants to meet you."

"Outstanding. That sounds good. I'll have the chance to thank him."

I attempted to recollect all that I knew about Captain Dragan. One of the prisoners sent out on a Luka work detail had brought back a Serbian magazine with a feature on Dragan. I read the article. Dragan was born in Serbia but had been orphaned at a young age. His adoptive parents immigrated to Australia when he was fourteen. In Australia his name was changed to Daniel Snedden. He attended an Australian military academy, then served in the Australian army for several years after graduation. Following his army service, he hired himself out in Africa as a soldier of fortune and a military instructor. A proficient open-water sailor, after his time in Africa, he captained ocean-going vessels for wealthy clients.

During the buildup to the Croatian War, Dragan returned to the Balkans by sailing to Macedonia. Once in Serbia he established a base of operations, organizing his own paramilitary force. They were identifiable by their red berets. After his unit's formation and training, the Serb leadership in Croatia's Krajina region welcomed in his legion. As the situation in Croatia spiraled toward war, the Red Berets organized local militias and began to forcibly occupy territory. They soon became feared for their aggressive ethnic-cleansing campaign against Croats. The inroads made by Dragan's forces were celebrated in Serbia, where he was applauded as a folk hero; he was literally a comic-book figure. One of his important supporters was Serbia's Princess Linda Karađorđević. Dragan also burnished his image with his Captain Dragan Foundation. The foundation received acclaim in Serbia for the assistance it provided soldiers injured in the Croatian War. Goods pirated from Croatia financed the foundation. As we drove to meet him, Dragan rode a crest of popularity and public approval.

Rade told me that after our conversation in Kosta's office, he had gone to the police station to get their opinion of me. "The reports were favorable. A police inspector, Petar Gavrilović, told me, 'Isak is a good person who has no bias against the Serbian people and wouldn't have anything against Serbs in the future.' There was one person, Major Milisav Milutinović, who was totally against your release. You know that he wields a lot of influence in Brčko."

I knew Milutinović. The JNA reservist had been my eighth-grade history teacher. Later, in technical school, I took a civics course from him that was preparatory to mandatory military service. I liked the history class and got along well with my teacher. The JNA preparatory class had a module on marksmanship that ended with a citywide competition. I had one of the top scores, which brought enthusiastic praise from Mr. Milutinović.

Thinking hard about a reason for his objection to me, I vaguely remembered a family story from thirty years before, when my brother Ramiz and some friends had gotten into trouble at school and been thrashed by a teacher. Ramiz came home hurt. My father had gone to the school to confront the teacher who, I now remembered, was Milutinović. That showdown would have been epic, and no doubt influenced the major's thinking. Knowing my competitive nature and bloodline, Milutinović must have wanted me out of the way.

Rade continued. "There was an argument. The major fumed and became red in the face, but couldn't give examples of your wrongdoing. Nevertheless, he was adamant that a decision had been made and that your execution must go forward as scheduled. I placed a call to Captain Dragan. He overruled Milutinović and approved your release. Captain Dragan is your benefactor."

After entering Ugljevik, a town of twelve thousand inhabitants, Rade parked the jeep in front of a multistory glass building. He went to the back of the vehicle, pulled out a cardboard box, and carried it inside. I watched him ascend the stairs to the third floor, then ring the doorbell. A man answered the door, taking the box.

Meanwhile, paramilitaries walking down the street noticed me sitting alone in the passenger seat of the jeep. They stopped, brandished their rifles, and demanded, "Roll down your window."

"What are you doing in this vehicle?"

"I am with Rade."

"Rade who? We don't know any Rade. Are you ours? Why aren't you in uniform? Get out of the car."

I did so; hoping Rade would show up soon. As the soldiers frisked me for weapons, Rade exited the building and hailed the soldiers. After receiving his assurances, they moved on.

Back on the road, the discussion went deeper than it had at Luka. I sensed an element of genuine curiosity from Rade as he asked about my family and political views. I told him I had been happy to be a Yugoslav. As I opened up a bit, Rade reciprocated. He talked about his origins in the town of Karlovac in northern Croatia, as well as his JNA military service. He was now a military policeman living in Belgrade.

He then took me completely by surprise. He began talking about the bridges in Brčko, saying, "I am going to tell you something that few Serbs know. I was in charge of the operation to blow up the two bridges. The operation went wrong. We watched the bridge for a week. The Croats had been letting the first pedestrians cross every day exactly at five a.m., so we set the timers for much earlier."

The Red Berets had rolled up to the Brčko crossing-guard station at four fifteen a.m., balaclavas covering their faces. They quickly overpowered the police, disabled their communications, and set timers on charges that had been placed weeks before.

At the onset of the Croatian War, Croatian forces had damaged the roadway on the Croatian side to prevent the bridge from being used by JNA and paramilitary convoys. The bridge had been restricted to pedestrian use for months. Refugees arriving by bus had to disembark before crossing on foot. Every day pedestrians queued up on the Croatian side waiting for an early morning release. Border guards on the Croatian side released one hundred and fifty pedestrians at four forty-five that morning. Many approached the Bosnian side just as the charges detonated.

"Something went wrong with our timers. They were delayed. I can't believe the damn Croats let all those people go early. Once we realized what was going on, it was too late; there was nothing we could do. What happened is terrible."

Rade's declaration surprised me. It seemed confessional, that he was truly troubled. He continued, saying, "These are hard times for Muslims; your leaders have put you in a difficult place." I thought, but didn't say: *Bosnia's Muslims have long felt like Serbia's bastard children, treated as outsiders and unwanted until a need for our support arises.* I also thought back to the downtown scene that was the aftermath of the bridge's destruction, and about the young boy who had lain there, torn apart.

While I had a sense that Rade was being genuine and had a conscience, I was wary of the confession. I now possessed knowledge that implicated him and his superiors. As a professional soldier, he would follow orders. I wondered again about his commander, Captain Dragan: *What does he want with me? Will this strange trip really lead to reunion with Jasminka and Adna?*

— 21 —

MY DINNER WITH CAPTAIN DRAGAN

As we neared Zvornik, Rade said, "We are going to the Vidikovac Hotel. We will meet Captain Dragan there." I knew the place; it was famous for its view of the lake formed behind the hydroelectric dam. As we drove beside the lake's vivid blue-green water, I recalled the Drina River's many beauties. Now the Drina, like the Sava, also bore bodies—so many that they clogged the dam intakes. When we pulled up to the hotel, which served as the headquarters for another paramilitary group under Dragan's command, a group of soldiers gathered out front asked Rade, "Who is he? Is he a prisoner?"

"No. Isak is with us," he said.

As we climbed the steps to the hotel entrance, Captain Dragan emerged from the building—a short, trim, dapper man, dressed in civilian clothes. He had alert eyes. Seeing me with Rade, he gave me a quick appraisal. A once over. Something prompted him to smile. I thought, *Stay on guard.*

I had seen Dragan once before, when he, Arkan, and Šešelj visited Brčko prior to the war. At that time, the three paramilitary leaders had been assessing the tactical force needed to overrun my city.

Dragan walked down the stairs toward us, nodding to Rade before extending his hand to me and saying, "I have heard many good things about you." A journalist from *Illustrovana Politika* (*Politics Illustrated*) accompanied him. The journalist's presence reflected the public's interest in Dragan. A woman who worked for Dragan's foundation completed his entourage.

Our group climbed into the Pajero with Rade driving. I sat in the backseat between the journalist and the foundation secretary. At the border crossings between Bosnia and Serbia, the guards on both sides of the Drina recognized Dragan and waved the car through. On the Serbian side, soldiers asked to be photographed with him. Despite the journalist's cajoling, I stayed in the jeep, out of the picture.

After getting underway, we stopped at a roadside café in the town of Muzice. I was on my best behavior, observing and listening intently to avoid any misstatements. I traveled in the company of strangers who controlled my fate. Jasminka was now known to Dragan—and at potential risk. As we returned to the car after our break, Captain Dragan traded places with the journalist, sitting in the back on my right. Once underway he said, "Your wife impressed me. She is first league. She really supports you and made strong arguments for your release."

Not knowing the backstory, I said, "Yes, Jasminka speaks with passion. She is from a good family. I appreciate your kind words."

The foundation secretary then chimed in, saying, "Captain, I've never before heard you pay a woman such a high compliment."

"Well, you should have seen how she fought for her man!"

Dragan then addressed me in a low voice, almost whispering, "You saw what it was like at Luka. There a human head is worth no more than a head of cabbage. I am sure you understand, and can appreciate, how precious life is. Life in these times can be so precarious. You need to be very careful what you say and very careful what you do. You have much to live for. You have a family, and I will deliver you to them. No worries there. I do, however, have a favor to ask of you."

"What is that?"

"I need a report of what you saw and experienced at Luka. For instance, did you see any killing there?"

Sensing the question was a snare I said, "No."

"That is good. Good for you. When you get to Belgrade, I want you to rest and recover for a few days. Then, when you are stronger, I'd like you to put pen to a couple of pieces of paper and write down what you saw in Brčko from the 30th of April until today. Also let me know who arrested you, as well as what happened while you were at Luka. Did you witness killings? Was there torture? The reason for the report is I want to know and document what is going on in Brčko. I want to have more control over the situation there. So just do this for me. Just bring your handwritten document to my office. I will let my staff know you will be coming. They will be expecting you."

"Yes, I will write you a report in the next couple of days."

"Were you given any documents when you left Luka?"

I gave Dragan my ID and the document from Kosta that said I had been released into the custody of Rade. Dragan said, "I'll keep the release," then asked, "Where should we drive you in Belgrade?"

"To the Golden Paddle Restaurant in Zemun, if possible."

When we arrived at the restaurant, Mirko sat out front with several of his customers. He greeted us warmly, inviting us inside for drinks or dinner. At first Dragan demurred, but then agreed to stay on. It was the dinner hour and the restaurant was busy. As our group entered, several of the diners recognized Dragan. They began to applaud. Soon the entire restaurant followed suit. As we settled in, a member of Mirko's staff called Jasminka to let her know that we had arrived.

I felt a great sense of relief upon seeing Mirko. My friend was relaxed and in his element here. Having him nearby increased my confidence that I was truly free. The seeming normalcy of life in Belgrade also impressed me. Here were people out for a good meal on a nice evening. The fresh air wafting up from the Danube mixed with aromas from Mirko's kitchen. After the sights and smells of Luka, this was ambrosia.

Dragan liked the restaurant's atmosphere. He took Mirko up on his dinner offer. Mirko pulled out all the stops. At the table, Dragan and Rade sat on my left, with Mirko and the journalist across the table. The chair to my right awaited Jasminka's arrival. The journalist saw that he had the makings of an article that would add to Captain Dragan's luster. He questioned Mirko and me about our sports careers and friendship. I expressed my gratitude for Dragan's assistance.

Jasminka arrived as meals were being served. Seeing me, she flew across the restaurant and we embraced. Dragan roared his approval, "See what I mean! She is first league! See how happy she is to see her man!" To Jasminka he said, "Here is your man! I told you I would bring him to you!"

While the meal was fine—and necessary under the circumstances—I felt relieved to get to Mirko's home. I no longer had to tiptoe through a conversational minefield with dangerous strangers. On the way to Mirko's, Jasminka asked, "How are you physically—and emotionally? You have lost weight, there are bruises on your forehead and face, and there is a wound and caked blood behind your ear. You look very tired."

"I am tired, as weary as I have ever been. I need a bath, and a good night's sleep. Don't worry. They didn't demolish me. Our life together can go on as before. It is so good to be here with you. I can't wait to see Adna and how much she has changed."

Relaxing a little on Mirko's divan, a wave of warmth washed over me. I could barely believe my good fortune—the change that had occurred for me over the past six hours. I also felt a pang of guilt. There were others at Luka who experienced much worse than me, and who remained in its foul grip.

22
FRIENDS INDEED

While I'd been able to piece together some of the story behind my release, there was much I didn't know. I wanted to understand it better. I asked Jasminka and Mirko for the details.

Mirko said, "I received a phone call three days ago. The man on the phone said, 'The life of your friend Isak Gaši is in danger.' When I asked him to identify himself, he said, 'It doesn't matter. I am a Serb in Brčko. You need to believe what I am telling you. The situation is serious; his wife has forty-eight hours to accomplish something. After that he will be killed. The only person who can help him is Captain Dragan. You must get him involved.'"

Hearing this, I told Mirko, "I gave your business card to one of my interrogators, a young officer from Ugljevik. It must have been him that called. Was that the first time you heard I was in prison?"

Jasminka responded, "Mira called me here saying you had been arrested and then taken to Luka. Ever since, we've been trying to secure your release. Every agency I went to either said no, or sent me to another office and another dead end. After the man's call, we at least knew whom to contact. I had read about Captain Dragan in the newspaper. Mirko found the address for his foundation, and we drove there the next morning. The offices were in the Beograđanka, the big skyscraper. We checked in with building security and were escorted upstairs to the thirteenth floor. The receptionist there was not encouraging; she wouldn't tell us Captain Dragan's whereabouts or availability. A man in the office recognized Mirko. He told us to take a seat in the lobby, saying he would do some checking.

"The man came back fifteen minutes later and said, 'Captain Dragan is away in Bosnia, but he will return to this office tomorrow morning. That will be your best chance to catch him.'"

Mirko interjected, "I returned to work and closed the restaurant at two a.m. Four hours later, Jasminka woke me up. I tried to put her off."

"I wouldn't let him. I wanted to get to the foundation bright and early. We left after a quick breakfast, arriving at the office building before seven a.m. Once on the thirteenth floor, we waited. No one was at the front desk. Office workers had just started to arrive when I saw a man who looked like Dragan exit the elevator. He wore civilian clothes—a red topcoat. Four big men who looked like bodyguards accompanied him. I called out 'Captain Dragan' to get his attention, and rushed over to him. From his reputation, I expected him to be bigger. He wasn't much taller than me. I took his arm and began to explain. It was spontaneous. Dragan's bodyguards were about to react when he told them, 'It's okay.' He then turned to me and said, 'Slow down, I will listen to your request.' That's when Mirko introduced himself and vouched for us. I told Dragan that you were an innocent man who had been imprisoned at Luka, and that you were going to be killed in two days. I asked him for his help."

As Jasminka related this conversation, she grew animated. I could see she relived it. I also saw how our separation had affected her. As she spoke, her face and neck were uncharacteristically blotched and flushed. Her auburn-colored hair had begun to streak white, and she was thin from lost weight.

I asked, "What was Dragan's reaction?"

"He challenged me, asking what if you had killed, or there was good reason for your being in prison."

"What did you say to that?"

"If Isak has killed someone, and you have the evidence, then take him. But I know my husband. He wishes no one harm and is innocent."

Mirko added, "Dragan liked Jasminka's response. He invited us into his office and called for his secretary. He asked Jasminka to go over your story so the secretary could take it all down. He asked Jasminka to be very specific about your background and where you were imprisoned. After she finished he said, 'You are the first wife who has reached out to me. Because you are so passionate for your husband, I tend to believe you. I need to do some investigating. Please wait in the lobby while my staff attends to that.'

"An hour later, Dragan walked out to the lobby and told Jasminka he wanted to reunite the two of you. When Jasminka sounded disbelieving, Dragan reassured her and said he would bring you to Belgrade. After that, we thanked him and left the office.

"When we were on the elevator, another passenger overheard Jasminka tell me that Dragan's promise might have been made to make us go away. The man said he worked for Dragan and that he was a man of his word. He was certain that Dragan would deliver you."

All I could say to this was, "Wow, you two really did the job." I told them about my interview with Rade at Luka earlier that morning, and about my release and the drive to Belgrade. "It is like we swam in separate rivers and met where they came together."

Jasminka said, "I have never been so nervous as today. This afternoon I received a call from Mira. She said you had been to the apartment with two soldiers who seemed friendly toward you, and that you left with them carrying two packed bags."

The hour had grown late. Mirko begged off and headed to bed. When we were alone, I asked Jasminka, "How have you and Adna been faring?"

"The last six weeks have been terrible, really trying. I've been desperate for news from Brčko, worried sick about you and my parents. I've been on the phone with Mira every day. Mirko has been great, paying all the long-distance charges. The news has been so discouraging; every day Mira tells me of someone we know who has been killed. My anxiety was bad when Mira told me you were at Elektrodistribucija. I almost fainted when I heard you were at Luka. The worry since then has been 'round the clock. It is like nothing I have ever experienced. It is good I have had Adna to care for. It sometimes takes my mind away from what was happening to you and my parents."

This helped explain her physical changes. Hearing her story, and seeing the effect it was having, told me of my wife's resolve and love. For me, after Luka, this was a powerful antidote—her concern was a good medicine.

It made me think back to when I first met Jasminka in December 1982. That evening I was having coffee with a friend, Zvone, at the Premier restaurant. An attractive young woman arrived with friends. She worked with Zvone in the business offices of Bimal. When she stopped by our table, he made a show of announcing, "Isak, this is the girl for you!"

Introductions and a light-hearted exchange followed. Though Jasminka was the same age as I, we had attended different schools. She knew that my father and brother worked at Bimal and that I was an athlete. That fact didn't necessarily work in my favor. When I attempted to follow up on the introduction, she was busy. The pattern repeated several times, but I persisted. She eventually asked

Zvone for the straight story on me. He must have said something positive, because we started seeing each other.

We proved to be well suited. I found myself smitten early on. One evening, double dating with Zvone at a supper club, I was especially struck by Jasminka's spiritedness and by how attractive she was. She wore her hair short, unusual in Brčko at that time, but I was really taken in by her eyes. They sparkled but could turn serious in a flash. The next day Zvone asked, "How did it go? What do you think?"

"It was all good. You know, for a while there I felt like I was in the bar in the movie *Casablanca*, talking to Ingrid Bergman's character."

"Well we'll see if you fly off with the girl or get left on the runway."

After several months of work and training, meeting Jasminka downtown every evening, walking her back to her parents, and then hiking back across town to my own place, I told her, "This is too much. I am wearing out. Let's put an end to this dating and get married."

Jasminka agreed, and so we were. Perhaps auspiciously, spring 1983 arrived like a lion on our wedding day, dumping eight inches of snow. Despite the harsh weather, my friends Mirko Nišović and Matija Ljubek were in attendance with their wives.

Before we turned in that night at Mirko's, Jasminka let me know that Matija Ljubek had offered her fifty thousand deutsche marks if it would help win my freedom. I now knew. My wife and my friends had succeeded in saving me. Given the looming deadline, and the Damocles sword that had hovered above my head, a number of stars needed to align—and they had.

23

FILING A PARTIAL REPORT

Over the next three days I slept and took long walks along the Danube with my family, savoring both. After Luka, freedom felt strange. It was hard to fathom my good fortune. Much had changed for, and in, me during the past six weeks. My daughter Adna had also experienced changes. She had been crawling when I saw her last. She was now pulling herself up and taking first steps wherever she could find some support. Her smiles at the accomplishment matched my own.

I mulled over the account I would provide Captain Dragan. On June eleventh, Mirko and I drove to Dragan's office. I had written a three-page report. I knew—which Dragan's comments in the car confirmed—that it would be folly to highlight the murders I had seen. I limited myself to detailing some of the mistreatment I had experienced, as well as the midnight song sessions, the beatings with batons and brass fittings, and the broken bones and sad condition of Jovo, the Muslim reputed to be a sniper. My statement also included the mistreatment administered to Ibrahim Lević, the man who slept beside me at Luka.

Ibrahim was forty years old. He had worked as a Luka warehouseman for years. One afternoon a paramilitary interrogator from Bijeljina stormed into the warehouse saying he wanted Ibrahim. The paramilitary called himself "Enver the Četnik." He ordered Ibrahim to stand. He then grabbed him by the hair, forced him against the warehouse wall, pulled out a knife and carved a cross into his forehead.

"I am not baptizing you, just marking you so that others know." Ibrahim slumped to the ground, where Enver kicked him twice. The intersecting cuts bled profusely. Several other prisoners and I tore up cotton batting to wash out and bind the wound. It was more flesh wound than an assault meant to do grave damage. Ibrahim survived, but with a nasty scar.

Upon arriving at the foundation, we were ushered into Captain Dragan's office. Dragan read my document. When finished, he nodded approvingly saying, "You made a good effort. Excellent."

Dragan then called in his secretary, asking her to type the document. While she did this, we three conversed. Dragan turned the conversation to the war in Bosnia. While I said nothing, Dragan expounded. He had a lot to say and was highly critical of General Mladić, who led the Bosnian Serb army.

"Mladić is a dumbass. If he is not careful, he is going to get himself prosecuted for war crimes." He also criticized Mladić's generalship, saying, "He's a madman who doesn't understand military strategy. The shelling and siege of Sarajevo make no military sense. If it doesn't stop, he is going to provoke the European Union into a military response."

After thirty minutes Dragan's secretary returned with the typed report. Dragan placed a phone call, saying, "This is Marty. I have a report that will interest you. I will fax it. I'd like your immediate opinion of it."

During the interlude before the return call, we fell back into conversation. It was not serious—sports and the like. After fifteen minutes the reviewer called back. Dragan asked, "What did you think of the report?" After hanging up he said, "The report will suffice. It gives us a better picture of what is going on in Brčko. You are free to go. If you need help with documents or approvals while you are in Belgrade, my staff will help you."

Driving home, I thought about the report. It bothered me that while accurate in its examples, it was far short of complete. I knew a comprehensive report would accomplish nothing other than my return to prison or worse. I expected the report would be used for window dressing or to provide Dragan and his higher-ups with cover. Having recently seen the pride that paramilitaries like Mauzer and Jelisić displayed when proclaiming their actions, I knew Dragan could get a proper report from his men in Brčko whenever he wished.

Back at Mirko's, I got through to Ramiz by phone. The five men living at my father's place were low on supplies. They wanted to escape Brčko, but this had proved impossible. Ramiz told me my father had slept outside on the concrete patio when he heard I was imprisoned, feeling that doing so would connect him to what I experienced, helping him sense whether I was in mortal danger.

Hearing this moved me. I'd received a great gift, an affirmation of my father's love. I hoped a day would come when I could tell him in person what this meant to me. To Ramiz I said, "Tell the others I'm fine, and that I hope you all can leave soon. I'll get supplies to you through Mira. She will find a way."

As we closed Ramiz said, "Take your family and get out of Serbia as quickly as possible. You are not clear of danger there."

Events soon revealed he understood the situation—and me—better than I realized.

—24—

BELGRADE DAZE

During the weeks we were separated, Jasminka saw the hatred that non-Serbs could experience in Belgrade. Serbians were fighting, dying, and losing loved ones in Croatia and Bosnia. The local populace expressed anger, both in private conversation and in the media. Jasminka felt lucky to be under Mirko's protection, realizing he swam against the tide of public opinion sheltering her. To be less of a burden, we planned to rent an apartment from one of Mirko's cooks, who was leaving for Australia in September.

Two weeks after my release, Jasminka was visited by our downstairs apartment neighbor and benefactor, Vera. She'd come to Belgrade for a break from the conflict in Brčko. The two longtime friends went out. When Jasminka returned, I asked, "How are Danilo and Vera getting on?"

"Vera says it is hard. Much worse than she expected. Their restaurant is struggling. Business is way down, and supplies are in short supply and expensive. They don't have their old Croat and Bosniak customers, Serbs aren't eating out, and the paramilitaries demand meals and don't pay. It sounds like they spend their days seeking information about the war just as we do."

"Jasminka, you used the word 'expected.' Did Vera say she knew about the war before it started?"

"She did. When I asked her why she didn't let me know, she said, 'You would have told all your friends.' I told her most of them had been her friends too. It made me angry, but I didn't want to start an argument. I told her I appreciated what she did getting Adna and me out of Brčko, but that I've been worried sick about my parents and sister, that I don't know if they ever got out. She told me there was only so much she and Danilo could do—that helping us was risky. I let it drop, but it makes me crazy. How can good people just go along when others are in danger? Why do they obey someone like Karadžić—who has never done anything for them—when it harms people they know? It's like people just obey, or just look the other way."

"Well, I thought the same thing watching the police shoot innocent people in the street. They can't all be psychopaths. There must be something strange in human nature. We want to fit in, to be part of the group. We are afraid of being isolated. Maybe it's instinctual—we think we need the group for survival. Whatever the reason, it is a weakness that can be exploited by those in power."

Working in Mirko's restaurant, I had recently seen one of Serbia's power players. The restaurant was popular with athletes and politicians, particularly politicians associated with the Serb Radical party. The head of the party, Vojislav Šešelj, arrived one day with a group of his supporters. I waited on their table. After a few drinks, they grew open with their comments. Their discussion turned to the war in Bosnia. I was amazed by their brazen declarations. The group discussed their Četnik paramilitary force, the prison camps, and the tactics of ethnic cleansing. They were disdainful of Bosnia and cavalier about the deaths of civilians.

On another occasion, a kayaker came into the restaurant. He had been a member of the Yugoslav national team before Mirko and me. He was in his early forties, dressed in a camouflage uniform. After a few beers, Mirko began teasing him about the war in Croatia, where the soldier had seen action.

He corrected Mirko. "You don't know. It is serious business, cutting the throat of another. The first time was difficult, but after that you block it out and feel nothing."

The restaurant was located a city block from Belgrade's main Catholic church—the Franciscan Church. A week into my stay I thought, *The church will want to know about the priest and nuns in Brčko.* I walked to the cathedral, where a nun introduced me to a senior priest. I told him, "Brčko's parish priest and several nuns were imprisoned at Luka. They may still be there."

The priest responded, "I see. We have had no word from Brčko for weeks. Thank you—the information is helpful. It may help us secure their release."

A network of Brčko expatriates developed in Belgrade. Most were in mixed marriages and had an ethnic Serb connection. Hungry for news, we met in the lounge of the Hotel Moskva or in the restaurant at the bus station when the bus from Brčko arrived. We wanted to learn about our city and fellow citizens, retaining hope that the situation in Brčko would resolve. Every week Jasminka put together care packages, sending parcels to Mira, who delivered those intended for my father.

We received Belgrade IDs that brought city resident status and its associated benefits. A downside for me could have entailed being drafted into the JNA to fight in the Bosnian War. Press gangs of military recruiters rode Belgrade's public transportation looking for draft dodgers. While I was never drafted, I generally avoided the bus system.

Many Belgrade men served as weekend warriors, heading to the front on Friday afternoon and returning late Sunday night. As the war became entrenched, the number of Serbian casualties increased, especially once the Bosnian and Croatian armies gained weaponry and competence. These losses caused attitudes in Belgrade to harden even more.

Serbia's state-controlled media stoked popular anger with a relentless propaganda campaign. The message that was communicated:

"Remember 1389 and Kosovo Field. The Turks slaughtered us then and are trying to slaughter our brother Serbs now. Bosnia's Muslims and their SDA party are Islamic extremists. They started the war. Because of what happened before, and their plans now, we are justified in killing them. Seizing the initiative is good defense. We must push them out."

Having been an SDA insider, I knew the facts and the stunning inaccuracy of the news reports. I was amazed at how susceptible the citizens of Belgrade were to fear-mongering and calls to violent action. The barrage of misinformation fueled fear and hatred of Bosnian Muslims. Since we today, whether Bosnian or Serb, were descendants of the survivors of Kosovo Fields, our ancestors were the fortunate ones. How could something centuries old be justification for atrocities now? The attitudes were like those I experienced at Luka. Muslims were portrayed as a great danger, but also as sub-human—without rights—as a people of no consequence.

I asked myself, *Is there anything I can do?*

Late in June, sitting at a restaurant table with Mirko, someone approached me from behind, placing his hand on my shoulder. The man wore civilian clothes. It took me a moment to recognize Rade Božić.

"Good to see you again, Isak. You are looking much better. I'm here with a friend. I'd like you to meet Bojan Stojanović." Stojanović was a photographer who worked for Reuters. His presence with a Red Beret like Rade seemed odd, a tangled web. I asked myself, *What is going on here?*

We all shook hands and sat down together. It was the lunch hour, so we ordered meals. Rade stated the reason for the visit: "I'd like your help in identifying the sites where some pictures were taken." He opened a folder, taking out a dozen eight by ten photographs. "The pictures are horrible," he warned.

One series showed a bulldozer working the ground at the mass gravesite near my workplace. The second set featured Goran Jelisić dressed in a police uniform. Jelisić carried a Scorpion machine pistol equipped with a silencer. He stood outside the Brčko police station in the same area where I had seen paramilitaries and police gun down thirteen civilians on May 6. In the sequence of photos, he shot two civilians from behind. Subsequent photos showed their blood pooling on the city street. The men looked lifeless.

Stojanović said, "I took the pictures of the policeman and his victims. I came upon the scene by accident. I've taken so many pictures of the conflict in Bosnia, I can't remember where they all were taken."

Rade knew both sets of pictures came from Brčko. He and I drove by the mass gravesite on our way out of Brčko. Stojanović surely knew where he "accidentally" took pictures. I wondered, *What are these two up to? Checking to see if I'll spill the beans about Brčko?* I decided that their visit was a test.

"Well, the pictures might have come from Brčko, but I'm not sure. I can't recognize the places."

The two men stayed for an hour. Rade asked me many questions. Knowing he was military police and a skillful interrogator, my responses were upbeat and superficial. I did not want him deducing that I thought deeply about the war or harbored resentments. Between the disturbing photo images and the complicated conversation, I had little appetite. For appearances, I finished my meal. I felt relief when the two departed. We parted congenially. I hoped Rade thought me straightforward and uncomplicated, someone satisfied with my present status. I also hoped there would be no future meetings.

The pictures I was shown soon received worldwide publication. Those of Jelisić won Stojanović the World Press Photo of the year in the spot news category. The award included a ten thousand dollar prize. When first published, the photo captions contained outright lies: "Muslim Police Shooting Serb Refugees from Krajina in Brčko" and "Muslims in Brčko Burying their Bosnian Serb Victims."

The pictures actually showed Serbs killing and burying Croats and Muslims. I thought, *Serbia is an alternate reality—a place where up is down. How long will the truth stay buried?*

Three days later, on July 16, I received a call from Mira. There had been a roundup of all Muslim men under the age of sixty-five in my father's neighborhood. My brothers Ramiz and Mirsad and my nephew Faruk had been taken by bus to a prison near Bijeljina. My nephew Jasmin had also been arrested, but, because he was only sixteen, was released. My father had been spared; Jasmin was with him. Mira also told me that two of Brčko's prominent Muslim citizens, the surgeon Sakib Edhemović and the attorney Osman Vatić, had been killed. When we closed, I asked Mira to find out what she could about the prison near Bijeljina.

After hanging up the phone, I thought about the dangers my brothers and nephews were exposed to. The deaths of two of Brčko's leading citizens deepened my concerns. I recalled Dr. Edhemović and my auto accident a decade earlier. I arrived at the emergency room in shock. Dr. Edhemović was on duty and had taken charge, just as he had when I was an eight-year-old with a nicked artery. After I had stabilized, he assessed the damage to my left arm. X-rays showed it had broken in three places.

"For the sake of your sports career, we will try to avoid surgery. I'm going to set the breaks." The surgeon placed his hands on the injured area, closed his eyes, and assessed the fractures by feel, gently working the bones into position.

When satisfied that the fractures had set, he put my arm in a cast. At the elbow, he affixed a lead weight to provide traction. The bones healed well and without noticeable difference to my right arm, although I experienced nerve loss. I had no strength in my left hand. The local neurologist recommended neurosurgery in Belgrade. Dr. Edhemović urged me to hold off, predicting that paddling would be a form of rehab that would eventually restore full function. He had been right.

The sixty-eight-year-old Vienna-trained surgeon had brought the town nothing but excellence, and posed no threat. His crime was competence. The same was true for Osman, the attorney who had asked me at Luka, "Do you know me?"

The double amputee was no danger on the battlefield. When Bosnia emerged from its current torment, he would no doubt have been a potent witness and a truth teller. This, apparently, could not be tolerated.

The next day Mira called. She had many local connections. The prison my brothers had been taken to was located on a large agricultural complex three kilometers from the village of Batković. Having traveled through Batković several years before, I tried to recall its geography.

Armed with this information, I went to Captain Dragan's foundation, hoping to secure the release of my relatives. I was initially told, "We will look into the situation." On my third attempt to follow up, I was told, "There is nothing to do. Stop making claims regarding a prison that does not exist."

I felt powerless. Jasminka had also grown very frustrated with attitudes in Belgrade. After seeing automobiles from Brčko being auctioned in Belgrade's public market, she began carrying a small flask of gasoline in her purse. She said, "If I see our Fiat up for auction, or parked on a city street, I'm going to set it on fire."

Hearing this, I realized that a long stay in Belgrade would not be best for my partner, the budding anarchist—or me, for that matter.

We discussed leaving Serbia, hoping to find a place in Europe or North America where we could wait out the war. I wanted to do something useful, perhaps finding a situation where I could do some canoe coaching. Jasminka scheduled an appointment at the Canadian embassy, having heard they might accept immigrants. During her visit, she learned that the Canadians required sizeable financial resources and a Canadian relative or sponsor. Both provisions were beyond our reach. We knew that the U.S. was not taking Bosnian refugees. With those avenues closed, she asked, "What about your aunt, Mensura?"

Mensura, my mother's sister, lived in neighboring Macedonia. She had lived with my family before her marriage. I was a young boy then, and we were close. Over the years we had maintained a strong family bond. Still, I thought that there would be few opportunities for me in Macedonia; its economy was in recession. In addition, Macedonia had declared its independence from Serbia and Yugoslavia. There was potential for war with Serbia. To me it looked like leaping from a frying pan into a fire.

Seeking an alternative, I tried the passport route, as we lacked the documents that would have enabled travel to a Western country. I made an appointment at the Ministry of Internal Affairs, which controlled travel documents. Upon arriving, the front desk attendant asked for my ID, retaining it. I met with a passport official in his third-floor office. Our interaction was cordial until I was asked my nationality. I said, "Yugoslav," thinking that response was better than Bosnian Muslim or Bosnian Albanian. My answer flipped a switch with the official.

"Where is your Yugoslavia now? It has collapsed. This is Serbia, and you want Yugoslavia. There is no Yugoslavia. So now you come here wanting a Serbian document and the approval of the Serbian people. You won't receive one."

The man's words and attitude stung like the blows at Luka. The pressures that had built there, which I had successfully quelled, still smoldered down deep. They ignited. I fired back, "You don't know what you are talking about. I hope that Serbia experiences precisely what the rest of Yugoslavia has." The encounter ended with the two of us glaring at each other.

I had lost my cool, letting my emotions take charge. Dread soon displaced anger. I had let a Serb in authority glimpse my inner thoughts and feelings. I wondered if the official was provoked enough to call downstairs, telling the front desk to retain my ID. Approaching the security guard, my heart raced and my temples pounded. The next minute would be crucial. I would either be free to depart or would be called to account within the hostile fortress that was the Ministry of Internal Affairs. I was mightily relieved when the guard returned my ID.

Outside the building I paused, leaning against a tree. I began shaking. It was all I could do to control the tremors. When I finally calmed down, I told myself, *You need to keep it together. People are relying on you.*

—— 25 ——

PETITIONING THE UNITED STATES

"And speech is an act, and what an act. Had you stolen, hit anybody, or done any harm, they would probably have forgiven you. But you had to go and talk about things any sensible person stays quiet about. That is what they won't forgive." —Meša Selimović

In mid-June, a week after my release from Luka, the International Red Cross (IRC) issued a warning to Western governments that genocide might be taking place in Bosnia. IRC staff stationed in Belgrade worried that they would be imprisoned or killed as a consequence of the warning.

The alert added credence to rumors that thousands of Bosnian men had disappeared into grim prison camps. Serb authorities dismissed these reports as disinformation designed to trick Western states into intervening in an internal Bosnian affair.

Luka prison closed in early July; its inmates transferred to Batković. I learned from Mira that during Luka's final days, prisoners cleaned up evidence of the camp's existence. Bullet-scarred walls were patched and painted, bloodstains were hosed and scrubbed away, and the facility was returned to a warehouse function.

Reports of prison camps in Bosnia had not been corroborated, as reporters were denied access to alleged sites. There had been no definitive coverage in the world press. In mid-July, I watched a Serbian TV broadcast that "investigated" alleged mass killings in Brčko. The broadcast concluded that reports of killing were bogus. Later that month I read an article in the Belgrade daily newspaper, *Borba*, that said the International Red Cross had visited Luka in the company of Serbia's Minister of Information, Velibor Ostojić. The article went on to state that the Bosnian government had manufactured accounts of atrocity and that Luka was never a prison. While the false report sickened me, I was surprised by the intensity of Jasminka's reaction. She was incensed, and prepared to fight back.

At this time, the world's attention was on Barcelona and the upcoming Summer Olympics. On July 25, Belgrade TV broadcast the opening ceremonies. I couldn't help thinking about life's swift turns, and the fact that the ancient Greeks stopped their wars for the Olympic games.

While the press and world leaders extolled the Olympic ideal, Western governments turned a blind eye toward the situation in Bosnia. Not wishing to be drawn into a Balkan conflict, they stonewalled, saying they lacked information to confirm reports of war crimes.

The misinformation disturbed me, as did references to Bosnia as a "former republic" in Serbia's media. I wanted the world to know what was occurring in Bosnia. I faced the problem of living in the country perpetrating the war and its atrocities, but which strenuously denied both. I kept waiting for the news blockade to break so the world realized what was occurring. When it didn't, I wondered, *Should I come forward?*

I knew that individuals attempting to expose Serbia played an exceedingly dangerous game, particularly if they lived in Serbia and lacked travel documents and an escape route. I knew the safe choice for me, and for my family, was to lay low and stay invisible.

Borba was the one Belgrade paper that had a reputation for being semi-independent of state propaganda. One morning I picked up the phone and called. My heart pounded as I asked to speak to the editor—I knew I was edging toward a slick and dangerous cliff. The sensation was both terrifying and exhilarating. The person answering the phone passed me off to an editorial assistant who asked, "To whom am I speaking?"

"A person who survived Luka prison camp."

"Can I have your name?"

"No, that would be dangerous. I want you to know that your paper got the Luka story wrong. There were several hundred civilians who lost their lives at Luka, in addition to many more civilians at other places in Brčko."

"We can't run your story, but I know reporters at the Reuters news agency who would be interested in talking with you." I was provided a contact and a phone number.

I telephoned Reuters. Similar to the British Isles, where English is spoken in dialects that identify the speaker's place of origin, dialects also indicate the home republic of those speaking Yugoslav (also known as Bosnian-Serbian-Croatian or BSC). When I called Reuters, the person answering the phone spoke with a Serbian dialect. Thinking they would not be sympathetic to my report, I excused myself and hung up. This happened several times over the next few days. Finally, a woman who spoke the Yugoslav language with an English accent answered the phone.

We talked about my experiences and whether the European Union or the United States would intervene in Bosnia. At the end of our conversation, she advised, "Call Henry Kelly at the U.S. Embassy. He will be interested in your story and has some influence." She gave me a phone number.

As I was striving to correct press reports anonymously from within Serbia, the American paper *Newsday* broke a story entitled "Bosnia's Camps of Death" on August 2. The article, authored by Roy Gutman, was based on refugee-center interviews conducted with two prison camp survivors, one from a camp at Omarska and the second from Luka. Gutman's article captured international attention; it accused Bosnian Serbs not only of mass deportation and imprisonment, but also of executing a deliberate plan for extermination. *Newsday* ran the article despite the fact that Gutman had not received access to either alleged camp. He convinced his editors that the two survivors were truthful.

Several days later, following intense international diplomatic pressure, observers were allowed into Omarska, confirming its existence. They had no such opportunity in Brčko, as Luka camp had been closed and whitewashed. The fifteen hundred or so imprisoned at Batković were still hidden to the world. I had information about both Luka and Batković. While I wanted the truth to come out, I knew that my next available step—contacting the U.S. Embassy—risked exposure. Doing so required a leap of faith. Jasminka encouraged me to take it.

After delaying several days, I finally called the U.S. Embassy, receiving an appointment to meet with First Secretary Kelly on August 10 at ten a.m.

During the intervening hours, an inner voice regularly sounded an alarm. It advised against getting involved. It said, *Don't go. You will be discovered.* In going to the U.S. Embassy and trying to expose Bosnia's situation, I thought, *My words will mean nothing against Serbia's power.*

However, as a prison camp survivor, I also felt an obligation to those still incarcerated—that I should at least try.

My nature has always been somewhat impulsive—my life never following a grand strategic plan. Jasminka had similar tendencies. We decided to plow ahead, keeping the appointment. A friend once told me, "People act when the pain of inaction exceeds the pain of action." Perhaps that is what happened with us.

On the morning of August 10, Jasminka, Adna, and I drove to the U.S. Embassy in Mirko's car. The embassy was located on Belgrade's long Kneza Miloša Boulevard. A neighboring building housed Serbia's Ministry of Internal Affairs, where I had argued with a passport official several weeks earlier.

Parking the car, we saw that police from the Ministry of Internal Affairs ringed the U.S. embassy. They checked the identification of all who crossed their line. As we approached the embassy sidewalk and the police line, my stomach tightened. A policeman asked, "Where are you going?"

"We have an appointment at the U.S. Embassy."

"What is the purpose of your visit?"

"We are applying for an emigration visa."

"Let's see your IDs." The policeman then wrote our information in his notepad.

"Who is your appointment with?"

"Henry Kelly."

"Oh yes. I know him. You must be someone important if Henry Kelly is seeing you on an immigration question. Let me walk you to the embassy entrance."

He did so. As we parted, I felt certain he would check us out.

Inside the building we were met by a Serb woman in reception. She too asked the purpose of our visit. I was not comfortable divulging our real intent—she could have been an informant—and continued with the emigration story. For a receptionist, she seemed to take unusual interest in us, asking questions about our origins and reasons for being in Belgrade. She made me uncomfortable. My discomfort grew when the clock showed ten forty-five, yet no Henry Kelly.

Kelly finally arrived, holding a notebook under his arm, expressing apologies for having kept us waiting. "Something important came up, but you now have my full attention."

I still felt uneasy. That increased when Kelly suggested we talk in the embassy restaurant, located in an adjacent building. We would have to walk outside, and again be seen by the Serbian police.

Once inside the restaurant, Kelly found an empty table in the corner, brought us coffee, and began the interview, taking many notes. He was proficient in BSC, so our conversation shifted back and forth between my language and English. I drew maps of what had occurred in Brčko, describing how the city had been overrun. Responding to his questions, I estimated that eight hundred to one thousand Muslim and Croat civilians had been murdered, and that ninety-five percent of Brčko's Muslim and Croat populations had fled or been driven out of the city.

I asked his government to get involved: "If any government can stop the bloodshed in Bosnia, it is the United States. Don't believe it when people here tell you it is a civil war between Bosnia's people. Go to the graveyards here in Belgrade and look at the inscriptions. People do not lie on the tombstones of loved ones. You will see that many speak to recent army service and dying in specific Bosnian communities. Serbia and the JNA are actively supporting the Bosnian Serbs. They are deeply involved in the war. The prison camps are real and horrible. I saw repeated evidence of Serbia's and the JNA's involvement at Luka camp."

I also told him what I had heard about Batković prison camp.

"That is very interesting. There is an American reporter in Belgrade, Jonathan Landay at United Press International, who is trying to confirm accounts of concentration camps in Bosnia. He would be interested in your story."

We talked for three hours. I eventually warmed to the task, forgetting about the police outside. At the time, it felt cathartic—I had unburdened my conscience about those I had left behind—doing what I could to help.

When finished I asked Kelly, "Please do not publish my name in any public documents. My father in Brčko and brothers at Batković would be in danger. My being here could be their death sentence."

"Yes, yes. I'll respect that. The information you have given me today is helpful. It reinforces and brings into focus other information we have been receiving. Because of what you know, Serbia is a dangerous place for you. Have you considered going somewhere else in Europe?"

"My story to the police was that we came here for information on emigration. Is it still true that the U.S.'s standard process is in place?"

"It is. I can't help you much in that regard."

I knew the process was deliberate, taking many months or even years.

"I'd appreciate it if you walked us out and made sure we get to our car."

"Yes. I'd be glad to."

At the edge of the embassy grounds, we parted. I left with a very favorable impression of Kelly. He seemed sincere.

Trudging toward the car, I saw the Serbian police in the distance. The one who'd taken our names motioned to me. I wasn't about to walk over and engage with him. As we crossed the street, I expected to be stopped.

The route back to Mirko's place in Zemun would take us back to the policemen. Driving straight ahead would put us into Belgrade proper. It was the wrong direction and would cause all kinds of routing problems. I chose it. Pulling away from the curb I looked in the rearview mirror. I saw that Kelly had stayed to watch us drive off.

As I drove, my mind raced. I had a bad premonition. I imagined being arrested by the interior ministry's police. Interrogated back at their fortress, I expected to hear, *We saved your skin and asked only that you be trustworthy and appreciative. This is how you repay our trust. They were right—you are arrogant—too arrogant for your own good. We will fix that for you.*

After driving for five minutes I pulled over to discuss the situation with Jasminka, saying, "I think a steamroller is bearing down on us." We decided to leave Serbia that evening, my Aunt Mensura's home in Macedonia our only option. That choice had its problems, as Macedonia had stopped taking refugees from Bosnia. Once at the border, provided we made it that far, we would have to figure something out. Our documents were a concern. We didn't have Serbian passports. Would my Yugoslav passport be recognized? Jasminka's Yugoslav passport was out of date. We had no travel documents for Adna, only a birth certificate.

Arriving at Mirko's apartment, I asked Jasminka to pack and to be upbeat with Mirko's wife. "Tell her we intend to visit relatives for two weeks."

I made a call to United Press International, scheduling a meeting for four thirty that afternoon. I drove the ten miles to the UPI office. The office was located in a downstairs walk-up.

Descending stairs, I entered the first of two office spaces. A Serb named Goran, who worked for UPI as a driver and interpreter, sat at a desk. I asked for Jonathan Landay, who, hearing his name, stepped out of the second office space. A trim American, about my height at six-foot-two, Landay wore his hair in a ponytail. That image caused me to flashback to my encounters with Ivan Repić and his brass firehose fitting at Luka.

I introduced myself. Landay asked me into his office. After we sat down, I provided him with an abbreviated version of the account given to Henry Kelly. Most of our conversation took place in English. Goran filled in as translator when needed. He took down a transcript of the conversation on a computer, pausing the conversation several times to change floppy disks.

Landay expressed keen interest in learning about both Luka and the mass graves. "If I travel to Luka tomorrow, will I find any prisoners there?"

"No, you won't. They have cleaned up and closed the camp, moving the prisoners elsewhere. The Serbs also arrested men in town and bussed them to Batković camp."

"Mass arrests? How do you know this?"

I relayed phone conversations I'd had with Mira and my father. Ramiz, Mirsad, Faruk, and Jasmin had been arrested at my father's home. Following their arrest, my father called me from the home of a Serb neighbor.

"Tell me about this place—Batković."

I told him what I had heard from Mira, including her statement that there were fifteen hundred to two thousand civilians incarcerated there. I drew him a map with driving directions from Belgrade to Batković.

As we finished, Landay thanked me. As with Kelly, I asked that my name and those of my brothers not be used, emphasizing, "With this you must be serious."

After our meeting, Landay called another journalist, Peter Maass of the *Washington Post*, and discussed making a trip to Batković. With an interpreter, Hvaltka Mihelić, they left the next morning at nine a.m.

Two days later, on August 13, the *Washington Post* published an article written by Maass titled, "The Search for a Secret Prison Camp: Reporters' Questions Provoke Angry Serb Response." The article described the two reporters' dangerous attempt to access the camp and confirm its existence. Though unsuccessful in reaching the site, they did talk to locals who acknowledged the prison's existence and harsh reputation.

As a result of the publicity, Serb authorities admitted that a camp existed near Batković. Two days later, on August 15, they allowed the International Red Cross in. Upon their arrival, the Red Cross registered and attempted to interview prisoners. Fearful, prisoners declined. The registration process did, however, provide a record and a level of accountability for their safekeeping.

Two weeks later Maass and the *Post* published a follow-up article, "Illusory Serb Prison Camp Materializes," confirming to the wider world what had been occurring at Batković and in Bosnia. Those incarcerated at Batković were in rough shape. Conditions in the camp were terrible. Prisoners shied away from talking about their treatment, so the Red Cross had to rely on observation. Unsurprisingly, the food and guard behavior were decent while they were on site. In the wake of the Red Cross visit, there was a changing of the guard. Local townspeople became overseers, treating prisoners more humanely.

With a few of the hundreds of prison camps now emerging into world view, journalists and diplomats began pushing Bosnian Serb authorities hard to provide access to other sites.

After meeting with Landay, my focus shifted to leaving Serbia with my family. I felt certain that our visit to the U.S. Embassy was known and that a shoe would soon drop. That evening at nine p.m., we left Mirko's apartment for the restaurant. I asked Mirko to drive us to the train station. Taken by surprise, he tried to talk us out of the trip.

"Are you leaving because you think you have overstayed your welcome? We aren't friends like that. The cook's apartment will be available in a couple of weeks. That will make things better for the three of you."

When this proved unsuccessful, he said, "You haven't thought things through, Isak. You don't have a good plan for your family's future. There is nothing for you in Macedonia. Things can work out for all of you here in Belgrade."

I tried to reassure my friend, saying, "We are just going to Skopje to visit relatives. We will be back in a couple of weeks."

I was not being straight with Mirko, which troubled me. I could feel my throat tighten as we talked. Mirko gave up trying to change my decision and drove us to the train station. I accepted his offer to buy our tickets. As we boarded the train, he handed me a roll of Serbian currency, bidding us a safe journey.

Until war broke out in Croatia, the train we boarded had been known as the Orient Express. Its route shortened, it was now called the Half Orient Express. The train left Belgrade station at 10:30 p.m. We were scheduled to reach Skopje in seven hours. Mirko had purchased us a compartment in a sleeper car, a boon for Adna. For Jasminka and me there would be no sleep, but at least our nervousness, invisible to other travelers, would not arouse suspicions. I told her, "Tonight will be our version of the Agatha Christie book. Let's hope the train agents aren't as skilled as Inspector Poirot."

— 26 —

NIGHT FLIGHT

The train rolled through the dark countryside, stopping at four stations. At a quarter past four the train slowed without a station being called. I peered out the window. A fog hung low. We were stopped in a cornfield ten kilometers short of the Macedonian border. The train fell silent, except for an occasional release from its air brakes. Jasminka and I listened intently. After ten minutes, loud voices broke the silence.

Uniformed officers of the Serbian police had taken several passengers off the train and were haranguing them: "What kind of Serb are you? How dare you desert and sneak out of the country when your nation needs you?" The men were led away to waiting cars. I whispered to Jasminka, "We must stay calm; otherwise they are going to figure us out."

We waited in silence. Time ground on slowly. After fifteen minutes, we heard officials checking the occupants of our car. Soon there was a knock on our compartment door. Jasminka had picked up Adna, who was asleep. She sat with her under the cover of a blanket. I answered the door, feigning grogginess from interrupted sleep. Two policemen stood in the doorway. They asked for our identification and our destination.

As they reviewed the documents, one of the policemen demanded, "Whose baby is this?"

Jasminka answered softly, "Adna is our daughter, our first born. She is ten months old. This is her first train trip."

"Let's not disturb the baby. Let's allow her to sleep," said the other officer. The two men agreed to move on.

We had passed the first challenge. Adna had proven a godsend. After a forty-minute delay the train got back underway.

At the border town of Kumanovo, we confronted Macedonia's border police. As the train pulled to a stop there, I could make out the shapes of dozens of travelers in an open field beside the platform, sitting on or sleeping beside their luggage. They were Bosnian refugees denied entry into Macedonia. They camped in a no man's land. I did not want to join them.

The Macedonian language differs from Bosnian, but I knew enough of it to get by. The border police took some time with our documents. They debated whether to send us back to Belgrade. I was called into a small office. The man in charge asked, "Why are you trying to enter Macedonia?"

"We are displaced by the war and want to visit relatives who are Macedonian citizens."

He then asked in Albanian, "Are you Albanian?" Albanians comprised twenty-five percent of the Macedonian population, and were Macedonia's largest ethnic minority.

Momentarily startled by the language change, I replied in Albanian, "I have Albanian roots. My father is a Kosovo Albanian." My cultural heritage and the fact that we had Macedonian relatives seemed to win the day for us. At times our heritage was a blessing, at others a curse. I thought of my grandmother. We conversed in Albanian for my first fifteen years.

The border captain finally said, "We are making an exception because you have relatives here. You and your family can enter Macedonia."

I'm sure I smiled as the official stamped my passport. I had fond memories of past trips to Macedonia, especially staying on the shores of Lake Ohrid, one of the world's deepest lakes and a World Heritage site. Jasminka had also loved the mountain setting, the secluded beaches, the crystal-clear waters, and the shops of Ohrid's old quarter. On one trip, I had used my race winnings to purchase her an Ohrid pearl.

When I returned to my family, Jasminka looked drawn and pensive. My absence with the border officials had been another source of worry. Through the ordeal of recent months, my partner had been supportive and resolute. As she looked at me expectantly, I could see how difficult and wearing it had all been. I finally had good news. Hearing it, she threw her arms around me. I could feel her trembling.

The train left the border and twenty-five minutes later arrived in Skopje. Once we had stepped down, I got directions to the bus station. It was two kilometers away. We set off on foot. Between the session at the U.S. Embassy, the meeting at UPI, taking leave of Mirko, the stop in the cornfield, and the uncertainty at the border, it had been a long day. We had not slept.

At the bus station, the ticket seller informed me that Serb dinars were not accepted. I had no other currency. Jasminka and Adna rested on a nearby bench. I told Jasminka, "I'm stepping outside to get some fresh air and to consider what we do next." I thought to myself, *We have had problems on top of problems. Tetovo is fifty kilometers away, too far to walk.*

As I stood outside, a cab pulled up to the curb. Leaning over to the passenger side, the driver called through the open window, "Hey man, how is it going?"

"Well, right now it's not going that good."

"Are you a refugee?"

"Yes, from Bosnia. I'm here with my wife and baby daughter. They are inside resting. They had a long night."

"Why don't you go inside and get them? You can all sit in my cab."

"The only currency I have is Serbian."

"Dinars! They aren't worth shit. Get your family anyway."

"All right. I'll fetch them."

After we climbed into his cab, the driver asked, "Where is your destination?"

"Tetovo."

"Why Tetovo?"

Before I could answer, the cab driver asked, "Are you Albanian?"

"I am, on my father's side."

"Good to meet you, countryman. I am going to drive you there."

Tetovo is a good-sized city, with a population that is seventy percent Albanian. I had visited my aunt there ten years earlier, bringing my teammates to her home for dinner following a competition. I remembered enough from that visit to find her neighborhood, but the high walls that surrounded each residence stumped me. Not wishing to inconvenience the cab driver further, we thanked him for the great favor and unloaded.

He responded, "No problem, and good luck. I've seen many in your situation since the war started."

After the cab departed, I approached an elderly man asking, "Sir, I'm a bit lost. Can you point me toward the house of Kerim and Mensura Arifi?"

"What is your business with the Arifis?"

"Mensura is my mother's sister. I want to introduce my infant daughter to a favorite aunt."

The old man lit up. He asked me to wait, walked to a house four doors away and knocked on the front gate.

My Aunt Mensura came to the gate. The old man made a show of explaining that he was about to deliver some important guests to her. Seeing us in the distance, Mensura beamed. She knew the situation had deteriorated in Brčko. For months, she'd tried without success to establish contact. She had begun to fear the worst. She told the man, "My prayers have been answered."

She rewarded the bearer of good tidings with a chicken, sending him happily on his way. She opened her home to us. After our journey and its uncertainty, it was a safe haven—a dot of an island in a threatening sea. We spent the afternoon and evening catching up, renewing our family tie. After dinner Jasminka and I retired early. While we welcomed sleep, Adna nestled in the capable arms of her great aunt.

—27—

THE EXTRADITION REQUEST

When in Belgrade, I had received a Serbian ID that listed Mirko's address as my residence. The next morning, at six a.m., about the time our train pulled into Skopje station, Mirko later told me he was awakened by a knock at his door. Two men in civilian clothes waited outside. One man, Đorde Jovanović, was a patron of Mirko's restaurant. The men showed Mirko their badges. They were state security police, the Serbian equivalent of America's FBI. Jovanović asked to speak with me.

"Isak was here, but left last evening. I'm surprised you are here so early asking for him. What's the reason?"

"Gaši has been to the U.S. Embassy. We need to speak with him regarding that visit. We need to know where he is."

"All I know is that he traveled to Skopje to visit relatives."

"Skopje! Do you have an address or phone number? Do you expect him back?"

"I don't have an address or way to contact him. His belongings are still here. He will be back. He said something about a two-week trip."

Looking displeased, the policeman handed Mirko a card with a phone number saying, "Let us know if Gaši makes contact or returns to Belgrade. It is imperative that we speak with him, and soon."

As they prepared to leave, Jovanović reiterated, "Keep us informed."

He returned the next day, visiting Mirko at his restaurant. Mirko could say that he had not spoken with me. More forthcoming on this visit, Jovanović said, "Gaši went to the U.S. Embassy and talked bad about Serbia. That ingrate—we save his ass and this is how he repays us."

Later that day I called the restaurant. Mirko informed me about his two encounters with the police and their aggravation about my visit to the U.S. Embassy. He said, "They seemed serious," then asked, "Why did you visit the embassy?"

"We went there to see if there was any opportunity to emigrate to the U.S."

Mirko absorbed this and didn't press me further, instead counseling, "Man, they are after you about something else. Don't even think about coming back to Belgrade. There is big trouble for you here."

In Tetovo, relations were easy with Mensura and her husband, Kerim. Mensura was completely taken with Adna, much as she had been devoted to me when I was young. Despite the fact that Macedonia's economy struggled and their finances were currently tight, they shared everything with us.

Muslims in Tetovo practiced a version of their religion more conservative than in Brčko. Women rarely left the family compound, and when out of doors spent the majority of their time on their second-story balconies. Jasminka was not about to restrict herself in this way. She toured Adna through the neighborhood in her stroller. Adna was a magnet. When neighbor women saw her approaching, they came to their gates with small gifts. News that the Arifis had refugee guests spread to local shop owners; they regularly refused payment when Jasminka shopped for Adna.

Kerim was also taken with Adna. He would arrive home each evening with his pockets filled with treats. Discovering their whereabouts became a game of treasure hunt between the kind older man and the one-year-old. Both were delighted by her discoveries.

Kerim's occupation was commercial painting. His formal education had ended after eighth grade. He and his brother had a friend, Ferid Muhić, who was a professor at the University of Saints Cyril and Methodius in Skopje. Their initial bond was great affection for Šarplaninac shepherd dogs. Professor Muhić was doing research for a book he would eventually write on the dogs and their breeders.

He regularly stayed in Tetovo. I met the professor during one of his visits. My family had always had Šar dogs—my uncles in Kosovo bred them. Over the years, we had the pick of several litters.

It turned out the professor and I had more in common than a love of Šars.

Born and raised in Bosnia, Muhić had been in Tito's inner circle. He expressed profound interest in the Bosnian War, both because it overlapped his academic expertise in cultural anthropology and political philosophy, and because of its severe impact on our countrymen. When he learned of my experiences, we fell into deep discussion regarding Bosnia's situation.

In the professor, I found someone allied with my cause. During the coming months and years, he would be a strident voice calling for international action to end the war. He opposed the conventional European view that this was a civil war with neither victims nor aggressors, instead arguing that the aggression was planned in advance and intended to eliminate both Bosnia as an independent republic and its two million Muslims, so that Bosnian territory could be divided between Serbia and Croatia.

It was encouraging to find someone with Muhić's credentials and keen intelligence speaking out.

At this time, I confronted other difficulties. Two weeks into our Macedonian stay, one of Kerim's cousins, an officer on the Tetovo police force, invited Kerim and me to coffee.

At the restaurant, the policeman said, "You need to know that the Serbs are looking everywhere for you. At the station we received a fax from Serbian State Security asking Macedonia about your whereabouts and seeking your extradition."

He pulled a folded sheet from his pocket and showed it to me. It was the fax. Though this Serbian initiative was not entirely unexpected, I still felt a surge of adrenaline and apprehension. I stared at the policeman wondering, *What next?*

"This looks serious, but I'll protect you here as much as I can."

"Thank you. I appreciate the information and your support. I am innocent of any wrongdoing but know too much for Serbia's comfort."

Sobered by the news, I shifted into problem-solving mode. I called Henry Kelly to ask his advice. Kelly thought I was in some difficulty. With Macedonia the route by which Serbia circumvented the international embargo, he said, "Many forces are in play. If you have a chance to emigrate, take it. The Scandinavian countries have begun taking refugees and may be a good option for you."

"Since Scandinavia has opened up, has there been any change in U.S. immigration?"

"Getting to the United States is a complicated process. It would take time. However, with time of the essence, we can arrange immediate emigration to the United Arab Emirates."

Having had no personal experience with the Middle East and with good memories from trips and competitions in northern Europe, Jasminka and I talked over our options. We set our sights on Scandinavia. The United Arab Emirates would be our backup if Serbia closed in.

Henry Kelly also provided information about the Batković prison camp, relaying what he had found out following the visits that the International Red Cross and the human rights group Helsinki Watch had made. He said, "The Red Cross has registered each prisoner and will serve as a conduit for communications."

I seized on this news, contacting the Macedonian Red Cross with a message for my brothers. In late September, I received a reply from Ramiz. His communication was short but reassuring. He wrote, "Mirsad, Faruk, and I are good, not to worry. Let the rest of our family know we are alive. Send my love to Suada, Fatmir, and Melita. Tell them how much I miss them."

This news was a great relief. Now that Batković was at least known to the world, I was encouraged that, having survived so far, my brothers and nephew would find a way out.

We hoped to arrange a safe passage to Macedonia for Ramiz's wife, Suada, and her two children. They were currently in Croatia. My friend Matija Ljubek came to their rescue. He purchased them ferry and train tickets to Tetovo. We reunited at Mensura's. I now needed to find a Scandinavian safe haven for six.

We applied for refugee consideration through the Macedonian Red Cross, visiting their offices in Skopje to begin the process. The application fee was $1,200. Jasminka sold some heirloom jewelry to raise the funds. We faced additional hurdles, as Jasminka's passport had expired and Adna had none. Kerim had a contact that possessed the stamps, seals, and passport blanks from the Yugoslav days. For a fee, again financed through a jewelry sale, we obtained documents that looked sufficiently Yugoslav to pass scrutiny.

I had a follow-up phone conversation with Henry Kelly, who had checked on the Danish option and encouraged us to go there. "If you encounter any difficulties on arrival in Scandinavia, call the U.S. Embassy and say that you know me. They will help you."

Two months after leaving Serbia, we again took to the road, departing Skopje in a two-bus caravan on October 12, 1992. Our immediate objective was Swinoujscie, a seaport in Poland. The refugees in our caravan departed, uncertain of our final destination and refuge. At the ferry terminal in Swinoujscie, after presenting documents, we would discover exactly what our options were, as each Scandinavian country had established distinct requirements.

The bus route to Poland was circuitous. After leaving Macedonia, we planned to cross Bulgaria, followed by Romania, then through Hungary to Poland. At their border, the Hungarians turned us away; they would not permit our buses to transit. When the bus driver announced his intention to return to Skopje, we implored the Red Cross agent accompanying us to find an alternative. After a series of calls, she said we would backtrack through Romania and try an alternate route through Moldova, the Ukraine, and finally Poland. She said, "The route is untested. There are no guarantees."

Each border crossing presented difficulties. The Red Cross agent was a marvel. She charmed, cajoled, and likely paid bribes to facilitate our progress, halting as it was. Road surfaces in Moldova and Ukraine were often poor. Speeds were slow, the ride jarring. Scenes in some remote areas looked unchanged from the Middle Ages, with primitive technologies and living conditions.

Moldova and the Ukraine were still recovering from the breakup of the Soviet Union. There were reports of corruption and lawlessness. At the Ukrainian border, our buses were stopped for ten hours. We finally received permission to travel through the country. Several hours later, our buses were pulled over by armed men at a checkpoint in the middle of nowhere. We were shaken down. The final demand of one soldier was a digital watch. No one on the bus had one. My Bulova would not suffice. I then remembered a training aide, a Finnish heart rate monitor, packed in my luggage. It was digital and a watch among other functions. Satisfied, the soldier allowed us to get underway again.

The forests of Ukraine awed us. They went on unbroken, a vast ocean of green. Driving through them at night in absolute darkness was spectral, reminding us again how alone and disconnected from the world we were. For me that was a hard night, with many disturbing thoughts. It was a sensation like Luka—I felt like I struggled underwater and didn't know the way to the surface.

Altogether we traveled for five and a half days. There were no showers and few opportunities to change clothes. Before departing, we had been told to pack food for three days. While we had plenty of baby formula for Adna, constituting it required hot water, which we ran out of in Ukraine. Most of us arrived in Poland having fasted for at least a day. The bus agent again came to our rescue, buying gallons of juice and several cartons of energy bars at the first opportunity. After a long drive across Poland, our two buses pulled up to the seaport in a driving rainstorm. It was five a.m. The bus driver asked us to disembark, but in the darkness and gloom it appeared that we were nowhere, so we refused. At daybreak, the outlines of the harbor and a large ferry terminal were visible in the distance. The seventy of us hiked to the terminal and waited for the ticket office to open at 7:30 a.m. Sleeping in the building were dozens of Bosnian refugees who had arrived lacking documents considered necessary by the Poles.

At the ticket counter, I learned that the ferry options were Gothenborg and Malmo in Sweden, and Copenhagen, Denmark. The Copenhagen ferry connected to Norway. I had been impressed with Denmark when racing there two years earlier, and had discussed Henry Kelly's recommendation with Jasminka and Suada. All three of us were set on Denmark. Suada's Yugoslav passport presented a problem. The Danes and Norwegians were only accepting refugees from Bosnia. The passports for Jasminka, Adna, and I were stamped as having been issued in the Bosnian city of Brčko. For some reason, Suada's passport had no city or republic designation. Although Suada had lived her entire life in Brčko, she lacked the documentation that the ferry officials required. They would only offer her family tickets to Sweden.

With Ramiz in Batković prison, I had responsibility for his family's safekeeping. Therefore, we had to stay together. I noticed a young, attractive Polish woman working with the refugee groups. She appeared to have some authority. I approached her, summarized our dilemma, and asked for her help.

She said, "I'll try, but don't get your hopes up. Problems like these are the reason so many people are camped here without tickets."

Over the next forty-five minutes she made our case, engaging in shuttle diplomacy, getting additional facts and assurances. I could see that she was turned down several times. On what she called a "last ditch" attempt, she asked me to accompany her, relating Suada's life story and the family's need to stay together. Her persistence paid off. The ticket agents finally said, "We will issue tickets to Denmark. If anything in the story turns out untrue, the resulting problems will be yours."

Hearing that, I told them, "My family thanks you from the bottom of our hearts. You have been tremendous to us."

Waiting for the ferry's departure, I thought back over the twists and turns of the past five months. There had been a yin and yang to our situation. Despite the dangers, everyone in my family was intact. At virtually every obstacle, there had been someone willing to provide an assist; these decent people were of all ethnicities. They were people willing to stick their necks out for others.

I recalled my coach Čonda's statement, "When you are ready, the coach will appear." We weren't ready for what happened in Brčko, but others helped us in hours of great need. We had good fortune. Our old life was lost, but we had this chance to regroup and to move on. Many others in Bosnia were given no chance, or were still in harm's way.

I again considered Milošević and the perversity of his 1987 statement in Kosovo that "never again would Serbs be beaten." That speech had launched his political rise in Serbia. He soon used the state's power to control and cow the media. Now, only five years later, Milošević had undertaken the beating, torture, and killing of a civilization. To me, he was a master manipulator who had broken the JNA to his purposes and transformed it into the army of Greater Serbia. He had possessed a detailed design for Bosnia and had pulled strings that the Bosnian Serb leadership danced to. The fact that Milošević and Brčko's outside attackers had so many local accomplices made the situation worse. Local participation made the tragedy personal. That impact was also part of Milošević's master plan—do things so terrible to your neighbors that they will never return to live beside you again. In driving populations from their birthplaces, and then leveling the homesteads and villages where they had lived for centuries, Milošević intended that there be no homes for Bosniaks and Croats to return to.

He had, however, underestimated how hard Bosniaks and Bosnian Croats would fight to stay. Most of us had no place else to go.

In Macedonia, I made a decision to take part of family Gaši to Scandinavia rather than returning to fight on Brčko's front lines. I had the military training and had been provided sufficient motivation for the second option. But I'd made a choice, and I felt a responsibility to make that choice worthwhile. As our ferry left for the Danish coast, I wondered if there would be any opportunity in Denmark to be of help to my now very distant and beleaguered homeland.

— 28 —

REFUGE IN DENMARK

We set off into the Baltic in a rainstorm. Swinoujscie was located in an archipelago of forty-four islands. Forested, with beaches and high moraine hills, it was a tourist destination during other seasons. I felt great relief to be departing. For a time, I stood on the deck, watching Eastern Europe recede, breathing in fresh air that smelled of balsam and the sea. Once we cleared the last island and its breakwater, the ferry turned, bearing into high winds. Our crossing was rough. Other than that, the seven-hour trip passed uneventfully. We had a sleeping compartment with a shower, which felt luxurious after the long bus journey. Famished, we were down to our last hundred deutsche marks. The restaurant staff told us the note would cover whatever we needed.

Danish immigration officials and police officers met us at the harbor in Copenhagen, asking us to form lines by ethnic nationality. Following a registration process, we entered a hall that offered a cornucopia of fruit, soups, sandwich meats, and Denmark's dense black bread. Our hosts had rolled out the welcome mat. They seemed interested in, and somewhat astonished by, the Balkan people who had arrived on their shore.

After processing, we boarded buses and were driven to a school in the suburb of Gentofte. It was our home for the next two weeks. Beds were cots and bunks from the Danish military. Men and older boys slept in a gymnasium, separate from the women and children.

The school overlooked Lake Bagsværd, where I had raced the world championships two years earlier. The next afternoon I walked down to the boathouse to meet the local paddlers. Several remembered me. Two days later an official from the Danish Canoe Federation visited me at the school. We had a good discussion about canoe sport and mutual friends, reminding me of happy times. As we parted he said, "The Federation extends its welcome. Please let us know if there is anything we can do to help."

The Danes also provided us with medical services. My ears had rung ever since the beating with the brass fitting at Luka, and the top of my head still hurt, so X-rays were taken. They showed that my skull had fractured, but was healing. The tinnitus in my ears faded after a few more months.

At the school, English served as the common language with our hosts. Since our English was passable, Jasminka and I kept busy interpreting. On our third day in Denmark, Jasminka developed a fever. It was like a dam burst from the tension she had been under. Her body seemed to recognize she now had the time to be sick, letting down overworked defenses. After several days in the infirmary and a course of antibiotics, she rebounded. Through all the changes and upheavals, Adna remained happy and healthy.

On November 1, we were in a group of one hundred Bosnian refugees that traveled west by bus and ferry to Jutland. From the bus window I saw a highway billboard that proclaimed, "All Colors Are Beautiful." Its background displayed a radiant collage of colors, while the center space showed a multiracial group interacting. I pointed it out to Jasminka, saying, "I think we have come to a good place."

Our destination was a Red Cross facility in Ødsted, a village eleven kilometers from the city of Vejle. The setting was rural, agrarian. Our home for the next three and a half years was a room in what had been a motel. For the first two months, it accommodated all six of us; then Suada and her children received a room of their own. We shared a large communal kitchen and dining area with the other residents.

Everyone, Bosnians and Danes alike, hoped that our stay would be temporary, with Denmark a safe port from a tempest that would blow itself out. As the weeks wore on and discouraging reports from the war in Bosnia came in, those hopes faded. Our war was a storm that fed upon itself.

As refugees, we were afforded the necessities of life, receiving stipends to purchase food, clothing, and toiletries. Since we were not expected to stay permanently, there was no instruction in the Danish language, no opportunity for work, and no integration into Danish society. The children were ineligible for Danish schooling. To fill that void, we established a school at the center, utilizing several teachers in our company and whatever teaching materials we could photocopy or otherwise create.

Overall the atmosphere at the center was good. A strong sense of community developed within our group. We hailed from many regions of Bosnia. With lives uprooted, worries about loved ones trapped in the former Yugoslavia, no opportunity to work or progress in careers, no educational options, and little opportunity to leave the confines of the village, we had to resist a sense of loss and stagnation. We had great hunger for news about the war, news that was endlessly discussed and debated.

Once the novelty of our new situation wore off, many of us experienced a flood of repressed memories and post-traumatic stress. The Danes were attuned to this, providing counseling services. Jasminka experienced the various stages of grief for friends, relatives, and a good life lost. Adna provided her with an important counterweight. Maternal focus trumped all for my wife, and she had the company of other devoted mothers.

I experienced vivid nightmares after Luka. They had gone away during the bus trip and the early weeks in Denmark. They returned with a vengeance in Ødsted. Two dreams recurred. In the first I heard the screams of women at Luka, then them calling out for my help. I was never able to come to their aid. I moved like I was in molasses and was constantly opposed or diverted by my jailers. While I was sidetracked, terrible things occurred. In my dream, I felt great guilt.

The second dream took place in Denmark. In it I met Bosnians who said they had relatives who had been taken to Luka and were unaccounted for. They asked me about them. I could neither recall their relatives, nor provide reassurances. Here too, I experienced an awful feeling of having let others down.

I would awaken from these dreams drenched in sweat, often thinking I was back at Luka. Finding Jasminka asleep beside me let me know that I was, indeed, free.

At that time, I had a couple of sessions with a Danish psychologist, whom I asked, "Do these dreams mean I'm mentally ill?"

The psychologist responded, "You aren't, but you are troubled by what has happened. Your subconscious is trying to make sense of something senseless: humans being inhumane."

The dreams persisted despite the counseling. I hadn't exercised for months. I started to feel caged in at the refugee center and knew I needed to be back in motion.

Just before Christmas, I received a reprieve. One of the workers at the center knew my paddling background. She had a close friend, Jytte Vodstrup, who was a member of a row and paddle club in Vejle. Jytte visited me at the refugee center. She was a middle school English teacher, so we communicated easily in English. She invited me to her club's Christmas and New Year's gatherings. Though the club didn't own racing canoes, they talked with the Struer boat company and had one delivered to their boathouse, which was on a bus line convenient for me. I was back to canoeing, with time available for training.

Vejle is a port city located on a large bay of the Baltic Sea. People in the local club did not paddle racing canoes because conditions on the bay were too windy and rough. For me the turbulent bay posed a challenge. I was not foolhardy, generally staying within swimming distance of shore. Even so, capsizing would have been dangerous during the cold weather months. Keeping my narrow canoe upright and dry required total concentration. Thinking about Luka or my brothers or of Bosnia's plight was not an option during my hours on the water.

Paddling was good for me. Being on the water and around the boathouse provided a connection to my past life as well as a means to forge a new one. The hard, physical effort satisfied a need I have always had. My fitness improved, showing I still had vitality and capacity. After a morning of hard training, I felt emptied, but in a positive way. The physical work, the fresh air, and the daily battles with the waves were centering. It reminded me of good times in my life. The club also provided me, and to a lesser extent Jasminka, with an entrée into Danish society. Both of us needed the stimulation and the added human connections.

The club seemed pleased to have a member with my background. After being degraded at Luka, receiving acceptance from these Danes meant a lot. The club asked me to help coach its junior racers. I developed friendships and learned Danish. This broke down barriers. One of the club members, Michael Fjeldvig, was a gifted athlete who had national-team coaching aspirations. We became good friends and coaching confidants. His father, Tomas, was the president of a prestigious boating club in Copenhagen.

The following summer, Tomas invited me to train at his club for several weeks, offering one of the club's apartments to my family. For us, release from the confines of the refugee center plus the chance to experience a city like Copenhagen was wonderful. The city's vigor and cooperative life reminded me of what we Yugoslavs once had, and somehow lost.

29

TELLING MY STORY

The Danish Canoe Federation asked me to lead a junior development effort in Jutland. I enjoyed working with the young athletes and their coaches, appreciating their enthusiasm. Coaching provided me an avenue to pay forward the support I had received so many years before from Čonda and the Brčko club.

The canoe club in Vejle gathered Wednesday evenings for a potluck and social. One evening the group's attention was drawn to a television special on the war in Somalia and Denmark's Somali refugees. Several club members expressed their displeasure with the government's decision to provide refugee relief to these African people with their strange language and Islamic faith. After the conversation got underway, several club members remembered that I came to Denmark as a refugee. One said, "We didn't mean you. You are much different."

Bowing to the outspoken side of my nature I said, "I'm not so different. I have much in common with the Somalis. I know some of what they went through. I can relate to them."

After the gathering, Jytte drove me home. On the way she said, "I appreciated the way you provoked our thinking this evening," giving me a fist bump.

The Danes I met often expressed curiosity about the Bosnian War. They would ask about my prison experience or the siege of Sarajevo they saw reported on the nightly news. I felt an urgency to have the story of the Bosnian War understood and accurately reported. My motivation was straightforward: I wanted the killing to stop, and I was convinced the carnage would not end in the absence of intense international pressure. When I recounted what Bosnians were going through, most Danes were incredulous and somewhat disbelieving. Relating these extraordinary events to the average Dane ended up being frustrating. Fellow refugees told me of similar experiences.

From the time of our arrival we had tried to connect with our extended family. Early in 1993 the Red Cross gave Jasminka the phone number of a refugee center on the island of Losij in the Adriatic. Her father, Salih, and mother, Ankica, had taken shelter there with her younger sister, Đordana. Jasminka made contact with her parents, encouraging them to join us in Denmark.

Working through the International Red Cross, Jasminka's family reunited in Ødsted two months later. Their arrival did wonders for Jasminka's spirits. A man who could find the good in every situation, her father sought out those from his generation at the center, quickly making fast friends. A lifelong horseman, he was soon volunteering at a nearby riding center.

I tried to contact my mother without success, then asked the Red Cross for assistance. In March they provided a phone number. When I dialed it, a clerk in a military unit near the front lines in the Croatian War answered the telephone, then passed it to the officer in charge. Though the interruption annoyed him, he listened to my story. At its conclusion, he said "Well, I will try to help you." He asked for my phone number, then said, "Never call this number again."

Two weeks later, I was summoned to the refugee center telephone. The caller was my sister, Jagoda. It had been a year since we had spoken. They had found refuge in Croatia. They had been staying in the home of my father's Second World War colonel, an ethnic Serb. The Croatian army eventually commandeered his house. At that point Jagoda, her twin daughters, and my mother relocated to a sanctuary in the local Catholic Church.

I told them about refugee life in Denmark, encouraging them to join us. Jagoda talked it over with my mother, but they decided against leaving their roots. They were intent on getting to Mensura in Macedonia. To finance their travel, Matija Ljubek wired them money. They remained in Macedonia until late 1994, when they reunited with my father behind army lines in northwestern Bosnia. My father and Jagoda's son, Jasmin, eventually received permission to leave Brčko in a prisoner exchange. They were driven to the front line by a policeman and exchanged for several Serbian soldiers.

Muslim and Croat populations in Bosnia continued to face grave risks. Muslims in particular had no place to go. The Bosnian Serb leader Radovan Karadžić had been serious when predicting their annihilation. Backed into geographic corners, Bosnia's army, primarily Muslim fighters, was motivated to fight to the bitter end.

The cycle of violence promised to be brutal and interminable—a Bosnian Alamo. International intervention was needed to break the cycle. I strove to convey this in interviews given to Danish national television and the national newspaper, *Jyllands-Posten*.

In autumn 1993, journalist Lars Kaaber from the Danish national newspaper, *Politiken*, visited me at the refugee center. His paper published an article about my having competed in the world championships hosted by Denmark before returning to the country as a refugee. The article was entitled "On Escape from the Memories."

Kaaber wrote, "Far out in the country, outside Ødsted, the Danes have built some little houses with nylon carpets and doorframes made from plastic. It is nice, cold, and silent. The children play and laugh. Most grown-up faces walk silently around—trying to remember and forget at the same time."

In response to a question about Yugoslavia, I said, "We were brought up to regard Yugoslavs as one people, where religious differences didn't matter so much. Our different nationalities were considered an advantage. We were Yugoslavs first, trying to build our own destiny on the ruins of the Nazi occupation."

We looked through a photo album that had recently arrived through the mail. Our friend Mira had retrieved the album, along with the Olympic torch, from the Serb family occupying our apartment. The journalist saw the many good memories represented in the album, asking me to compare them to the things experienced when Brčko was overrun.

We also discussed refugee life. I acknowledged that my situation was better than for many other refugees, as I had the connection to the canoe club in Vejle and the fellowship of other sportsmen.

Kaaber wrote that I could "both smile and laugh, but that I also needed to talk about what happened to Bosnia." We spoke about the contradictions in that experience—the crimes that seemed to be inspired by jealousy and fear on one side, set off against the assistance and courage of many others, like Mirko and Mira, on the other.

The journalist noted that earlier that morning I had paid my last visit to the psychologist, who asked if I felt hatred or the need for revenge. I said, "No, I tried hatred, but it didn't fit with me."

I asked the psychologist if this was normal. He said it wasn't. Mulling this over, I said, "With one hundred thousand Bosnians having perished since the war's outbreak, perhaps this means something died in me too."

The journalist concluded the article noting that Adna had "fallen asleep on her bed. His wife is sitting on the floor smoking a cigarette. Her eyes are angrier than Isak's. The sun is low over Ødsted as I leave."

Eleven months later I was one of two Bosnian detention-camp survivors featured in an article written by Steve Coll for the *Washington Post Magazine*. Coll traveled to Ødsted to meet with me. He was surprised to learn that Jasminka and I had seen the movie *Schindler's List* the week before. He described our meeting:

> Steven Spielberg's holocaust film might be described as a brave or foolish entertainment choice if you consider that Gaši is a rare survivor of one of the most lethal of Serbian detention camps… Gaši endured beatings, a mock execution with a pistol thrust in his mouth, and grim labor carrying corpses of the executed for dumping in a nearby river. His memory is precise. He can draw diagrams and explain what he saw in each direction at various points in his narrative. He gave two days of testimony at one point to war crimes investigators from Washington; he has become an effective witness… He was—and is again as a refugee in Denmark—an internation-al-level competitive kayaker. Tanned and muscled, he tells his story dressed in a striped boating shirt and blue slacks, as if he has just stepped over from the yacht club.

Coll's sixteen-page article carried the title "Bosnia in the Shadow of the Holocaust." The piece featured photos taken when journalists first gained access to the Omarska detention camp. A photo of Fikret Alić, the other survivor that Coll interviewed, showed his emaciated frame set against barbed wire fencing. It was published worldwide.

The article also featured two photos taken by Bojan Stojanović. One is of Goran Jelisić shooting a Muslim civilian in the back outside the Brčko police station. The other shows a bulldozer piling dirt on Muslim civilians at the mass grave opposite my workplace. This was the mass grave that I had observed when working on the power pole. Both photos had been in the packet shown to me in Belgrade when Rade Božić and Stojanović paid their surprise visit. The caption in the *Washington Post* article noted that the photographer was "considered a traitor by many fellow Serbs and now lives in hiding in the Netherlands."

Stojanović had been a hero when Serbian media printed captions on the photos stating that Muslims were killing and burying innocent Serbs. When the international press eventually got the story straight, Stojanović transformed into a traitor.

Coll's story included a discussion of the International Criminal Tribunal for the Former Yugoslavia (ICTY) that had recently been established to investigate and prosecute war crimes. He discussed international law while comparing the Bosnian situation to that which inspired the Nuremburg trials. Coll noted that in the former situation, the Allied victors had full access to records. In Bosnia the situation was much different. Our war raged on. Evidence resided primarily in areas held by Bosnian Serbs. Investigators would "need the permission of crime subjects to look for evidence against them. They will not have supreme powers of search, arrest, or detention in the former Yugoslavia."

In pressing the United Nations to establish the International Tribunal, the American ambassador Madeline Albright stressed that the international community "must establish the historical evidence before the guilty can reinvent the truth."

The war-crimes court would be looking for witnesses with specific facts who could demonstrate that careful planning had preceded the Bosnian conflict, and that it involved—and relied upon—the JNA and other federal powers of Yugoslavia. In a trial setting, physical evidence and paper trails would be difficult to acquire. In that context, Coll discussed the implication that circumstantial evidence linking atrocities to higher-ups in the power structure would play an important role. This was a role that experiences like mine could help fulfill. In this regard Coll quoted Richard Goldstone, the South African jurist who would be the tribunal's chief prosecutor: "It does seem to imply that any political leader who possessed power during the course of a series of atrocities, and who failed reasonably to intervene and prevent them, is criminally responsible."

Coll concluded his piece saying that my experience helped make "an irrefutable connection between Bosnia and Nazi Germany: emotive, primal."

30

SAID AND ADMIR

In May 1993, I traveled to Copenhagen to talk with representatives of Human Rights Watch and the Helsinki Committee. Their interest was violations of basic human rights as established in the 1972 Helsinki Accords.

Later that year, I met with M. Cherif Bassiouni, a law professor at DePaul University and the founder of the International Human Rights Law Institute. He had been appointed Special Rapporteur Gathering Facts for a United Nations commission investigating the Bosnian War. He later became chair of the commission and was nominated for the Nobel Peace Prize for his leadership in the human rights law arena.

At the conclusion of our interview, he asked, "Do you know a Said Muminović from Brčko and his current whereabouts? We have been looking for him in Croatian refugee centers without success."

"I know Said well. We've been friends since childhood. After he and his family escaped from Brčko they landed in Croatia. From there, with the Red Cross' help, they came to our refugee center in Ødsted, Denmark. He is there now."

Said was the best man at my wedding and my best friend growing up. As kids, we were on the same wavelength. We enjoyed sports and were both devoted to swimming, soccer, and team handball before we found canoeing. We were canoe partners as juniors, and were swift together. Said expressed great self-confidence. We regularly sparred, both intellectually and physically. While Said was stronger, I could lure him into endurance contests and prevail.

My first television experience was with my father watching a boxing match between Sonny Liston and Muhammad Ali. The bout was broadcast on a screen set up in the employee restaurant at the Bimal plant. Afterward I told my father, "Ali is just like Said. They both say, 'I'm the greatest.'"

The war took some of the starch out of Said, as it did all of us. While in Croatia he had written an eight-page letter to President Bush of the United States. The State Department forwarded the letter to Bassiouni. Several months after its writing, Radio Bosnia-Herzegovina broadcast the letter. We listened to the broadcast at the refugee center.

Said lost his father during the war. His father had gone out walking with Serb friends during Brčko's occupation. At that time, Muslims and Croats were required to wear white ribbons on their arms, while Serbs wore blue. It was a crime for a Muslim to wear blue. Said's father had done so during his walk. He was arrested and was never heard from again. A decade later, forensic pathologists found some of his DNA in a mass grave. Such was the Bosnian War's exchange rate: two desiccated shoulder bones for a whole, vibrant human being.

When war descended on Brčko, Said came close to suffering his father's fate. He wrote to President H.W. Bush:

On May 5, a representative of the Yugoslav army in a radio broadcast instructed the citizens in my part of town to go the army barracks. We were told the army would organize an evacuation to a safer place.

I knew that the Serbs used special groups to massacre civilians. These groups of lunatics and psychopaths go from apartment to apartment, cellar to cellar, and, hidden behind thick walls, commit crimes against the powerless civilians. Under these circumstances, going to the army barracks seemed like a better chance to leave this town in which one could already smell death. Upon our arrival at the barracks, we realized we were all in a trap.

Said must have been in one of the lines that I observed from my apartment balcony. I didn't comprehend then what those in line were about to experience.

At gunpoint we men were put on a bus. We were taken to one of Brčko's places of execution, a physical education hall in the center of town... For the couple hundreds of us locked up, the long hours of torture began. When this ended, they took four of us out for execution. We were selected by Ranko Češić... He put one of us against the wall, and shot him dead. Looking at the holes in his back, my whole life passed in front of my eyes. I thought I would never see either my wife or family again... My eyes closed, I lost consciousness, and my body crumbled onto pieces of glass.

Said's fainting awakened a bit of humanity in one of the Serbs. He was taken back inside. The next day he was put on a bus with a group of women and children and allowed to leave Bosnia.

He concluded his letter to President Bush asking, "For God's sake, please do something."

While in Copenhagen for the interview with Professor Bassiouni, I met Admir Karabašić, a nineteen-year-old Bosnian Muslim. Admir and his father had been detainees at a collection center near Trnopolje in Bosnian Serb-held territory. They were in a group of two hundred and fifty fighting-age men who were put on buses for an alleged prisoner exchange. Escorted by policemen from Prijedor, they were driven into a mountainous area. The buses stopped at the edge of the Korićani Cliffs, overlooking a steep ravine with one-hundred to three-hundred-meter drops.

The soldiers took the men from the buses in groups, lined them up in two rows at the edge of the ravine, and made them kneel. Admir knelt in front of his father and beside his brother. The police began shooting into the mass of kneeling prisoners. When the firing started, Admir's father shoved him over the edge. He tumbled down the ravine, landing on a pile of bodies. Soon afterward, the police pelted the pile with grenades.

Admir survived the fall and the grenades with a badly broken leg. He crawled out of the human destruction into a forested area. A streambed led him to a watermill. He remained there two days, slipping in and out of consciousness. In the meantime, authorities attempted to destroy evidence of the massacre, setting fire to the bodies. Two hundred and twenty-eight civilians lost their lives there, including his father and brother.

Admir eventually struck out from the watermill, following a trail along the streambed. After some time, he came to a dwelling occupied by Serb soldiers. By this time, he was delirious. The soldiers thought he was a Serb youth hurt in a bad accident. He was taken to a field hospital and treated for his injuries, which had become infected. In a feverish dream, he called out for his father (*babo*) as Muslims do, giving his heritage away. This caused great consternation among the field hospital staff.

Luckily, he was transferred to the central hospital in Banja Luka, where a Serb physician provided lifesaving care. His right leg was amputated below the knee. When he was strong enough, he was released to the care of a local humanitarian NGO, the Muslim Merhamet, where he and six other survivors of Korićani Cliffs received shelter. A local Serb police inspector provided protection, as the perpetrators from Prijedor wanted to kill the survivors. Alerted to their existence, the International Red Cross arranged safe passage to Croatia. From there Admir went to Germany for rehabilitation treatment, eventually settling in Denmark.

To me he seemed to have recovered well, persevering despite many losses. I was humbled by his calm demeanor and by his ability to endure and move forward.

I also had interviews with the U.S. State Department and with the Danish Special Police. Eventually it got to the point where those conducting the interviews said, "You are anticipating our questions!"

Early in 1994 George Alldridge visited me at the refugee center. Alldridge was a vice-consul at the U.S. Embassy in Copenhagen and connected to the U.S. Congressional Commission for Human Rights. He interviewed me regarding Luka. We struck up a friendship, and he later brought his family to Ødsted to meet mine.

I asked him whether the U.S. truly had strong interest in Bosnia, where it seemed so reluctant to intervene. As a candidate for the presidency in the fall of 1992, Bill Clinton had drawn attention to what he termed "the genocide" occurring in Bosnia. Since becoming president, however, he had been equivocal.

The international arms embargo remained in place and we lacked weapons to defend ourselves. Croatia partially circumvented the embargo by purchasing weaponry in Hungary. Bosnia had to rely upon Iran and our erstwhile ally Croatia for arms.

With the fall of the Berlin wall and the dissolution of the Soviet Union, I learned from Alldridge that Yugoslavia had been downgraded as a strategic priority for the United States. The Pentagon had cautioned that intervention could be costly in terms of American lives, as Yugoslavia had Europe's fourth largest military in 1990. America's leadership considered the war a European problem, turning responsibility for its resolution over to the European Union.

Alldridge said, "Great Britain's John Major and France's Mitterrand oppose military intervention in Bosnia."

We discussed reports that the UN's peacekeeping forces were exposed and trapped in Bosnia's "safe areas," posing little or no deterrent to the Bosnian Serb army.

I also expressed my wish that President Clinton would heed the open letter Britain's Margaret Thatcher had sent to him and other world leaders in September 1992. Mrs. Thatcher did not pull punches, writing, "In Bosnia, the democracies have used the need to deliver humanitarian aid both to excuse their own inaction and to keep the recognized multiethnic state of Bosnia outgunned and therefore itself unable to protect its civilian centers from slaughter by a dictator bent on making a Greater Serbia."

She observed that Croatia was now piling on a beleaguered Bosnia. Smelling blood and the opportunity for territorial expansion, it too waged war against the Bosnian army.

I asked Alldridge to encourage his government to step up the pressure on both Croatia and Serbia.

Living in Denmark and striving to have some impact, I could only wonder how my family back home fared. I feared for my two brothers, Ramiz and Mirsad, and my two nephews, Faruk and Jasmin, who remained caught in the vortex of the Bosnian War.

— 31 —

MY BROTHERS' WAR

Before leaving Macedonia, I had received a message from Ramiz, still held captive at Batković, saying that they were together, intact, and hoping to be part of a prisoner exchange. By the time he sent that message, conditions in the concentration camp had improved. Even so, he would later tell me, "I would have traded a twenty-year stretch in a Danish prison for the five months I spent at Batković."

What follows is what he related about their experiences during and after Batković.

When he, Mirsad, and Faruk arrived at Batković in the middle of July, camp operations were in full swing. Busloads of prisoners arrived regularly, often from other camps that were about to be discovered by the outside world. The prisoner population swelled from seven hundred to double that number and more.

Getting a taste of what was in store, my relatives were beaten with rubber truncheons as they stepped off the bus.

On their second day in camp, guards made a sweep, asking to see prisoner identification. They were looking for former JNA soldiers, who would be singled out for the worst treatment. This posed a serious problem for Faruk, who had attended military college before becoming a member of JNA Special Forces. His military ID indicated that. He would be blackballed and ineligible for prisoner exchange. With his background and experience, he could look forward to being one of the several dozen who were beaten to death that summer.

When the guards' intent became apparent, Mirsad asked Faruk for his ID book. Melting toward the back of the crowd, Mirsad tore the paper and cloth document into small pieces before swallowing it. When Faruk could produce no ID, explaining that it had been left behind when he was arrested, he was cuffed severely. He considered that a small price to pay.

Like others, my three relatives were beaten. For Ramiz, the hardest part was seeing his son sent off, only to return badly hurt. His inability to protect Faruk was a psychological torment. He had seen what happened to prisoners who lost their cool, and forcibly kept a rein on his anger.

To fight the boredom of incarceration, my relatives volunteered for work parties. Though slave labor, the work offered some variety, plus the meals were better than those served at the camp. Meals at Batković were inadequate. During Ramiz's imprisonment, his weight dropped from seventy-eight to forty-nine kilograms (170 to 108 pounds).

In late November, Ramiz and Faruk were offered the option of a prisoner exchange.

Both the Bosnian and the Bosnian Serb armies exchanged prisoners with the expectation that those rescued in this way would serve as soldiers. Mirsad was out on a work detail when the exchange took place, missing the opportunity. When he returned to the camp, Ramiz and Faruk were gone. His own exchange came five months later. Having survived a harsh winter in the unheated barn, he leapt at the chance. After repatriation, Mirsad was assigned as an infantryman to the 108th Motor Brigade in the 2nd Corps of the Bosnian army.

The 108th fought in the Brčko theatre. Soldiers in the Bosnian army were assigned to their home regions where possible; they knew the terrain and were resolute in their efforts to regain lost territory and their former lives.

In the 108th, Mirsad was reunited with Faruk, who had his own squad of handpicked special operatives. The focus of Faruk's unit was reconnaissance and disruption. Faruk was a tremendous soldier. His unit captured seven Serbian battle tanks. The captures were a major addition to the Second Corps' armament. For actions like these, Faruk was awarded the Golden Lily, Bosnia's highest military honor. On the eve of one of the war's decisive battles, near Brčko, Bosnia's President Izetbegović traveled to the front in an effort to rally the troops. He met with Faruk, later inviting him to join his security detail.

Ramiz was an officer in the Croatian army. My nephew Jasmin served under him. Ramiz's command was outside Brčko. After the Serbs pushed the Muslim and Croat resistance out of many areas of Brčko proper, the fighters fell back to the southern villages, joining their respective armies. In the Brčko fighting theater, the Bosnian and Croat armies cooperated, even as the two armies clashed for a period of time farther to the south.

In Brčko the opposing armies dug in, engaging in trench warfare. Croat and Bosnian forces established a front line within a sector of Brčko's city limits and held it. The fighting in the Brčko area was brutal. Ramiz and his squad fought from filthy, rat-infested trenches.

They experienced regular artillery fire. On multiple occasions Ramiz lost men to mortar rounds. Faruk was himself injured by a mortar. Soldiers lived in mortal fear of the white flash and incendiary heat. Ramiz said, "Life in the trenches was Russian roulette. It was random and deadly. The psychological pressure was really intense."

Mirsad also fought on the front lines, firing artillery, converted anti-aircraft guns, and heavy machine guns. From his trench he could see the silos of Bimal. He was decorated following a January 1994 action when Serb forces massed to breach his unit's area of the front line. His squad was in danger of being overrun. Spotting an overwhelming force approaching, the commander of his unit asked for a volunteer to man a forward machine gun position.

Mirsad's name means "peaceful" in Bosnian, but he volunteered anyway—provided that he had an ammunition bearer who would stay with him to keep the gun continuously fed. His close friend, Hajrudin, stepped up. The two men rushed forward to the gun emplacement. Once in place, they laid down a barrage with the Browning heavy-gun to devastating effect. Bosnian soldiers in the trenches could hear a Serb officer calling frantically for artillery support, shouting that his squad was being cut to shreds. Mirsad and his bearer shot relentlessly for five minutes, then took off running. Thirty seconds later the machine gun placement was demolished by an artillery barrage. The Bosnian line held and the Serb force retreated.

Several weeks later, Mirsad's position was again threatened. Fighting throughout the afternoon had been sporadic in his area but fierce a kilometer farther south where the Bosnian Serbs had concentrated forces in an attempt to break the Bosnian army's line. Late in the afternoon the fighting in front of Mirsad's position picked up. One of his fellow soldiers noticed several armored personnel carriers approaching from behind their line. Mirsad radioed field operations asking, "Do we have any APCs?" When the response came back, "No, the Serbs must have broken through," he said, "Damn, this looks bad."

The situation grew more serious several minutes later when he heard the motor roar and clank of tanks. Three T-55 tanks took up a position in front of the APCs. They began firing on the Bosnian army line. Mirsad's colleagues snapped off a couple of RPG rounds, which got the tanks' attention. The turret of one of the tanks pivoted toward Mirsad's position, firing its cannon. A berm of riprap projected directly behind Mirsad's trench. The tank ordinance exploded into it, with the berm absorbing some of the blast. Mirsad was thrown into the air and knocked unconscious.

When he came to, ten feet from where he had been standing, his back was in fiery pain. He knew he'd been hit. Two of his companions had been tossed completely out of the trench. They lay in the open, dead. His friend Hajrudin lay on his back in the trench. His abdomen had been torn open, with a portion of his intestine draped over his side. Hajrudin's right arm was damaged near the elbow; his hand had turned 180 degrees to the orientation of his upper arm. Mirsad went to his friend, tucked his intestine back in, and pressed the abdominal wound shut. He used Hajrudin's damaged arm as a compress, laying it on top of the wound, cinching it down with his belt.

He began dragging Hajrudin by his jacket collar. The trench exited into a deep ditch that drained the farm field. The ditch sheltered their retreat. It emptied into a wooded area at the edge of the farm field, three hundred meters away. As dusk descended, Hajrudin came to and began moaning. With Serb soldiers advancing, his groans posed a major problem.

Mirsad lay down beside Hajrudin, speaking low: "Listen to me, Hajrudin, and listen good. I am hurt too. If you don't stop making noise, we'll both be killed. If you shut up, I'll get you out. If you don't, at the next sound from you, I'm leaving you here."

Hajrudin complied. After reaching the woods, Mirsad found a hiding place. The two of them waited until well past dark, when Mirsad began pulling Hajrudin toward the safety of the Bosnian army's second line, a kilometer away. When they got within fifty meters of the trench, Mirsad heard voices. He called out, "We are Bosnian army and hurt."

A heated exchange ensued between Mirsad and those in the trench. He was told to stay put. When he had established his Bosnian army bona fides, three men rushed out in the dark to help him with Hajrudin. The two injured soldiers were taken to a field hospital and operated on. Mirsad had sustained a wound to his neck. He also had three pieces of shrapnel removed from his back. Hajrudin was stabilized and flown to Germany for life-saving surgery.

As an important battle loomed in May 1994, Roger Cohen, a war correspondent for *The New York Times*, embedded with the 108th and wrote about the soldiers' preparations for the coming fight.

> A Bosnian army officer, Mevludin Hasanović, stood today… close to the most sensitive line in the Bosnian War and delivered an impassioned message to the kneeling throng. "Clinton won't help you, Boutros-Ghali won't help you… After Goražde," he said, harking to the recent Bosnian Serb blitzkrieg of the United Nations safe area there, "we know that we must fight for victory alone."

Cohen noted, "The Bosnian forces, many of them refugees fighting to go home, appear driven by an implacable determination to take Brčko."

His article concluded with Hasanović telling his troops, "We have to clear our brains of the bad idealism that somebody will come to help us… Only we can save ourselves. We have to shoot the Serbian Četniks before they shoot us. That is the level of our existence."

Such was the existence that my two brothers and my two nephews experienced.

The war came to a negotiated settlement eighteen months later with the signing of the Dayton Accords on November 1, 1995. During negotiations in Dayton, Ohio, Serbian President Milošević represented Bosnian Serb interests. It was a demonstration of who had called the shots from the beginning.

Several developments contributed to reaching the agreement. In April 1994, bowing to intense U.S. pressure, the Croatian army ceased its war against Bosnia and the two countries reinstituted a military alliance. The U.S. started supplying arms to the Bosnian and Croatian armies. In the summer of 1995, the combined force began taking back wide swaths of territory from the Bosnian Serbs, putting that population to flight. The reversal was so swift, and the methods so intense, that the Western powers pressured the Bosnian and Croat armies to stand down.

By this time, the West's economic sanctions had begun to bite hard enough that Serbia grew interested in seeing the war end.

As these pressures built, the Bosnian Serbs overplayed their hand, doing something so terrible that it could not be overlooked or reasoned away.

In July 1995, the Bosnian-Serb army overran the United Nations safe areas in Srebrenica, Žepa, and Goražde. UN peacekeepers did not have the means—or the orders—to resist, so they stood by. At Srebrenica, Bosnian Serb forces under General Mladić captured and then murdered more than eight thousand Bosniak men and boys. Mladić proclaimed the act "a gift" to the Serbian nation, payback for atrocities allegedly committed by Turkish forces during what came to be called *The First Serb Uprising* in 1804. The outside world at last comprehended that Mladić and Karadžić intended to make good on their threats to annihilate Bosnia's Muslims. The outrage required a response. In August, NATO retaliated with intensive air strikes after four years of idle threats. The combination of NATO airpower and the Bosnian-Croat counteroffensive changed the facts on the ground. This war's diplomatic course had always been dictated by those facts. The new reality, and surging Bosnian-Croat capability, brought the parties to the Dayton bargaining table.

The ceasefire in Bosnia was tenuous, eventually requiring an international peacekeeping force of sixty thousand troops. An

International High Commission was created to settle disputes and to initially do the lion's share of Bosnia's governance. Karadžić's Republika Srpska ended up with forty-nine percent of Bosnian territory, while the Bosnian-Croat Federation controlled the remaining fifty-one percent.

Negotiations over Brčko's status failed. The parties agreed to submit the question of its future to international arbitration. The arbitration panel decided that Brčko would be separate from both Republika Srpska and the Federation. Brčko's governance would reflect the interests of all three constituent nations. In the early postwar period, with the potential for renewed conflict high, the U.S. established Camp McGovern on Brčko's city limits to support a peacekeeping force. With the Brčko bridges blown, the U.S. army constructed the world's longest pontoon bridge to span the Sava. The bridge provided U.S. troops with heavy equipment and weaponry in defense of their mission.

For my countrymen and my city, these interventions finally marked an end to the madness.

32

WAR CRIMES INVESTIGATORS

As the war careened toward its conclusion in 1995, requests for my story continued. It was considered useful in prosecuting individuals high and low for crimes against humanity. I hoped that by adding my story to those of others, justice would be served and act as a deterrent against such crimes in the future. The International Criminal Tribunal for the Former Yugoslavia called to mind the Second World War's Nuremburg trials. The ICTY represented the international community's first effort since Nuremburg to hold the perpetrators of war crimes accountable. The trials promised major courtroom confrontation against men—and one woman—accused of murdering their way to power and territorial gain.

I agreed to play a role. I would not escape my memories, but would instead present them to those on trial. I was about to enter a new and adversarial arena, facing some of the world's best defense counsels—my memory against their best professional efforts to call my experiences into question.

In April 1995, that journey began with a trip to Copenhagen. At its central police station, FBI agent Fred Buckley and Susan Castro, a forensics specialist from the U.S. Air Force, interviewed me for two days. The two Americans were on special assignment to the ICTY, investigating the Bosnian War as a potential crime scene.

The investigators heard a common refrain from the Bosnians they interviewed; they had told their stories over and over and asked what purpose would be served by telling them yet again. I challenged Buckley and Castro in this regard, saying, "I don't want to dredge up difficult memories if it will accomplish nothing."

Buckley responded, "Information provided by Bosnian refugees fueled media coverage that shined a light on what occurred. That coverage led to the formation of the tribunal. Where the tribunal finds hard evidence, it will take action."

In Copenhagen, I gave a thorough account of what I had seen and experienced. I described witnessing the shooting of civilians on the street, at the police station, and at Luka camp. I talked about the mass grave, about bodies overflowing the dumpster at the Partizan Sports Hall, and the federal army's direct involvement in the distribution of weapons, the administration of prison camps, and the blowing up of bridges.

"If your account is true, it will lead to indictments," said Buckley.

Over two days he and Castro repeatedly tested me. I think they found me consistent, with good recall for details and spatial relationships. I drew them maps and diagrams of the places where I had observed important events.

After the interview, Buckley returned to Tuzla, Bosnia, and his work with a four-person investigative team there. Tuzla was behind the front lines in territory controlled by the Bosnian army. In Tuzla he continued to interview refugees while waiting for the war to end. With the cessation of hostilities, his team would be able to enter Brčko, conduct crime scene investigations, and corroborate or rule out witness statements.

Once the war ended and NATO peacekeepers were in place, the investigation got under way in Brčko. This required coordination with the local police force, which was now composed entirely of Bosnian Serbs hostile to the probe. Buckley later told me, "The police denied my team access to Luka. I let them know that U.S. troops would back me up—that we would force our way in if necessary. They argued that angry Bosnian Serb citizens would endanger us. I invited them to come along if they thought it necessary to keep the peace. After that discussion, we entered Luka without incident."

At Luka, which had been cleaned up and repurposed as a warehousing facility for the past three years, he found landmarks as I had described. They went to my sleeping space in the warehouse and looked out through the openings in the metal door, taking pictures that showed I could see what went on in the street. They drove out to the area near EDB and exhumed the mass gravesite. Although Serb authorities had dug up many bodies, moving them to other sites to hide evidence, DNA evidence remained. The investigators scaled the power pole, taking photos that showed its view of the gravesite. In the downtown area, they used metal detectors, unearthing spent shell casings in the alleys I had described. At the police station, they went to the top floor, assessing the view it provided into the parking lot in back of the building. Buckley told me, "What we saw matched your descriptions and drawings."

The Bosnian War did not occur in an era of smartphones and selfies. Luka was not Abu Ghraib where jailers shared videos of their misdeeds on social media. At war's end, Buckley traveled to Bijeljina and met with Goran Jelisić's mother and sister to obtain a photograph of his suspect. The only photo Buckley possessed was Bojan Stojanović's prizewinner, taken from behind. In keeping with Bosnian hospitality, the two women offered him coffee and produced a photograph. Buckley said, "The hospitality ended when Jelisić's father arrived on the scene. He was enraged, but by then, we had what we needed."

Buckley later described meeting Jelisić at The Hague. "He was of good height, thin and baby-faced. My first impression was, 'This is the guy who did so much? You've got to be kidding!'"

33

RETURN TO BRČKO

Almost six years passed before I returned to Bosnia. My father-in-law, Salih, and I flew to Sarajevo in January 1998. We then drove a rented car to Brčko. The journey on snow-drifted mountain roads was slow and bitterly cold. The extended time provided an opportunity to take in the scenery. There were thousands of signs alongside the roadway warning of landmines. For me, having left Bosnia before the war's destructiveness got into full swing, the devastation to homes, businesses, and infrastructure was eye opening. Images of bombed out and neglected factories and shell pocked and roofless houses repeated in virtually every community on the long drive to Brčko.

Salih had fought in the Second World War. Then, an outside enemy had caused the destruction, the need to rebuild. What occurred from April 1992 to October 1995 was self-inflicted; it was literally beggar-thy-neighbor. We both commented on the colossal stupidity of it all. Our war gutted the economies of Bosnia, Croatia, Macedonia, Montenegro, and Serbia. Something substantial—the Yugoslav free-trade-zone—was atomized into republic-sized portions that were almost inconsequential. During the war, local citizens and outside paramilitaries looted Bosnia as a criminal enterprise. That enterprise masqueraded as a flowering of ancient glories and Serbian honor restored. It featured the standard propaganda and symbolism of those beating the drums of war, but anxious to have others do the fighting and dying.

As we approached Brčko, Salih asked, "How could a modern and educated people have been so gullible?" We both knew the stereotype within Yugoslavia that viewed Bosnians as likeable and hospitable, lacking in subtlety and diplomacy, but capable of enduring suffering like no others. Seeing the devastation that the war had wrought, as well as the depopulation of previously vibrant areas, I said, "We Bosnians were cynically played, and we fell for it."

The reunion with my family took place at Mirsad's home in an outlying village. Living in Brčko proper was not an option for any in my family at that time. Before I arrived, Ramiz warned me that Mirsad would challenge me over my pre-war insistence that we all stay in Brčko.

"He is going to make you answer for the ten months he spent at Batković."

I looked up Mirsad as soon as I arrived. If there were going to be problems, we needed to get over them.

Seeing me, Mirsad broke into a big grin. "You don't know how many times I wanted to slug you when I was in prison. Later I thought you did me a favor. If I'd joined the Bosnian army at the start of the war, back when it fought tanks with hunting rifles, I probably wouldn't have survived. It is good to see you again, my brother."

After six years away, reuniting felt tremendous to me, like a giant weight lifted. I met Mirsad's wife, Hata, for the first time. She and Mirsad met during the war; she was a cook for the Bosnian army. My sister, Ramiza, was also there. She and her young family spent the war years in the Mostar area, where they were trapped in a region with heavy fighting.

My parents lived in a nearby village. (They would not be able to reclaim their Brčko home until late 2001.) I bunked with them during my three-week stay, sleeping in the living room next to the wood-burning stove.

That arrangement conjured up satisfying memories of my youth. My parents had been strict but caring, insisting that their five children be honest, hardworking, and a credit to our family name. I admired my father for his strength and work ethic. I was a middle child who generally had his approval, but who knew that my older brother, Ramiz, would always be his favorite.

In many respects, I was also my mother's son. Fair-haired as a boy, I regularly heard, "You favor your blonde mother." She called me her "shadow and protector," as I often followed her at a distance to town and the marketplace. Her day began at five thirty a.m., stoking the stove to prepare breakfast. I would rise with her to help, viewing that time with her as special. Even as an eight-year-old I enjoyed sitting with her over a cup of coffee, dipping a cake or a lump of sugar, and having her undivided attention before we both started our days.

Thirty-plus years later, I again rose early with my mother to stoke the stove and to talk.

We discussed what had occurred over the past six years. She was philosophical, having the perspective that in the long run, events tended toward peace—not so much because people are inherently peace-seeking, but because we run out of energy and eventually see the futility of war. My father's input was different. He thought history's lessons faded fast, that every fifty years came a new generation who, lacking an understanding of the past, could be steered toward violence.

My parents expressed their deep, abiding relief that their five children had survived the war. This was the fact that mattered to them. They were not consumed with regret or thoughts of score settling. My long conversations with the two of them were therapeutic. I could sense my anger over the war waning.

I made two trips into Brčko during my visit. The drives into the city center were sobering. The city's outlying residential areas had been badly damaged, with evidence of destruction everywhere. Arriving downtown, I found it in better shape. On my first trip, I parked and walked to my apartment, but did not confront the Serb family living there.

From the apartment, I hiked to the neighborhood where I grew up, in the shadow of the Bimal plant. Our old house had been damaged, and stood vacant. As I sat on an abandoned bench in the backyard, a torrent of family memories came flooding back.

At the end of the Second World War, my father was assigned to the military intelligence service. He joined a joint military and police force maintaining safety and security in the Brčko area and was responsible for one of the larger outlying villages. During that assignment he met, and in 1948 married, Šemsa Sabuljić.

My mother was four years older than my father. She grew up in a Bosnian Muslim family in a village located seven kilometers from Brčko. After her schooling, she worked as a nanny for a prominent Jewish family, growing close to them.

Following the Second World War, she was the first Muslim woman in Brčko to drop the veil. Although the communist leadership in the community—who promoted a society devoid of religious requirement—viewed this positively, her choice was personal. There were consequences. She was derided and spat upon by some in the Muslim community. Nevertheless, she was undeterred. Soon many others followed her example. For me, my mother was a tolerant iconoclast, resolute in her convictions.

By the time I joined the family in 1957, my parents had worked hard to establish a foothold in a country recovering from war and occupation. My father had left the army. Both he and my mother worked for Bimal, a company that processed vegetable oil and other agricultural products. It was the largest economic concern in Brčko, employing more than one thousand. My father was the plant's safety officer and a fireman. To provide for our large family, he regularly took on extra—and hazardous—maintenance assignments at the plant.

Bimal families populated our neighborhood. Back then, our community water supply was delivered by metal pipe, with one spigot to each city block. We had a large yard with a vegetable garden and wine grapes. Brčko winters were harsh, and bringing home logs to stock the family woodpile was year-round work for us.

My grandmother lived with the family until her death at age 103. She was from Albania and spoke only her native tongue. We were close, and she taught me her language.

My father and I both loved dogs. We had a Šar shepherd dog named Dickie. He had all of that ancient breed's strong characteristics. Šars could be left alone in the high country to protect their flocks without human supervision. They were sturdy and courageous enough to take down wolves and drive away bears. With us, Dickie had a flock of five goats and was vigilant looking after them.

I thought he shared many traits with my father, as both were devoted, smart, and calm until called into action. As a boy, I cherished being asked to go with them on my father's evening rounds at the Bimal plant. As he brought us around to meet his coworkers, I could sense my father was proud of Dickie, and of me.

Back home, my mother complained that I was high-energy, banishing me to the out of doors. I liked that, spending time there with other kids from the neighborhood. We made up games, played sports, and explored.

When I was eight, one of those outdoor escapades almost ended badly. Roughhousing with friends on a winter afternoon, I fell. We played near the spigot that delivered hot water to the neighborhood, courtesy of the Bimal steam plant. Someone had attempted to fill a glass jug in the cold air, neglecting to clean up the mess after it shattered upon exposure to the hot water. I went hands first into the glass, nicking an artery. Most of the neighborhood's adults were at work. With the uncanny sense possessed by all mothers, my grandmother was outside looking for me. She found me being helped home by friends, blood spurting from my wrist. Running toward us, she tore off her scarf, using it as a tourniquet. She rushed me to a nearby clinic, where the staff called for an ambulance. The wound was deep, requiring a surgeon.

At the Brčko hospital I met Dr. Edhemović. He acted very calm, looking me in the eye and talking to me like an adult. "You look strong. Is that true?" I said I was.

"That's good. That will help me. Closing this wound will take some time, so we both need to be patient. If we are, everything will turn out fine." He gave me an injection to dull the pain.

My grandmother had questions for the doctor, which I interpreted. Dr. Edhemović talked to us throughout the procedure. Halfway through, my father arrived, escorted by a nurse. By his manner I could tell he had a good opinion of the surgeon, and that they were acquainted.

After many stitches the surgeon said, "The repair is good and complete. You were an outstanding patient. There will be a scar to remember your accident and our time together, but it will fade and be less noticeable after a few years."

He used surgical staples and made a cast from my hand to the midpoint of my upper arm. The staples and cast were needed to prevent the wound from reopening. On the way home, my father said, "I've seen Dr. Edhemović before, when we have brought in men hurt at the plant. He is very good. I think you are going to be fine. Brčko is lucky to have a surgeon with his ability."

At home my friend Said Muminović stopped by. The cast impressed him, as did hearing about my stitches. My mother invited him to dinner; she had made my favorite—burek meat pies. I fell asleep at dinner, exhausted from blood loss and the day's commotion. When I awoke the next morning, Said was back at our table, checking in on me.

Said and I spent many afternoons at the Radnik movie theatre. One of Ramiz's friends worked there, offering us tickets in exchange for cleaning the aisles between shows. The films and the scenes they portrayed got me thinking about seeing a world beyond Brčko. Once I started canoeing, I hoped that paddling would provide me that avenue to the outside world.

Most evenings I stayed up with my older sister, Jagoda, listening to jazz programs broadcast by Radio Free Europe, wondering about the lands and people where the music was made.

In 1971, we moved. The Brčko economy, like Yugoslavia itself, had made significant strides, and my parents bought a new house. It was comfortable and considerably larger. There was no more need to fetch water from an outdoor pipe for a quick bath or shower.

When I turned fourteen, my father occasionally asked me to work at the plant. In retrospect, he was prepping me for the work world, and for manhood. I would tend the fire hose when he and his coworkers were below ground cleaning out the plant's drainage and filtration systems, or I would keep ropes coiled and untangled at the top of the silos when they descended into them to scrape residue from their sides. For me the climb to the top and the view of Brčko from twelve stories high was outstanding, as was being around the workmen. When my father lowered himself into the silo wearing a mountaineer's harness and headlamp, he looked like a coalminer slipping into the earth. When he emerged following the dirty and dangerous work, the image was complete.

While I waited on the silo, I had a bird's eye view of my city. I could see the city's railway, bridge, and harbor connections, along with the outlying villages that doubled Brčko's municipal population. The view included great green fields of corn and soybean, quince and plum orchards, as well as the long, narrow barns of large livestock operations. The view gave me an appreciation for my city and its possibilities.

When I was fifteen I was invited to attend a special camp sponsored by the national police academy. Those invited had expressed an interest and demonstrated an aptitude for police work. The camp was a tryout of sorts, and could lead to leaving home and attending the police academy. I enjoyed the camp, and at its conclusion was called in to meet with the director.

He said, "You have abilities and some good qualities. You are enthusiastic, perhaps too much so. Your group was very boisterous on the rifle range. We waited to see if you would get them focused and under control. You didn't. You were also the recruit who asked the most questions. Some of the instructors wondered if you questioned their authority. In the police, we ask our suspects questions, and show our commanders respect. We think you need to mature. Think about what I have said. If you do mature, in a year you are welcome to apply again."

I had a similar, albeit far more heated, discussion with my father eight years later. Arriving home after training, my father confronted me. "When are you going to learn? Do you think that because you are some big-shot athlete, you can say anything? It was bad enough when you criticized Tito's legacy and got reprimanded by the JNA. Now, you've opened your big mouth and are in trouble with the communist party. I got pulled aside at work. I was told to warn you. You are on thin ice—you could lose your job. How can you do this to me? I fought for Tito, and the Party. Now you question them. You have done nothing, and know nothing, but school, and sports, and travel. You have no appreciation for the sacrifices we made, or for what happens to malcontents when hard times come. You had better wise up."

When I didn't seem to take what my father had said seriously enough, he slapped me—hard—on the cheek. Taken aback, I saw he was prepared to fight me, to impose his will. Still full of myself, I thought, *I push heavy weights three times a week. You're no match for me.* Fortunately, I didn't say this. I backed down, saying, "Okay, that's enough. I heard you. I'll button up—be more discreet."

Inside, I fumed, angry and embarrassed at being treated like a child. I left the house, and didn't see my father again for three weeks. By then, we had both cooled down.

Now, fifteen years later, and a father myself, I better comprehended what my father intended that day, and the emotional investment parents have in their children. That night, over dinner, I finally told my parents, "I am grateful for your example."

34

FRIENDSHIP RENEWED

The following day, I met coach Čonda at a restaurant. Seeing me, his eyes registered surprise, then teared up. He pulled me close, enveloping me in a bear hug. I felt a wonderful warmth. My eyes were also moist—showing relief and happiness. We were both intact—survivors. Being back in Čonda's company felt hugely satisfying. We had experienced so much together—and apart.

After catching up, we walked down to the boathouse, which had been demolished during the war. It had not been rebuilt. Seeing its status, I said, "The boathouse is in the same shape as our country. Look at what this stupid war accomplished. It took everything good, and leveled it. I can only hope that you will someday have a new building and athletes on the water. Brčko needs you back coaching."

We continued walking along the footpath. Coming to an area of concrete seating built into the terraced riverbank, Čonda suggested we sit down, dusting away a layer of snow. Dressed for the weather, we sat quietly, gazing out onto the Sava. A wan midafternoon sun shone, providing a bit of warmth and cheer. The Gunja Bridge was prominent five hundred meters downstream. It had been repaired, and was open to vehicle traffic.

As we sat reminiscing in the late afternoon sun, Čonda said, "I'm sure you remember the time the Hungarian national team came here for the Memorial 10K. Was it 1983? I think so."

"Yes, it was the August before our Winter Olympics."

"That was some day. Six thousand people sitting here, and crowding onto the bridge to watch your race. The atmosphere was something else—crackling, electric. When they introduced each of you, it was like something out of the Roman Coliseum—gladiatorial. You were sure the favorite that day—with people chanting 'Gaši, Gaši' throughout the race.

"I remember that. I also knew wagers were being made, and that before long I was either going to be a hero or a goat. Even though Mirko was entered, and the Hungarians were very good, I felt calm. I always felt confident racing on the Sava."

"Well I was nervous for you. You should have heard the crowd when you started accelerating on the last lap."

"Believe me, the noise carried over the water. The one Hungarian kept it close though. It was a relief when he fell away in the last two hundred meters."

"Yes, that day you were 'the boy who won his town the race.' I had people coming up to me for days afterward, wanting to talk about 'The Race' and congratulating me for being your coach.

"As good as that day was, your race to win the first Yugoslav marathon championships and to qualify for the worlds in 1988 was better.

"When you came by the grandstand at 5K in fifth, and trailing that group of Ljubek, Mirko, and Sabjan, we all thought it was over. They were world champions and working together. You were isolated, having to eat their waves. We waited almost three hours to see what happened.

"Finally, we could see two paddlers way out in front. When they passed under the bridge and into better view, I knew it was Mirko and I thought the other paddler was Ljubek. Jasminka said, 'No, it is Bison (Mirko's nickname) and Isak.' It turned out she had better eyesight than me. When you started pulling ahead, my assistant, Samid, got so excited he ran into the river and got stuck past his knees in the mud. We left him to go congratulate you. When we came back, he was still stuck. He said seeing you win was worth it. That was a great day for all of us."

After several more stories from our shared vault, we stood stiffly and began walking downstream, toward Luka. Čonda turned more serious, saying, "I lost six of you during the war. That was really hard. I was so grateful when you made it out. I heard it was by a hair's breadth.

"We all know Elvedin is gone. What else could have happened? It is as if he vanished from the face of the earth. I've heard you may have seen him."

"I'm sorry to say, I probably did," I replied, as the memory of my fallen friend in the bloodstained yellow shirt came rushing back.

"Was it because he had been a paratrooper? Because someone thought he was a danger? You know what makes it so hard? Just days before the war started, I saw his wife and his son down at the train station, waiting for Elvedin's train to pull in. He waved to them from his locomotive. The boy was so excited. And his wife was pregnant. You could just see the pride she had in Elvedin and the hopes she had for their family."

"Well, they are in the United States now—Kansas City. She is working as a pharmacist."

Our talk turned to the many others we knew, and had lost.

When it was time to depart, Čonda asked, "When will you be back, hopefully for good?"

"I'll visit next year. I'm just not ready to live here permanently. It has been great seeing you though—this was something I really needed."

On that first trip home, I could not bring myself to walk down to Luka. Doing so would have fanned memories that were still too difficult.

Two years earlier, former Swedish Prime Minister Carl Bildt had something similar to say as he assumed the role of high commissioner for Bosnia:

> My first visit to Brčko came as a shock. The southern end of the town made it look as if the world had come to an end. Snow covered the ruins, which stretched as far as the eye could see. But what made the greatest impression was not what could be seen, but what the ear could not hear. There was absolute silence. Life always involves sounds—a dog, traffic

on a distant road. But here there was nothing, just silence and ruins.

I made my way down to the Brčko harbor. At one time coal from the mines in Tuzla was shipped by barge to the steelworks in Serbia. Now the harbor was destroyed, the mines closed down, the bridge with a gaping hole in the middle … But the harbor was also a prison camp and execution site when the Serb campaign of cleansing began. From here bodies were flung from the quay down into the river. Executions took place in the warehouse. The police accompanying me looked around, resigned, ashamed, and confused, as I walked in silence between the quay and the warehouse. I did not want to enter the building.[13]

Despite the war's devastation, Brčko eventually came to be viewed internationally as an indicator city for measuring Bosnia's recovery and the effectiveness of international peacekeeping efforts. In a world still torn by nationalistic strife, Brčko remains a global social laboratory for testing reconciliation efforts.[14]

I made a follow-up trip in 2000. At that time, I wrote to a friend: "Today I am in Denmark, having just visited Bosnia. The trip was excellent. It was great to be with family and to see my parents. I had a chance to canoe on the Sava River and it was a strange and wonderful feeling to be back on those waters after so many years. The boathouse has been restored and my club is functioning. My old coach is back leading the team."

Mirko visited me in Brčko during that 2000 trip. We walked down to Luka and took a photo together outside the warehouse. For me the photo evokes the movie *Stand by Me*, which is exactly what Mirko did for me during a time of great need. I expressed my thanks, both for sheltering my family and for interceding on my behalf with Captain Dragan. I had always thought that Mirko's reputation and influence was the principal reason for my release. I had expressed this in interviews with Danish press. In follow-up, one Danish paper, the *Jyllands-Posten*, sent a reporter to Belgrade and wrote an article about Mirko's friendship and assistance.

That day at Luka, Mirko said, "Yes, thanks. What else are friends for? I want you to know that Jasminka was the real star that morning with Dragan. I was there and probably helped, but it was ninety-nine percent Jasminka. She was incredible. You know, that woman really loves you, although it is a mystery to me why."

Matija Ljubek could not join us for this reunion, as he was in Sydney, Australia, watching his youngest son, Nikica, compete in canoeing at the 2000 Summer Olympics. Matija and I made plans to meet in the United States the next summer. He was an official in the International Canoe Federation and we scheduled a visit in Gainesville, Georgia, the site chosen to host the 2003 world championships.

As the situation in Brčko stabilized and the need for the peacekeeping force diminished, Jasminka and I regained our apartment. Eventually we sold it, using the proceeds to purchase property outside Brčko on a tributary to the Brka River. We had Mirsad build us a home nestled among working farms and plum orchards. The house sits at the end of a grassy lane. The setting is peaceful. Calls for prayer from a nearby mosque mix with the murmurings of the creek and the sounds of farm animals. Out there, in the country near Mirsad's home, I felt relaxed and connected to the Bosnia of my first thirty-five years.

Seeing Mirsad was always a highlight of our visits. Jasminka's face lights up whenever Mirsad is mentioned. Before our home was built, Mirsad and his wife would give up their bedroom and sleep outside on the patio whenever we came to town. Every week for years Mirsad gave money to a woman who sold religious tracts outside the White Mosque. Her name was Zinca. She once asked him, "Gaši, why are you so good to me?" He told her that someone in a distant land thought her special.

Mirsad and Mira's son became good friends. At first I thought this surprising, as they had been on opposing frontlines during the war. I later recalled something Hemingway said about those on the frontlines being the best soldiers and men. They had the most invested and shared a common trial by fire.

Jasminka and I never had the opportunity to see Mira again, to thank her face to face. She passed shortly after the war's end.

During one visit, Mirsad and I walked downtown. After we had passed another pedestrian, Mirsad nudged me, saying, "You didn't recognize your old friend Kosta." I looked back. It was indeed the backside of Luka's deputy commander, with the same hitch in his stride. I was tempted to shout to him. I had a curiosity about what made such men tick and wanted to see what he was like after the war. I thought to myself, *Perhaps another day.* That day did not come around anytime soon. The next morning Kosta was arrested and charged in a national court, eventually receiving a six-year sentence.

To my deep disappointment and grief, my reunion with Matija Ljubek never occurred. My friend died six days after his return from Sydney. He was shot and killed while defending his mother from an attacker.

35

MEETING MILOŠEVIĆ

While my extended family either took up old lives in Bosnia or fashioned new ones in Denmark and the United States, I maintained contact with the International Criminal Tribunal for the Former Yugoslavia. Though I eventually lived an ocean and nine time zones away (in the U.S.A.'s Pacific Northwest), I wanted to see that process through.

The process started with the witness statement taken by ICTY investigators Susan Castro and Fred Buckley. Many witnesses made their statements under a protective seal. I wanted my testimony attributed to me, and to meet the accused face-to-face in open court.

At one point Buckley warned me, "You are making yourself vulnerable. I'm surprised they haven't killed you. They have the means. You are a witness who gives an overall picture of what happened and who implicates those higher up."

In May 1996, the ICTY called me to The Hague, Netherlands, to testify in the trial of Dušan Tadić. His was the first trial by an international criminal court since the Second World War. I was the sixth witness. I arrived a day early and went over my witness statement with the prosecutors assigned to the case. That evening they drove me to the courthouse. Three special courtrooms had been constructed there for the ICTY. The facility had high security, with separate entrances and elevators for defense and prosecution. The visit was intended to give me an idea of what to expect.

Security at the hotel where witnesses stayed was strong and included a police escort on the drive to the courtroom the next morning. We passed through a police checkpoint on arrival, parking in a special underground lot. The courtroom, now packed with judges, attorneys, and international media, presented a scene much different from the empty room the night before. The charged atmosphere felt like my oral examinations as a university student, only multiplied fifty-fold. I was fitted with headphones for translation purposes and sworn in. I sat in the witness box directly facing the four red-robed judges, who sat above me. Each judge had two computer monitors. Directly below them and facing me were five black-robed individuals who supported the judges. Prosecutors were to my right, while the accused with his counsel were seated to my left. Translators were visible through glass in an upper room. Blue and gray curtains provided a backdrop for the television cameras.

The accused, Tadić, lived in the small northwestern Bosnian town of Kozarac. He was a karate instructor and café owner, as well as a leader in the local Bosnian Serb (SDS) political party. The changing political situation in Bosnia had provided him an opportunity to be the town's political strongman. When hostilities broke out, he became a daily presence in the nearby Omarska prison camp, where he was given free rein. Tadić practiced his karate on the prisoners. Much like Jelisić and Česić at Luka, he was alleged to have inflicted unconscionable acts. Eyewitnesses to his actions were scheduled to follow my testimony.

The prosecution called me as an expert witness who could show that there was a similar pattern between the atrocities in Luka and those at Omarska and that it was part of a widespread, systematic campaign against Bosnia's non-Serb population. Michail Wladimiroff, a prominent Dutch law professor and defense counsel, represented Tadić. Wladimiroff helped draft rules for the International Criminal Tribunal, knowing that these early cases would define new areas of international law. He participated to ensure strong representation for the accused. Following my testimony, his cross-examination primarily tested my knowledge of the various uniforms Serb forces wore as well as the designations that signified whether war equipment belonged to the JNA or to paramilitary forces.

Although my testimony went well and the cross-examination was relatively straightforward, the courtroom experience took some toll on me. I relived my Luka days as they were introduced into the court record, remaining keyed up for several days after returning to Denmark. My Luka nightmares returned. Now invested in the outcome, I followed the trial as it ground along. It lasted a year. The court ultimately convicted Tadić of crimes against humanity, breaches of the Geneva Convention, and violations of the customs of war. He received a sentence of twenty years. On appeal two years later, his sentence was increased to twenty-five years. Reaction from the Bosnian government was muted. They pushed for those who had been indicted and who were higher up in the chain of command, individuals like Radovan Karadžić and Ratko Mladić, to be arrested and brought to trial.

In that regard, U.S. and NATO forces treaded lightly. Some of the indicted hid out in Serbia where the peacekeepers had no jurisdiction. Within the territory of Republika Srpska, where there was jurisdiction, there was a reluctance to pursue the big fish, fearing organized resistance from a supportive population and a return to violence.[15]

An individual less immune was my former jailer, Goran Jelisić. U.S. Navy Seal Team Six arrested him on January 22, 1998, as he walked from his home to his car. The farm machinery mechanic was grabbed, handcuffed, and pushed into an unmarked van. He was the first of those indicted by the ICTY to be arrested by U.S. forces. President Clinton authorized the operation and was notified of its successful conclusion. My witness statement had helped obtain Jelisić's indictment. News of his arrest was welcome; he had cut a wide swath at Luka, harming many.

The ICTY judges convicted him on thirty-one counts of crimes against humanity and of breaching the laws and customs of war. He was acquitted on a genocide charge. The judges concluded that he killed for the sheer pleasure it provided him, and not with intent to wipe out a particular population. He received a sentence of forty years and is imprisoned in Italy.

Serbia's President Slobodan Milošević eventually received an ICTY indictment. In October 2000, he called for early parliamentary elections and was unexpectedly defeated. The incoming regime ordered his arrest. After a standoff at his home, Milošević was captured and extradited to The Hague.

Traveling from the United States, I gave testimony in his trial in early September 2003. Milošević handled his own defense, providing me an opportunity to converse face to face with Serbia's former president. It was an exchange I both desired and was anxious about.

In the weeks preceding my testimony I was on edge. I would confront a man the international press had labeled the "Butcher of the Balkans," the man who had pulled the strings that caused the suffering experienced by so many of my countrymen. By reputation and actual performance, Milošević was an enigmatic genius. A lawyer turned international banker, and then national leader, he had held the international community off balance and at bay for years. He overplayed his hand in 1998 when his repression of Kosovo's Albanian population led to NATO intervention and an ICTY indictment.

I had long wondered how I would fare if I came together with Milošević, and what tactics he would use to overcome my testimony and experiences. It was a conversation and a confrontation that I needed. I wanted him to respond to my experience.

Ever since seeing him speak in Belgrade in 1988, I thought he was the man making the decisions that led to the Bosnian War. He was charismatic—when he spoke, people listened. He had a much stronger appeal and presence than did our Bosnian leader Izetbegović or the Slovenian leader Kučan. He could have been the Yugoslav leader to replace Tito and unite the republics.

Milošević gave the impression that something boiled inside him—that if you opposed what he was saying, watch out. In that regard, and in his physical stance, he reminded me of the pictures I'd seen of Italy's former leader, Benito Mussolini—imperial, self-assured, and belligerent.

I felt tense flying to Holland for the trial. I expected Milošević would be the opponent of my lifetime. I wanted to keep my composure and make my points.

After arriving in Holland, my testimony was postponed due to Milošević's illness. I spent several days cooling my heels at the hotel and touring The Hague. One of the other hotel guests was a woman from Zvornik, Bosnia, who also waited to testify in the Milošević trial. She reminded me of my mother, and we struck up a friendship. One morning she asked me to accompany her to the nearby Scheveningen beach. We spent a good day on the pier and in the museums. Walking on the beach at day's end, she asked, "Is it safe to wade in the ocean? I have always wanted to experience the Atlantic."

We kicked off our shoes and rolled up our pants legs to do so.

On the taxi ride home she told me she was nervous about going to court, even though she was a protected witness and would have a curtain separating her from the courtroom audience and television cameras. She showed me a photo of her husband and two grown sons. The war started in her city of Zvornik with artillery shelling from the Serbian town of Mali Zvornik, just across the Drina River. Her hometown was where I met Captain Dragan after being released from Luka.

From the trial transcript, I later learned that the woman, her husband, sons, and thirty neighbors had taken refuge in the basement of a large building. After twenty-four hours of hiding, the cellar door was blasted. Paramilitary soldiers led the basement's occupants outside. Women and children were separated from the men and marched away. After they had walked two hundred meters, the woman heard massive rifle fire from the building. She was not allowed to look back, but knew her husband and sons perished at that moment.

To help her maintain her resolve while testifying, I suggested she make a copy of her family photo and take it into the courtroom with her. "If someone tries to get tough with you, look at the picture of your loved ones. It will give you courage. I know you will honor their memory."

With my appearance delayed for a week, I traveled to Vejle, Denmark, to visit family and friends for several days. Upon my return to The Hague, a card and a present were waiting. The woman wrote, "I gave my testimony, and having the picture helped. Afterward, the judges asked to include it in the court record. I am relieved that my husband and sons are part of the permanent record and that they mattered to history. Thanks for your friendship to me. I hope your daughter likes the sweater."

When I entered the courtroom on September 11, Slobodan Milošević was already there. Despite having been ill, he looked good. He was well dressed, in a gray suit with a red tie. He sat back, with his left arm resting lightly on the back of his chair. He looked at ease. His receding hairline was combed straight back into a crown. His forehead dominated his face. He had large ears, sparse eyebrows, and alert eyes. As I sat down, our eyes met. His seemed to express a curiosity. I am quite certain mine did.

Meeting Milošević face-to-face, I soon learned that what I had heard was true. In his diction, manner and appearance, he was smooth, sophisticated, and charming. It was easy to see how he had operated effectively at the highest levels, with the Majors, Mitterands, and Clintons of the world. After I testified for the prosecution, Milošević had ninety minutes to cross-examine me.

He walked me through my witness statement, hoping to catch me in an uncertainty or a contradiction. He primarily insinuated that the difficulties I had experienced were caused by the actions of others from the local community, or at most, wider Bosnia. The questions he asked were probing, but expressed in a conversational way. I sensed he was prepared to pounce on any sign of weakness.

Relative to my witness statement implicating the national army's involvement, he stated, "Did you know that at that time, or even before that actual time, JNA units were not there at all?"

"What do you mean weren't there? I saw them on a daily basis. I saw the JNA at the barracks and at the JNA training ground near my work. At one point, Lt. Col. Malinković came with an escort. They came to EDB and I saw them at the gate."

"All right, but did you see any JNA soldiers killing anyone?"

"Well, Ranko Češić belonged to the JNA and he wore JNA camouflage when he shot two men in front of me at Luka."

Milošević later referred to my testimony regarding a Major Djurković of the JNA visiting Luka, and asked, "Was Djurković a major in the army of Republika Srpska and also a local inhabitant?"

"I don't know of him being a major in the army of Republika Srpska. The only army that existed in Brčko was the JNA. Now what it came to be called later, I really can't say. I think he said he was a native of Bijeljina actually."

Milošević later asserted that one of the Luka thugs, who called himself Enver the Četnik, must have been a Muslim rather than Serb. Enver was the paramilitary who carved a cross into the forehead of the man who slept next to me at Luka. In Milošević's mind, Enver was more commonly a Muslim name. "Well, if his name was Enver, I assume he was a Muslim, wasn't he? And I also assume he was a local inhabitant."

"He had patches on his uniform which denoted a Četnik, with the cockade—the double-headed eagle of Serbia. And he said his name was Enver and that he was a Četnik—that is to say, a member of the Serb Radical party. Now whether he gave his real name or not, I can't say. I don't know people and I can't recognize ethnic groups judging by their names."

"Well if he was … If his name was Enver, he couldn't have been a Serb."

"I can say my own name is George and I wouldn't be an American."

Milošević later cleverly posed a question regarding the mistreatment I received. He used a Bosnian word that would be translated as "torture" to the judges, but which in our language meant something more: "eternal suffering."

While I had been tortured, I had to answer no to a question regarding eternal suffering.

Later, Milošević tried to have me agree with the statement, "So there was general chaos."

"Well, as to general chaos, I wouldn't put it that way, because everything was nonetheless controlled by the JNA. I think everything was controlled from the garrison, from the officers stationed there."

When Milošević had no more questions, he told the presiding judge, "All right, Mr. May. I should like to thank the witness."

The judge told me, "Mr. Gaši that concludes your evidence. Thank you for coming to the tribunal to present it. You are now free to go."

That evening I wrote a friend, "Today it was D-day. I was in court and met President Milošević. Everything was good. After my testimony, he had ninety minutes for cross-examination. He tried hard, but ran out of questions. He didn't use all his time. After I finished in the court, the lead prosecutor came to the witness room and said that my testimony was outstanding. She was very satisfied. My race with Milošević is done."

To me, the contest with Milošević was far more important than any I had as an athlete. Even though it went well and I was satisfied with my testimony, the experience wore me out. Reopening the old wounds always did that.

36

LEAD WITNESS

In the years that followed, I returned to The Hague to testify in the trials of Vojislav Šešelj, Radovan Karadžić, and Momčilo Krajišnik. Like Milošević, these three were "Big Fish." Šešelj, the head of the Serb Radical party and the Četnik paramilitary group, was reportedly an outstanding attorney. He, like Milošević, conducted his own defense.

During my time with him, Šešelj was pugnacious and insulting with the prosecutors and the judges. His mouth was set in a permanent snarl—baring his bottom set of teeth. Beneath his crew cut, he had a bulbous nose and narrow, hooded eyes.

My responses to his questions and my unwillingness to concur with his contentions seemed to exasperate him. At one point, he steamed, rose angrily, and his face turned red. He accused me of being "arrogant." Perhaps the truth sounded arrogant when it contradicted him.

Šešelj had not wanted me to testify. A document from the Public Library of U.S. Diplomacy entitled *ICTY: Witness Troubles at the Šešelj Trial* states, "Šešelj's legal advisors are associated with a campaign of intimidation against at least a dozen witnesses who had agreed to testify for the Office of the Prosecutor (OTP)." I was one of those witnesses. Šešelj's associates tried to get to me through Mirko, threatening to burn his restaurant down. I informed the OTP about the attempted tampering. The OTP's Chief of Trials reported, "Gaši, a former Olympic kayaker, is tough and remains committed to testifying for the prosecution."[16]

For actions like these, as well as for revealing protected witnesses on his website, the court twice found Šešelj guilty of contempt of court. He received prison terms for the contempt charges.

In February 2004, I testified in the trial of Momčilo Krajišnik. Together with Radovan Karadžić, Krajišnik was a cofounder of the SDS and considered the number two political power in Republika Srpska. He was a member of its five-man presidency during the Bosnian War. Prior to the war, before the SDS pulled out of Bosnia's parliament, Krajišnik had been speaker of the parliament. He was a veteran politician who steered Karadžić, particularly in the period leading up to and throughout the first year of the Bosnian War. After that Karadžić gained experience and acted more independently.

In his opening statement, Krajišnik said, "I would like to state that I believe in God and in justice. I believe that truth will win and I will finally be a free man."

I met the prosecutor, Thomas Hannis, three days before the Krajišnik trial. We went over my witness statement. He said, "We picked you to go first because you were tried and tested in previous trials. We want to start with a witness who lived through things that were terrible; someone who can attest to murders, imprisonment, deportation—a crime-based witness."

Hannis told me the defense would focus on the first witness, putting significant time and effort into the cross-examination. "Expect to be challenged from the word go."

In his opening statement, Hannis stated that the prosecution would demonstrate that the "accused failed to take necessary and reasonable measures to protect from the offenses occurring or to punish the perpetrators" under his control. He also referenced the "solemn responsibilities imposed on us by the international community."

When attention turned to me, I agreed to "solemnly swear that I will speak the truth, the whole truth, and nothing but the truth."

Hannis then began presenting his case and leading me through my testimony. His responses to each of the defense counsel's objections were sharp and to the point. The two counsels went back and forth like Olympic fencers, even as they referred to one another as "learned friend." From his formidable and slightly mocking manner, I could see that my upcoming cross-examination by the English lawyer, Stewart, would be rigorous.

Our conversation would not take place that day. At 7:07 in the evening, after five hours of testimony, the court adjourned. The trial reconvened at two p.m. the following day, with Hannis taking more of my testimony. Anticipating that the defense would raise issues relative to the incomplete report I had provided to Captain Dragan, Hannis asked me about it. I testified, "I did not report everything because I wanted to save my life."

Hannis also had me establish that I was no longer a member of any political party at the time of Bosnia's referendum. I testified, "By then, I was independent, a free agent."

When it was Stewart's turn, he stripped down to the task, asking the presiding judge, "Your Honor, can I take my wig off? Because it is a lot easier. I hope your honor doesn't mind me being half dressed in the national style, but it is a bit ridiculous with the headphones."

Stewart knew that I had been an athlete, and he tried to draw out my competitive nature. Early on he began probing me hard and with an edge. I told myself, *He wants you to lose your composure. Don't get drawn in too deeply.*

As he asked me to review his first exhibit, Stewart said, "You are looking puzzled, Mr. Gaši. I want to make it very clear that on this particular point you are not under attack, there isn't any disagreement between us—whatever disagreements we might reach on other matters."

"I subscribe to everything I read in the exhibit. Is that your point?"

"I tell you what we will do, Mr. Gaši. We will continue with me asking the questions."

Later, Stewart attempted to poke holes in my testimony by portraying Brčko as so violently upset and confusing that no one could truly know what was going on.

To this assertion I said, "In my opinion there was no uncontrolled chaos in Brčko, but everything coming at us from the Serb side was controlled and coordinated." The actions came straight from the JNA's wartime playbook, a document that I and virtually every other Yugoslav man studied during our mandatory service.

Relating to the beatings I experienced on my first day at Luka, Stewart said, "I'm just suggesting to you, Mr. Gaši, that there's every possibility that you could get confused about these names and confused about these particular incidents. You don't agree?"

"You can be very sure that I know very well who interfered with me at Luka from day one."

Stewart told me I could not possibly have been working and able to see trucks deliver and distribute automatic rifles in outlying villages.

"Well the point I am making, Mr. Gaši, is you were there to do your work. Presumably you were getting on with your work. You weren't there to sit around and observe in detail what was happening in relation to weapons. So, you actually don't know to whom weapons were being issued."

"Listen very carefully, sir. I had plenty of time. I even had a coffee with these people. They even offered me a piece because they thought I was one of them, if that can help you arrive at the truth. I had time to observe everything in great detail and can remember everything."

Stewart asked about Croatian forces and many events outside Brčko that I had never previously testified to.

"You know that in April 1992 there was not just a question of Muslims and Serbs but there were also questions of army units from Croatia. That's right, isn't it?"

"I don't know anything about that, sir. I don't know that."

"Do you know anything about an attack on a village of Sijekovac in February 1992?"

"I don't know. I really don't."

He asked four more questions about Croatian incursions, receiving the same answer.

During my time with Stewart, I could never anticipate where he would probe next. I thought, *Milošević was prepared and clever, but this guy is something more. I see why he is Queen's Counsel. I can't wait for this to be over.*

Inside, I felt great tension, with a pain in my stomach. It was similar to the discomfort I'd so often experienced at the end of a canoe race, with muscles screaming for oxygen and denying oxygen to the brain and the gut.

I was relieved when Stewart finally said, "Your honor, I am finished." I could come up for air.

After that, prosecutor Hannis had several redirects, which did not elicit responses from the defense. I was also questioned by the judges. They asked about the shooting of civilians I'd witnessed on Braće Ćuskića Street, the Muslim 'sniper' incident, the distribution of weapons in Serb villages, and the tossing of bodies into the Sava River.

Judge El Mahdi then asked a perceptive question: "Since you explained to us in detail how you came to be released, could you please tell us: Do you believe that the guards who were at the camp were free to do as they wished, or was there—or were they actually just carrying out orders—in a fashion? Were they allowed to bring anybody they wanted there and could they release anybody they wanted to or was there some kind of authority, some kind of power who said, 'Well, this man should be freed, and this man should be detained?'"

My mind flashed to a document I had seen posted in Kosta's office at Luka.

"Let me tell you. On one occasion, when Kosta took me out to come to his office, after an interview when he asked me for names, as I was leaving the office, by the door there was a document in an A4 format. It was typed. It said that nobody was allowed to enter the camp and nobody was allowed to enter the hangar without the supervision of the commander, Kosta, and that inmates were not allowed to be eliminated without his permission. And this was signed by the commander of the camp, Kosta Simonović.

"Well I don't know how the actual organization worked. I can't tell you that. But I was taken out, I was freed, upon the orders of Captain Dragan. That's how it was. I don't know anything else."

"And this Captain Dragan, what was his function?"

"When I met him in Zvornik, he was their commander… Everybody referred to him as 'Boss.'"

Defense counsel Stewart did not want this to stand. The document I had seen indicated that there were policies and procedures in place that, coupled with Captain Dragan's involvement, might lead to higher-ups in Serbia and Republika Srpska, including his client.

In an attempt to thwart this, Stewart interjected, "Mr. Gaši, it's unreal what you just said, isn't it, to suppose that you, as a detainee in this camp, had any knowledge at all of procedures such as what documents needed to be signed in order actually to authorize a detainee's release."

"I didn't say that. I answered the judge's question—it was what stood next to the door for me to read when I left Kosta's office."

The presiding judge, Orie, then said, "This, Mr. Gaši, concludes your evidence in this court. The chamber would like to thank you for having come and for having answered questions of both parties and of the bench. It is important for this court to hear the evidence given by those who have been present at that time in the area. Thank you very much."

On the ride from the courtroom to the hotel, the adrenaline that had surged within me throughout the afternoon rapidly faded. When I got to my room, I e-mailed a friend: "I finished my testimony today at five thirty. Yesterday I was in the court for five hours and for almost four hours today. It was harder than with Milošević. The prosecutors told me I did a great job."

Though it was the dinner hour, I didn't feel like eating and lay down to rest.

— 37 —

A WOMAN'S EXPERIENCE

Awaking famished at eight p.m., I headed down to the hotel restaurant. There I recognized a woman who had been a nurse at the Brčko hospital. I had also seen her at Luka, interned in the office buildings. She was in Holland for the Krajišnik trial.

Witnesses could not talk with one another about their testimonies, but I was interested in finding out how she was getting on after the war. We had dinner together, talking about family and our new lives. After escaping Brčko, she relocated to the Midwestern United States, raising two children without her husband, who had fought in the Bosnian army and died in combat. Once in the United States, she requalified as a registered nurse. I filled her in on my family and other refugees from Brčko now living in the United States. We parted warmly. Seeing her made the trip to Holland especially worthwhile. She was courageous. I knew that the women at Luka had it much harder than we men.

After returning to the United States,[17] I waited for the trial transcripts to load onto the ICTY website. I wanted to know how the nurse's appearance had gone. She turned out to have been the witness who followed me on the evening of February 5, continuing her testimony the following day. Reading the transcript,[18] I wept for what she had endured.

During her testimony, the judges expressed concern for the emotional toll she experienced while reliving the events at Luka. Her statement in response was sublime: "May I say something, please? All my life was dedicated to working and helping people, and for the first time I met—I faced—something that was inconceivable. So, I experienced a terrible shock, and I still feel the pain. It was really a painful experience, and now having to go through this again just revives the pain. But I still want to continue with this testimony. I want to tell the truth and nothing but the truth. I want to inform you about the truth. I want the criminals to be punished. I want the crime to be punished."

Following the destruction of the Gunja Bridge on April 30, 1992, the Brčko hospital cared for pedestrians who survived the blast. Once the fighting broke out, the hospital also cared for combatants and civilians caught in the crossfire. On May 3, the hospital's ethnic Serb staff stayed home from work. After finishing her shift, the nurse stayed on. She testified, "I felt duty-bound to stay. I couldn't leave my patients unattended."

Later that day, Serb soldiers commandeered the hospital. The hospital was a tall building, providing a strategic vantage point. The army set up heavy weapons on the roof and began firing into the city. That evening Muslim and Croat members of the hospital staff were assembled. The paramilitary commander, Major Mauzer, addressed them. He told them he was in charge and that, "If anything was done without his knowledge, he would execute us."

Then, as Mauzer had done to me and my coworkers at EDB, "He went down the line, questioning the next doctor, asking what is your name? And then he also slapped more people. He was angry—he wanted to show his strength."

She continued. "My whole life was split between my work and my family.[19] So I did not have any political leanings or tendencies, and I did not have any religious leanings."

Despite being apolitical, she was arrested the next day and transported with three other Muslim hospital workers to Luka. The first person she encountered at Luka was my neighbor, Ranko Češić.

"When Češić returned to the office, he started shouting so much that the whole room was shaking. The blood vessels in his neck were tense. He was spitting with anger. He started cursing our balija mothers. He cursed us. He said he hated all Muslims. His every word was a swear word."

Češić beat his prisoners and made them beat each other. After the beating, she and others were marched across the street to the first warehouse room. There, "I heard the soldiers say that we should line up... At that point, I don't know why I turned... and that's when I saw that it was a column of approximately fifty people... Somebody came up to me and pulled me out of the line and then they pulled me past the soldiers ... As I was passing the soldiers I heard an order to fire and I could hear a terrible blast. I could hear the firing of a large number of rifles, and you could smell the gunpowder in the air. This smell of gunpowder and this smoke was very irritating to the eyes... Was it really possible that these people were killed? I heard the bodies as they fell, and I could hear the sounds, the sighs, and the moans of the people. As the people were falling, they were making these sounds, and you could hear the dull thuds of those fifty bodies falling to the cement floor."

She was saved from the firing squad to be Ranko Češić's plaything. "Then he told me that he had to play with me... that the first thing he wanted to do was rape me. Then he took a knife out. He had the knife in his boot, a very large knife with a serrated edge. He placed it on my neck..."

She also had encounters with my nemesis, Goran Jelisić. Her description of the first: "He said, 'I am Goran Jelisić, also known as the Serb Adolf Hitler. My duty is—I have been given the green light; my hands are free to do whatever I want because Muslims have a lot of children—my duty is to eradicate the Muslim people. My duty is to hate Muslims... Don't count on the Red Cross. Don't count on international organizations. They will not help you.' He said he was our god, and our lord... He said, 'Abandon all hope, because your destiny is in my hands'... and the way he spoke, he was so assured of himself that I felt convinced that what he was saying was the truth."

The man on trial, Momčilo Krajišnik, said he was not responsible for the actions of men like Češić and Jelisić. Prosecutor Hannis later described Krajišnik to me as "a very cold individual." He provided an example through Elvir Pasić, another witness for the prosecution. A fourteen-year old at the time, he and his family were captured in the forest trying to flee the Bosnian Serb army. They were held overnight at a school. The next morning women and children were placed on buses, where they watched the captured men being executed in the schoolyard.

Elvir eventually got out of Bosnia, moving to the large Bosnian refugee community in St. Louis, Missouri. By the end of his testimony, virtually all in the room were crying, including the three judges.

At the break the accused, Krajišnik, asked to speak to the judges, complaining, "Your honors, it is very difficult for me to have to listen to witnesses like that."

To this Hannis said, "Your defense is that you didn't know anything about this, that you were a legislator with no control over the army or police, but you also contest that the crimes occurred. Now when we bring in witnesses to show that the crimes did happen, you complain that it is hard for you to listen to it."

In trying defendants like Krajišnik, who maintained political control in Republika Srpska, prosecutors tried to obtain evidence in areas that were under the defendant's control. Hannis characterized the task as "really, really difficult. They were making things up, hiding evidence, and intimidating the people who were inclined to help us."

During the defense phase of the trial, Krajišnik maintained that he didn't know what occurred in the seventy percent of Bosnia that the Bosnian Serbs controlled, that when he asked for information he was lied to and that the Bosnian Serb government did not have control over their military, police, and judiciary.

Intercepts of Krajišnik's phone conversations with Radovan Karadžić contradicted his claims.

At the conclusion of the lengthy proceedings, Krajišnik received a sentence of twenty years. In their trial judgment relative to the *Takeover of Power and Crimes in the Municipality of Brčko,* the three judges cited my testimony in reference to the use of JNA tanks and other vehicles, maps for dividing Brčko on ethnic lines, the destruction of bridges, Serbian forces numbering more than one thousand invading the municipality, the execution of approximately twelve unarmed citizens in downtown Brčko on May 6, 1992, the beating of detainees, the murder of Stjepan Glavočević, dumping bodies into the Sava River, the existence of a black list of people to be executed, Kosta replacing Jelisić as deputy commander, and the transfer of detainees to and from other facilities.

The citations were personally gratifying.

Following his conviction, the tribunal transferred Krajišnik to an English prison. He received credit for time incarcerated while on trial, and when his sentence was two-thirds complete, received an early release in 2013. Upon his return to Bosnia's Republika Srpska he received a hero's welcome. To the assembled media he feigned surprise, saying, "After all, I am a war criminal."

My neighbor, Ranko Češić, received an early release at about the same time. Ranko was arrested in Belgrade in 2002 and taken to The Hague. He pled guilty to ten murders, including the two men shot in front of me at Luka. At his sentencing he said, "First of all, without any false sentiments I wish to express my deep remorse for the evil I have done. Looking back after so much time has elapsed… there is an enormous difference between my state of mind then and now. Now I would never do the things I did then, the things that took place in a time of euphoria, a time when all human dignity was abolished."

Before the war, it would never have occurred to me that when the barriers went down and laws were no longer enforced, individuals would describe themselves as feeling euphoric while harming others. Perhaps a psychiatrist like Radovan Karadžić better understood this, using that knowledge for his purposes.

—— 38 ——
OTHER TESTIMONIES

In 2009, I testified in the joint trials of two high-ranking police officials who failed to protect and serve. Hannis again led my testimony. The two men, Mico Stanišić and Stojan Župljanin, each received twenty-two-year sentences in 2013.

As he finished his cross examination of me in that trial, the defense attorney Slobodan Cvijetić asked, "My last question to you is, Mr. Gaši, when Kole took you out and told you that you were to go home, he said that you will again row for Yugoslavia, is that correct?"

"Yes."

"Would you have been glad to compete for Yugoslavia again?"

"Yes, I would have."

"I am glad to hear that and I see a tear in your eye which tells me that you are being sincere. Thank you."

Afterwards the defense counsel asked to meet with me in the witness chamber. The prosecution team told me, "This never happens."

When Cvijetić entered the chamber, he shook my hand saying, "I am from Bijeljina. We used to be neighbors, and I hope we are still neighbors. I hope you were not offended by my questions; they are part of my job. I know from your answers that you are passionate for Yugoslavia. I just want to say that it was an honor to meet you."

"Thank you. Yes, we are neighbors. Your words are meaningful to me. It was my privilege to meet you as well."

My marathon of Hague appearances continued with the trial of Bosnian Serb leader Radovan Karadžić in 2011. As with Milošević, this was a conversation I wanted to have.

Karadžić had been keen for war. The psychiatrist and poet came relatively late to political prominence. He seemed to relish it. I recall watching video footage of him during the war years. He had climbed atop a rock outcropping in his mountain redoubt near Pale and proceeded to recite his verse to the empty Bosnian landscape arrayed far below him. Karadžić claimed to be a descendant of Vuk Karadžić, the writer who had popularized Serbian mythology a century earlier. He was not a relative, but the story promoted the image he wished to portray.

As I entered the courtroom, Karadžić was standing. His characteristic mane of silver hair with its widow's peak had been trimmed and was parted down the middle. He stood tall, dressed in a blue suit with an off-white shirt and a red tie. Glasses covered his bushy eyebrows. He peered out from under his glasses, studying me.

After the prosecutor placed my testimony into the trial record, Karadžić handled the cross-examination. He questioned me on the Second World War and my membership in the SDA political party. His line of inquiry was puzzling. I felt some relief—he wasn't seriously contesting my testimony. Karadžić spoke in deep, sonorous tones— like an actor. He seemed to be performing for an audience other than the judges, perhaps for the TV cameras and his supporters back home. As time passed and I faced no real challenge to my testimony, I grew confident it would stand with the judges.

That sense increased when the judges warned Karadžić that his questions were frivolous and he risked squandering his available time. At one point Judge Kwon said, "And this is an example of how you are wasting your time. You could have put your case to the witness... Instead you read out all the documents that can't be admitted... Let's proceed." And later, "You have spent almost one and a half hours with this witness, who testified his experience he underwent at Luka camp, but you didn't ask a single question about it."

At the end of his time, Karadžić requested more, saying, "I'm asking for half an hour, and that is very little time for such an important witness." Karadžić was granted ten minutes—he ran over.

When the judges finally instructed him to stop his cross-examination, he closed with, "Thank you, Mr. Gaši, and I have no more time. It is possible that I spent too much time trying to paint a picture of Brčko, Excellencies, but it is necessary. I wanted to do that with a Muslim witness. I wanted to paint a complete picture of Brčko."

"Mr. Karadžić, a correction. I'm not a Muslim. My father is an Albanian from Kosovo, and my mother is a Muslim from Brčko, but I was raised a Yugoslav."

The judges then allowed a sharp exchange between Karadžić and me. He denigrated me for exercising my right to join a political party. I criticized him for falsely telling the world that Bosnia's Muslims were extremists intent on upsetting the European order. While I felt strong emotions well up during the exchange, I maintained my composure—even chuckling at one of Karadžić's misstatements before responding. On video replay I did see myself raising my finger to emphasize a final point. This surprised me—I was not aware of it. It signaled my deep-down feelings. I wanted to raise a hand in opposition to him and his political program.

I was the only witness called to establish Karadžić's connection to the crimes that occurred in Brčko. The prosecutors told me, "We think your testimony will suffice."

Jasminka accompanied me on this trip. It made the experience easier, and I wished I'd asked for this consideration earlier, as all witnesses were allowed one companion. Her presence left me feeling far more relaxed during and after the trial. It was an antidote; after reliving the old memories I could immediately reconnect with my family and our present life.

For Jasminka, the trip was also therapeutic. She got to view one of the Bosnian War's kingpins in the flesh and see how uninspiring they were when called to account. She was struck by how "fidgety" Karadžić was and by his inability to get traction. She said, "I expected more. He seemed cowardly, sort of pathetic. I'd heard he was crooked and ran a smuggling ring during the war. Seeing him in person, that seemed possible."

On March 24, 2016, the court provided summary judgment in Karadžić's case. He was found guilty of genocide. This was important to those who had suffered as a result of his actions. Relative to Brčko, the court found the "Accused bears individual criminal responsibility… for persecution, extermination, murder, deportation and forcible transfer as crimes against humanity; and murder, a violation of the laws and customs of war." Karadžić's sentence was forty years.

Of these powerful men from Serbia and Republika Srpska, Milošević was the only one who stood out to me as truly exceptional. All the defendants attempted to make eye contact with the witnesses, to make a connection that would affect the witness in their favor. For me their efforts were simple gamesmanship and easily shrugged off—except with Milošević. His presence was mesmerizing.

Milošević's performances made me think of how Joseph Conrad described his character Captain Kurtz, as "a shadow insatiable of splendid appearances, of frightful realities… and draped nobly in the folds of eloquence."[20] Milošević spoke so well, but his words were hollow.

After my testimony in his case, I was asked to summarize my own sense of Milošević. I responded, "Well, isn't the devil supposed to be the one who is the most charming?"

Milošević died at The Hague of a heart attack in March of 2006. Defiant to the end, he did not die of a broken heart, or decrying the horrors and the crimes he had inspired. The forces he set in motion did not die with his passing.

Dragan Vasiljković, the "Captain Dragan" who freed me from Luka, eventually left Serbia and returned to Australia to evade war crime charges. His wartime activities were exposed in a September 2005 article in *The Australian* newspaper. In response, Dragan sued the paper's parent company for public defamation—a serious miscalculation on his part. Bosnian and Croatian citizens traveled to Australia to testify against him, bolstering the paper's defense. One witness was a Bosnian woman from the Zvornik area who testified that Dragan imprisoned and repeatedly raped her.

The Australian court ultimately held for the paper, concluding that Dragan committed rape and torture. The court awarded the paper $1.2 million in damages. The court's conclusion seemed to influence the extradition request, which was approved in 2006. Dragan ran out of appeals in 2015. On July 9, 2015, he became the first Australian accused of war crimes ever extradited. He was ultimately convicted by a Croatian court, receiving a sentence of fourteen years.

Three days after his extradition, an international memorial service was held on the twentieth anniversary of the Srebrenica massacre. Victims from that massacre are still being discovered. The ceremony at Potočari Memorial Center was also to bury an additional 136 bodies recently unearthed. The ceremony was a solemn occasion with tens of thousands of spectators. Former U.S. President Clinton attended, expressing his deep regrets for taking so long to end the war. He praised Serbia's Prime Minister Aleksandar Vučić for being there.

When the crowd recognized Vučić, some of those present began to pelt him with shoes and stones. He was chased away from the ceremony. As a member of the Serbian Parliament in 1995, Vučić had made the following speech several days after Srebrenica, when NATO began bombing Bosnian Serb positions: "Come and bomb us. Kill one Serb and we will kill one hundred Muslims. And then we will see if the international community dares to attack Serb positions and treat the Serb people that way."[21] The one hundred-for-one threat was the same one used by the Nazis when they invaded Serbia in 1941.

Days before the memorial service, the United Nations took up a resolution to brand the Srebrenica massacre as genocide. The resolution failed following a veto from Security Council member Russia.

Ten years after his passing, Milošević's legacy endured.

— 39 —
The Wolves We Feed

One evening an old Cherokee told his grandson about a battle that goes on inside people.

He said, "My son, the battle is between two wolves inside us all.

"One is Evil. It is anger, envy, jealousy, regret, greed, arrogance, resentment, ego, false pride, and superiority.

"The other is Good. It is joy, peace, love, hope, sincerity, humility, kindness, empathy, generosity, and truth."

The grandson thought for a moment and then asked, "Which wolf wins?"

The old Cherokee replied, "The one you feed."[22]

Jasminka and I traveled to Brčko in 2012 to attend a special commemoration that the city of Brčko organized on April 30. The date marked the twentieth anniversary of the destruction of the bridges, and the commemoration recognized Brčko citizens lost during the war. Prior to the ceremony, I was asked to testify in a national court, in the trial of Branko Pudić, the policeman who attacked me upon my arrival at Luka prison. During the trial it was apparent that Pudić did not remember me—I was just one of the hundreds entrusted to him. At the conclusion of his trial, he was sentenced to two years, and lost his police pension.

At the ceremony itself, I witnessed something different. There I visited with another policeman, Galib Hadžic, who had been on duty when the bridge blew. He was one of those from the police station who ran to bridge and attended to the injured. Afterward, he collected belongings and evidence. He found a wallet belonging to a Bego Ramić from Tešnja, Bosnia, a community one hundred-fifty kilometers southwest of Brčko. Bego had been traveling home from work in Austria for the May Day holiday. He perished in the blast.

His wallet contained a photo of his wife holding a baby in one arm. A young, smiling daughter held her other hand.

Now, twenty years later, Galib said, "Excuse me, I think I see someone." He walked over to a middle-aged woman and asked, "Are you Mrs. Ramić?"

After the woman said yes, he explained, "I found your husband and his wallet on that terrible day. I don't think he suffered. I could tell from his photo that he had a happy family. I have always wondered what happened to you, and your two children. They were so beautiful."

"Well, thank you, sir. I can hardly believe you recognized me. You must be a good man. This young man is my son—the baby in the picture. I know he wants to talk with you. Thank you for giving us both this connection to my husband."

Standing to the side, just observing, I felt some of the emotions that seemed to wash over the three of them.

I last saw my mother the following year, in the summer of 2013. She was eager to meet friends of mine visiting from the United States. We stopped by her first-floor apartment in the group home where she lived. She was ninety-two at the time. Well-dressed, sitting on the edge of her bed, she held forth in a gentle, knowing fashion. The window to her apartment was open. Soon a crowd of ten residents and neighbors had gathered outside, eager to meet those she entertained. She had prepared for guests in Bosnian fashion. Soon coffee cake and cups were being passed through the window, and strong Turkish coffee poured from a long-handled brass pot. It was a pleasant, neighborly and multicultural scene—the Bosnia I knew growing up.

Later that day I visited the Ivici graveyard. It is where my father and brother, Mirsad, are buried. My mother would join them in six months. The graveyard had spilled over its boundaries and across the street as a result of the war. In July 2015 eight graves were added, as more bodies had been found in a recently discovered mass grave. As I walked through the sections of the cemetery holding the hundreds of wartime dead, I knew three quarters of them or more.

My companions asked me about a young woman who was buried beside her mother. They had lived near the Luka camp in a nice residential area. She had been a classmate of Ranko Češić. One day, coming from one of his rampages at the Partizan Sports Hall, he stopped by the home she shared with her mother. After raping both women, he slit their throats with the serrated blade he kept strapped to his boot.

War in an integrated community like ours became intensely personal. Some residents treated their neighbors terribly, acting on their own initiatives. Others followed orders from unconstitutional authorities. Nevertheless, without the assistance of the army and paramilitary soldiers from far-off republics, twenty-one percent of Brčko's population could not have wreaked, or countenanced, such devastation on the rest of us. Absent authorization and outside assistance, men like Ranko would never have gotten started.

As I walked through Brčko's downtown mall in August 2014, a man hailed me from behind. The man was Fadil Redzic, a former JNA major who had also been imprisoned at Luka. He was now a driving force behind a museum dedicated to the prison camps and victims of the Bosnian War. The museum was scheduled to host a group of foreign journalists in two days. It would be open the next morning to get ready. Fadil wanted me to see it. We agreed to meet at Luka the following morning.

I arrived at ten a.m. and was greeted by six other Luka survivors. Ours was a heartfelt reunion. Inside, one wall of the museum was covered with portraits of civilians known to have perished in Brčko during the war. This exhibit contained more than eight hundred photographs arranged alphabetically. As at the graveyard, the collective loss stunned me.

A man and a woman in their late twenties came to the entrance of the facility. A brother and sister, they asked to come in. Curious, I asked if they had relatives who had been at Luka.

"No, but we have three family members who are memorialized here."

Their father, uncle, and grandfather had been shot in their backyard during the early hours of Brčko's takeover. The two siblings were young at the time. Separated, the young man was raised in Germany, his sister in upstate New York. She had wanted to be at the twentieth anniversary remembrance I attended, but had just delivered twins and could not make the journey.

The siblings had walked down to Luka many times over the years, knowing that their relatives were remembered inside, but the memorial had always been closed. Their father had been an electrician and a good friend of Ramiz at the Bimal plant. They asked me to take a photo of them gazing at their father's portrait. The photo represented something tangible, as their father's remains had not been found. When they departed an hour later, the woman, Enisa Terzić, told Fadil, "Thank you for your efforts and the memorial. It means a great deal to see my family members remembered and our loss acknowledged."

Before leaving Luka, I walked with Fadil out past the train tracks to the place where guards made us throw bodies into the river. Standing on the site, the old, strange sensations crept back. Fadil saw that the back door to the second warehouse room, our former prison, was open. We entered through it. Floods had devastated this region of Bosnia and Croatia weeks earlier and the Red Cross had set up a distribution center in the warehouse. The organization's efforts at dispersing aid had been under media fire. When I walked in with a camera, someone in charge thought I was there to cause difficulty and asked me to leave. The attitude changed when Fadil explained our connection to the room. He showed me his old sleeping space; I pointed out my space next to the door. Swept clean, it looked innocuous enough. Seeing it and its lookout portal caused memories to cascade back. They had me in inner turmoil the rest of the afternoon. The trigger, after the passage of twenty-two years, was seeing my space. I did a lot of thinking, and experienced considerable torment there.

As dusk fell that evening, Jasminka, Adna, and I were upriver, walking on the promenade near the boathouse. It was still a daily gathering place for those with a connection to canoe sports. I encountered several of my old teammates. Soon we were laughing and reminiscing about shared good times. We laughed so hard there were tears. I think the tears were also for friends and a way of life lost, and now partially recaptured. The bitter mixed together with the sweet.

After nightfall, we crossed the Brka river bridge and headed up the hill to the downtown pedestrian mall, ending up at the Premier Coffee Bar, located fifty meters from where I once saw police shooting civilians. At the open-air Premier, two musicians set up for a performance. They played long into the night. We stayed for the encores. The music transported me back in time. It pulsed out into the quiet night full of hope and yearning, recalling fond memories. Jasminka had similar thoughts. On the drive home, she said, "What a great evening this has been."

The next morning, as we crossed the bridge to Croatia in a rented car, I saw a new placard dedicated to the Jewish people who lost their lives there in 1941. The previous memorial had blown up with the bridge on April 30, 1992. The new memorial acknowledged additional victims, the innocents killed that fateful day. The marker made me think of an unknown boy, then about six years of age, who lost his life here.

Below the restored bridge, on the Sava, a canoeist practiced. The young man, a local Serb, was training for the upcoming World Marathon Canoe Championships. Three days earlier I had helped him secure a plane ticket to Oklahoma City, where the competition would be held.

In Oklahoma City, I would be his team manager. There I would reunite with Matija Ljubek's youngest son, Nikica, who represented Croatia. When we had last seen each other, Nikica was nine years old. Now, a quarter century later, I couldn't get over how much he looked like his father, both standing on the riverbank and when paddling a canoe. I felt an immediate bond, and I think he did as well.

The Bosnian War enabled me to experience both good and evil. A psychologist friend has called me "watchful, an observer." I became more watchful and observant, and also less trusting and open, as a result of the war. Perhaps I returned to Brčko in April 1992 because deep down I wanted to know what was going on, to witness whatever was about to transpire. As a younger person, I thought my purpose in life was to be an athlete. In retrospect, athletics may have helped me survive and provided helpful experience for later responsibilities.

Our war was inspired and fueled by strident ideologies, propaganda, and through the repression of a free press. When the troubles came, there were still many in Bosnia whose humanity remained awake. My family and I survived as a result of their conscientious actions. The importance of such countervailing courage and decency was, for me, one of the war's great lessons.

The philosopher Will Durant wrote,

> Civilization is a stream with banks. The stream is sometimes filled with blood from people killing, stealing, shouting and doing the things historians usually record, while on the banks, unnoticed, people build homes, make love, raise children, sing songs… The story of civilization is the story of what happened on the banks.[23]

During the Bosnian War, people were torn from the riverbank and literally thrown into the river. This happened to my friend Elvedin Salkonović. At that time, Elvedin had a two-year-old son. Some years later, Elvedin's wife asked me to write a letter to her son, Eldin, as he had questions about his father and how his friends remembered him. Writing that letter was a great honor. Elvedin's then unborn daughter, Eldina, was also named for her father. She is currently a graduate student in Denmark. Her brother recently earned a PhD in astrophysics from the University of Chicago. I'm sure Elvedin would be proud that his children's sights are on the stars.

The Bosnian War and its mistreatment of civilians was an effort to destroy our civilization, to demonstrate something impossible: that Bosnia wasn't Bosnia. We had centuries of living together. My responsibility, once I was free of Luka, was to testify to what happened, to try and give those who were cut down some voice, some acknowledgement that they mattered—that they had consequence.

Throughout my journey, I hoped to see Bosnia's civil society restored. In that I had a guide and an example.

When my mother baked bread for those on the Jasenovac-bound train, and when she fed me coffee and cakes as a child and again on our last visit together, she nourished the Good Wolf that exists in all of us. I dedicate my story to her. May she, and Bosnia, enjoy peace.

AFTERWORD

After the Karadžić verdict in March 2016, I was interviewed by reporter Jefferson Robbins of The Wenatchee World. He asked me if there were lessons to be learned from Bosnia's experience. He quoted from my testimony in the Karadžić trial: "To create a state for Serbs only—it seems to me, I don't know, madness. I don't know what other term to use."

Nationalism, not unlike the destructive nationalism we experienced in the former Yugoslavia, is on the rise around the world. It was a prominent feature in the 2016 U.S. presidential campaign. Living in the United States, I heard its siren song daily. I told reporter Robbins that, in my experience, nationalism attempts to divide people. I see Yugoslavia's experience as a cautionary tale; it is my reason for telling this story.

Once the dividing started in Yugoslavia, it was amazing how quickly it spread. I don't think we Yugoslavs were unique in this; it is a problem for the human race. By any measure, we had good lives in Yugoslavia, yet we gave that life up. We humans are so easily manipulated by propaganda, by claims that we need to fear our neighbors. In our case, men who wanted power made these claims. They used the state apparatus, including our federal security services, to bring both the army and our independent media to heel. Democracies dispense with a free and unfettered press at their peril.

Once Milošević and his henchmen obtained power, they were intoxicated by it. So were the men who did their dirty work. In Brčko that work was done by individuals like Goran Jelisić and Ranko Češić. They too were drunk with power, declaring that they were gods and lords over the rest of us, that they were duty bound to hate us. At

Luka I got to know those men, and at The Hague I got to experience their leaders, to see what they were like under pressure—when they were held to account. In general they were cowardly—avoiding blame and trying to shift it to others. They rained destruction down on the Yugoslav people. I believe these kinds of people exist in every culture, awaiting opportunities to gain power and impose their will, confident that many ordinary citizens will want to fit in and will comply.

In Yugoslavia we had a constitution, police, laws, and a judiciary. They all gave way.

We Bosnians were not a restless or a migratory people. We tended to stay close to our hometowns, to our roots. The first reason was family. We lived in communities where we knew one another. That was one tragedy of the war. It pushed people out of homes and villages where there had existed for generations, even centuries. The mass graves ended up telling the story of close-knit Bosnian families; in many were found generations of the same family, literally bound together at the time of their death.

What happened to us can happen elsewhere. Unless societies are vigilant, there is no such thing as "never again."

The crisis we experienced also showed another aspect of mankind—the willingness to assist others. My family and I experienced this during Yugoslavia's breakup, and throughout our refugee and immigrant journey. For the past fifteen years I've worked in healthcare, in the midst of people who are healers. One of the physicians I work with references Margaret Mead, the anthropologist who argued that a healed femur was the first sign of civilization. According to Mead, in any other species a broken thighbone leads to death. Where we find one healed in man, we know that someone else provided for that person during the long healing process.

That physician's mother recently passed away. Her name was Madeleine Joan Justus. She was born in Transylvania in 1916. Like my mother, she lived long and experienced much. A student of Dr.

Montessori and a friend of Anna Freud, she came to the United States as a refugee following the Second World War.

In the U.S., she carved out a distinguished career as a Montessori educator. In her eighty-sixth year, the Washington state senate honored her for her contributions to childhood education.

Mrs. Justus didn't tell her American-born children about her wartime experience until they were grown. It came as a great surprise to them. She was an Auschwitz survivor—she didn't want her ordeal to impact their worldview. Her grace, stoicism, and life force represent the far superior side of our complicated human natures.

May those forces always surround us.

ABOUT THE AUTHORS

Shaun Koos & *Isak Gaši*

Isak Gaši is a former world-class canoeist who represented Yugoslavia internationally for more than a decade. His Bosnian War experiences propelled him into a prominent and ongoing role as a witness for the prosecution at The Hague tribunal. He has lived in the United States for the past sixteen years, working in a technical field. A devoted husband and father, he still canoes regularly, finding deep satisfaction in the interplay between a boat, a paddle, and the Columbia River's eternal flow.

Shaun Koos is a retired hospital executive who grew up in Minneapolis, Minnesota. After graduating magna cum laude from Carleton College, he earned a graduate degree from the University of Washington. He rowed in UW's graduate program, feeling some connection to the school's storied history and the boys in its 1936 boat. Shaun is a former member of the U.S. canoe and kayak team, and the former Secretary of USA Canoe/Kayak. It was through canoeing that he met Isak Gaši. His primary interests as a writer are in historical biography and in exploring the motivations, mindsets, and actions of individuals who confront and surmount great challenges.

INDEX OF CHARACTERS AND PLACES

Brčko—City in Northeastern Bosnia. Hometown of Isak Gaši. (Pronunciation: BERR-ch-koh)

Bijeljina—City in Northeastern Bosnia. (Pronunciation: bee-YEHL-yee-NAH)

Anto Čonda—Isak's canoe coach for twenty years. (Pronunciation: AHN-taw CHON-dah)

Mišo Čijević—Bosnian Serb policeman at Luka prison camp. (Pronunciation: MEE-show Sigh-YAH-vihch)

Ranko Češić—Isak's neighbor and jailer at Luka prison camp. Convicted war criminal. (Pronunciation: RAHN-koh CHEH-sihch)

Adna Gaši—Isak's daughter. (Pronunciation: AHD-nah GAH-she)

Fetah Gaši—Isak's father. (Pronunciation: feh-tah GAH-she)

Faruk Gaši—Isak's nephew and Ramiz's oldest son. Squad leader in the Bosnian army. Awarded the Golden Lily, the highest military honor in Bosnia. (Pronunciation: fahr-OOK)

Isak Gaši—Champion Yugoslav athlete and community leader imprisoned in a Bosnian Serb prison camp. Prosecution witness at the International Criminal Tribunal for the Former Yugoslavia. (Pronunciation: EE-sock GAH-she)

Jasminka Gaši—Isak's wife. (Pronunciation: YAHS-mink-ah)

Jagoda Gaši—Isak's older sister. (Pronunciation: YAH-go-dah)

Mirsad Gaši—Isak's younger brother. Soldier in the Bosnian army. (Pronunciation: MEER-sahd)

Ramiza Gaši—Isak's younger sister. (Pronunciation: rah-MEE-sah)

Ramiz Gaši—Isak's older brother. Officer in the Croatian army during the

Bosnian War. (Pronunciation: RAH-miz)

Šemsa Gaši—Isak's mother. (Pronunciation: SHEM-sa)

Alija Izetbegović—President of Bosnia-Herzegovina from 1990 to 1996. (Pronunciation: Ah-Li-Jah EEZ-eht-BEH-goh-VIHCH)

Jasenovac—Croatian concentration camp during the Second World War. (Pronunciation: yah-SIHN-oh-vahts)

Goran Jelisić—Notorious jailer at the Luka prison camp. Convicted of war crimes. (Pronunciation: GOHR-ahn YEHL-ih-sihch)

Radovan Karadžić—Co-leader of the Bosnian Serb party. Indicted for war crimes. Convicted of genocide. (Pronunciation: RAH-doh-vahn KAHR-ah-jeech)

Momčilo Krajišnik—Co-leader of the Bosnian Serb party. Convicted of war crimes. (Pronunciation: MOHM-chee-loh KRAH-yeesh-nihk)

Matija Ljubek—Isak's close friend. Olympic canoe champion in 1976 and 1984. (Pronunciation: mah-TEE-jah LOO-beck)

Slobodan Milošević—President of Serbia. Indicted for war crimes. Died during trial. (Pronunciation: sloh-BOH-dahn mee-LOH-sheh-vihch)

Milisav Milutinović—Isak's history teacher. Officer in Yugoslav army, ethnic Serb. (Pronunciation: mee-loo-TEE-noh-vihch)

Ratko Mladić—Ranking general in the Bosnian Serb army. Being tried for war crimes. (Pronunciation: RAHT-koh MLAHD-ihch)

Said Muminović—Isak's childhood sidekick and best man at his wedding. (Pronunciation: SIGH-eed MOO-MEEN-o-vitch)

Mirko Nišović—Isak's close friend. 1984 Olympic canoe champion. (Pronunciation: MEER-koh KNEE-soh-vihch)

Ivan Repić—Jailer at Luka. (Pronunciation: EE-vahn REP-ihch)

Ružica—Isak's female friend, also incarcerated at the Luka prison camp. (Pronunciation: ROO-zheet-sah)

Vojislav Šešelj—Serbian political figure. Leader of the Serbian Radical party. Indicted for war crimes. (Pronunciation: VOY-EE-SLAHV SHEH-shehl)

Constantin Simonović—Deputy commander of the Luka prison camp. (Pronunciation: kohn-stahn-TIHN see-MOAN-oh-vihch)

Srebrenica—Bosnian town where more than 8,000 male civilians were massacred in 1995. (Pronunciation: sreh-breh-NEET-sah)

Dušan Tadić—First person tried at the International Criminal Tribunal for the Former Yugoslavia. (Pronunciation: DOO-shahn TAH-deech)

Franjo Tuđman—President of Croatia from 1990 until his death in 1999. (Pronunciation: FRAHN-yoh TOOJ-mahn)

Ustasha—Croatian political organization that combined fascism, nationalism, and Catholicism. (Pronunciation: OO-stah-shah)

Dragan Vasiljković—Commander of Serbian paramilitary force known as the Red Berets. Also known as Captain Dragan. (Pronunciation: DRAH-gahn vah-SIHL-yeh-vihch)

Alexsander Vučić—Current president of Serbia. (Pronunication: VOO-chi-hch)

Stojan Župljanin—High-ranking Bosnian Serb police official. Convicted of war crimes. (Pronunciation: STOY-ahn zhoo-PLAH-neen)

HISTORICAL NOTES

During the seventh century BCE, Indo-European tribes inhabited the areas that are today Bosnia, Serbia, and Albania. The Greeks and Romans of that time called these people Illyrians.[24]

Over the intervening centuries, many different tribes and ethnic groups reached Bosnia. When the Slavic Croat and Serb tribes arrived during the seventh century AD, settling as farmers and herdsmen, they intermingled with existing Slavs, Vlachs, Romans, Illyrians, Celts, Avars, and Huns. Their Slavic language took root and eventually dominated.[25]

During the ninth and tenth centuries, Bosnia fell under the shifting control of Croatian and Serbian principalities.[26]

In Croatia, a kingdom existed from 916 to 1102. It entered into a union with Hungary in 1102.

During the eleventh century, the Hungarian kingdom and the Byzantine Empire vied for control of Bosnia.[27]

During the twelfth century, both Serbia and Bosnia escaped from Byzantine rule.[28] The two nations established separate kingdoms. Both kingdoms battled against the expanding Ottoman Empire during the fourteenth and fifteenth centuries.

In the areas that later became the Yugoslav republics of Serbia, Montenegro, and Macedonia, populations were strongly influenced by the Byzantine (Eastern Roman) Empire and the Greek Orthodox Church.

Influences on the Slavic peoples that lived in the areas that later became the Yugoslav republics of Croatia and Slovenia were different. These people fell under the sway of the Catholic Church, the Venetian city-state, and the Habsburg (later called the Austro-Hungarian) Empire.

Bosnia followed a third path. Located at the border between the Eastern (Greek Orthodox) and Western (Roman Catholic) branches of Christianity, Bosnia developed distinctly. During the thirteenth century, a unique, independent Christian church emerged in Bosnia.[29] The Bosnian church dominated Bosnia's religious life for the next century.[30] The Bosnian church was considered heretical by the Catholic church, which encouraged a series of crusades to stamp it out.

In 1340, the Bosnian ruler Stjepan Kotromanić invited the Catholic Franciscan order to establish in Bosnia.[31]

The period from 1353 to 1391 marked the reign of Bosnian King Tvrtko. This was the apogee of the Bosnia kingdom. Tvrtko's territory reached the Adriatic Sea and included portions of modern-day Croatia and Serbia.[32]

The Battle of Kosovo Field took place in 1389. Serbian forces, accompanied by soldiers sent by the Bosnian king,[33] battled with the Ottoman Turks. Both armies withdrew following devastating losses and the deaths of their commanders, Prince Lazar (Serb) and Sultan Murad I (Turkish). The Serb force was so diminished it had difficulty repelling subsequent Ottoman invasions.[34] By 1459, all Serb lands had been conquered by the Ottomans.

The Bosnia kingdom was invaded and conquered by the Ottoman Turks in 1463.[35]

Ottoman incursions during that time also reduced the Habsburg's Croatian territory. In response, the Habsburgs established a military frontier in Croatia to provide a buffer. They encouraged settlers from Serbia to populate and defend this frontier region. Serbian settlers did so, putting down roots and developing a warrior ethos.[36,37]

The Ottomans ruled Bosnia from 1463 to 1878. Many Bosnians accepted the Ottomans' Muslim religion.[38] In doing so, and in acquiescing to the Ottoman's administration and protection, Bosnia received relatively favorable treatment.[39] Bosnia became a largely self-governing province within the Ottoman Empire, retaining its historic name and territory throughout. The Bosnian kingdom, and then the Bosnian Protectorate, maintained intact borders for 700 years. Situated at the crossroads of the region, Bosnia experienced in-migrations of Catholic, Orthodox, and Jewish populations. Within Ottoman Bosnia, four of the world's great religious traditions coexisted, as did four semi-distinct cultural groups—Bosnian Jews, Bosnian Muslims, Bosnian Croats, and Bosnian Serbs.

Periodic conflicts broke out, both between the Eastern and Western branches of Christianity—and between Christianity and Islam—within the territories that later became Yugoslavia. Serbia chafed under Ottoman rule. Serbs viewed themselves as defenders of the Orthodox faith. They looked to another Slavic and Orthodox nation, imperial Russia, as a benefactor and ally. Over time, an alliance between Russia and Serbia formed. During the nineteenth century, a Pan-Slavic movement gathered momentum in Russia and the Balkans. Rapidly expanding its own borders during this period, Russia desired warm-water ports and political influence in the Balkans.

Serbia achieved partial independence following uprisings in 1804 and 1815.

By the end of the Ottoman era, land ownership in Bosnia was highly concentrated among Muslims, who owned ninety percent of the country's land.[40] Distance and Bosnia's mountainous topography provided its aristocracy with significant autonomy. For centuries they successfully resisted both peasant desires and Ottoman attempts at agrarian reform.[41]

A Bosnian peasant uprising in 1875 received support from Serbia, Montenegro, and Russia.[42] That coalition defeated the Ottomans in the resulting Russo-Ottoman War.[43] So much territory changed hands as a result of the war that the international order was threatened.[44] With the European balance of power destabilized, the Balkans became a potential flashpoint between the competing interests of that era's great powers.

In an attempt to restore international order, Germany's Bismarck in 1878 hosted an international conference in Berlin intended to address international grievances and redraw borders. Russia, Great Britain, France, Austria-Hungary, Italy, and Germany represented the great powers.

Out of that conference the following changes occurred: Serbia, Romania, and Montenegro achieved independence; Bulgaria became an autonomous principality within the Ottoman Empire but was required to return Macedonia to the Ottomans; Russia received territory and access to the Black Sea in present-day Moldova and Ukraine; Britain received Cyprus. The Bosnia Protectorate was transferred from the Ottomans to Austria-Hungary.[45]

At that time, the Austro-Hungarians envisioned Bosnia as a model colony that would thwart a rising Serbia and a growing movement to unite the southern Slav peoples.[46] To further these objectives, Austro-Hungary made significant infrastructure investment in Bosnia.[47]

Serbia was gravely upset by Bosnia's transfer to its Austro-Hungarian rival. Croatia supported the Austro-Hungarian efforts, thinking that Bosnia would become part of Croatia within the larger empire. Those hopes were soon dashed by Vienna and Budapest.[48]

While the Berlin Conference was hailed at the time as a diplomatic achievement, Russia felt betrayed. In addition, the aspirations of the Serbs and Bulgarians were unfulfilled, sowing the seeds of the First (1912) and Second (1913) Balkan Wars.[49] These bitter conflicts provided fodder for the First World War to follow.[50]

In 1908, concerned that the Ottomans were preparing to demand the return of the Bosnian Protectorate, the Austro-Hungarians requested international approval to annex Bosnia. The annexation was formalized the following year, again disappointing Serbia's desires.[51]

The First World War began six years after Bosnia's annexation. The war was triggered by the assassination of Austrian Crown Prince Franz Ferdinand in June 1914. A Serb nationalist shot Franz Ferdinand in the Bosnian city of Sarajevo. A month later, on July 28th, Austria-Hungary used the assassination as a pretext to declare war on Serbia. They invaded Serbia. Bosnian troops fought in the Austro-Hungarian army, sustaining heavy losses. Serbia's losses were staggering—750,000 in a population of 4.6 million.[52]

Serbia, however, fought on the winning side in the war, as a member of the Entente that defeated the Austro-Hungarian and the Ottoman empires.[53] The victory, and the settlement conference that followed, provided an opportunity to unify the southern Slav peoples. Serbia envisioned itself leading a unified effort. Croatia and Slovenia desired independence. Both countries worried that they would be annexed to Italy in the post-war settlement.[54] They agreed to a federal union with Serbia, anticipating that the new country's constitution would allow them significant autonomy.

Following the Versailles peace conference, a new country, the Kingdom of Serbs, Croats, and Slovenes, was established in December 1918. Bosnia was included in the kingdom. The kingdom's ruler, King Alexander, sought a centralized government headquartered in Belgrade, Serbia. He achieved that, despite the opposition of Croatia and Slovenia, during the 1921 constitutional congress.[55]

From its beginning, Yugoslavia was handicapped by fundamental differences in the aspirations and intentions of its Serbian, Croatian, and Slovenian constituents.

Interwar Yugoslavia (1918—1941):

The first incarnation of Yugoslavia featured regular disputes between Croats and Serbs over regional autonomy versus central control.[56] In 1929, the country's leader, King Alexander, banned political parties, declaring a dictatorship. He was assassinated in 1934 during a state visit to France. His assassin was a member of a Bulgarian dissident group that had ties to the exiled Croat Ante Pavlić and his separatist group, the Ustaša.[57]

Alexander's successor, Prince Paul, formed a government that made attempts toward democratization and a federal system.[58] Croatia exerted strong pressure for autonomy and additional territory. It received both in 1939. The Croatian banovina that was established included a large portion of Bosnian territory.

World War II (1941—1945):

On April 6, 1941, the Axis army invaded, rapidly overpowered, and occupied Yugoslavia. The Axis dismantled the Yugoslav federation. They annexed large portions of the country, assigning Yugoslavia's remaining territory to occupied zones.[59] Croatia declared its independence from Yugoslavia, aligning with the Axis. Ante Pavlić was recalled from his Italian exile and installed as the leader of the so-called Independent State of Croatia (NDH in Bosnian).[60] Bosnia was included in NDH territory. The NDH was ultranationalist and fascist. Its objectives included driving ethnic Serb influence from Croatia and Bosnia. Smoldering antagonisms between the Catholic and Orthodox religions resurfaced.[61]

The NDH endorsed the Catholic church and tolerated Islam. They attempted to stamp out the Serb Orthodox religion and to drive out Serbs from the territory they controlled. In that process massive war crimes, crimes against humanity, and genocides were committed.[62] This situation was later described as "the deranged expression of Croatian resentment at Serb domination of Yugoslavia."[63]

Using concentration camps and death squads, the NDH embarked on a murder campaign so vigorous that it took their Nazi overseers by surprise.[64] They targeted Jews, Roma, political opponents, and ethnic Serbs living in Croatia and Bosnia-Hercegovina. Ethnic Serbs suffered greatly, with several hundred thousand killed by the NDH during the war years.

Following the Axis invasion, the Yugoslav Communist Josip Broz Tito formed a resistance group, the Partisans. It was multi-ethnic and intent on driving out the Germans and the NDH as well as establishing a Communist state in Yugoslavia.[65] The Partisans also battled with a Serb nationalist group, the Četniks. The Četniks were loyal to the former royalist government and desired a Greater Serbian state. In a drive for ethnic homogeneity in the territory they controlled, the Četniks targeted Bosnian Muslims and Croats with extreme violence.[66] Within the context of the wider world war, a fierce civil war broke out in Yugoslavia between the NDH, the Partisans, and the Četniks.[67] With the Partisans headquartered in central Bosnia, much of Yugoslavia's fighting took place within Bosnia. The human cost was staggering.

The Allies eventually judged Tito's Partisans to be the most effective group opposing the Axis within Yugoslavia, swinging their support to the Partisans.[68] That support continued during the post-war settlement. In 1946 the international community again recognized a reconstituted Yugoslavia. The country looked to Tito as its leader. Tito was of mixed Croatian and Slovenian parentage. He was raised in the Catholic church, but did not promote a state religion. He advocated a philosophy of "brotherhood and unity" inclusive of all Yugoslavia's nationalities.

Socialist Yugoslavia (1945-1992):

In re-establishing Yugoslavia, Tito proved to be committed and ruthless;[69] an estimated 250,000 political opponents died in the early years of his regime.[70]

The new state included six republics. Bosnia-Herzegovina was one of six co-equal republics. The federal union of those six republics lasted for the next forty-seven years. This second incarnation of Yugoslavia made much progress in the years preceding Tito's death in

1980. While Yugoslavia included people from twenty-five different nationalities, Yugoslavia's constitution formally recognized five ethnic nations, affording them additional constitutional guarantees. The five favored ethnic nations were: Serb, Croat, Bosnian Muslim, Slovene, and Macedonian.[71]

During the Tito years, nationalist sentiments within Yugoslavia's ethnic nations were suppressed. It was his government's way of addressing the genocide that occurred in occupied Yugoslavia during the Second World War. That was unfortunate history that was literally and figuratively buried. Never fully addressed, these divisions lurked beneath the surface of Yugoslav society.

During the Cold War between the U.S. and the U.S.S.R., Yugoslavia became a principal organizing force behind the international non-aligned movement. The West considered independent Yugoslavia a crucial geographic bridge to its strategic allies Greece and Turkey, lavishing development loans on the country. Yugoslavia leveraged the Cold War adversaries to its advantage. As a result, its economy grew, in part on borrowed money, during the 1960s and 70s.[72]

In 1974 a new Yugoslav constitution was adopted that provided increased autonomy and authority to the six republics. Two regions within Serbia, Kosovo and Vojvodina, were also recognized as semi-autonomous provinces.[73] These changes upset many Serbs. The 1974 Constitution has been described as "neither federal nor confederal. The center of power was not defined. The center of power was Tito, and the problem came with his demise."[74]

Tito died in 1980 without naming a successor. Lacking a replacement of Tito's stature, it was determined that the Yugoslav presidency would revolve annually between the presidents of the six republics and the two provinces.[75]

Following Tito's death, nationalist sentiments re-emerged. Seeing these sentiments as a means to political power, political operatives in Serbia, Slovenia, and Croatia fanned nationalist flames. The rise of nationalism in Yugoslavia threatened to break the bonds that had held the country together.[76]

In 1987, Slobodan Milošević, a Communist party official closely aligned with Serbian President Ivan Stambolic, visited Kosovo. During this visit he addressed a Kosovo Serb demonstration and realized that rising Serb nationalism was a political phenomenon he could tap into and encourage.[77] By the end of the year he had ousted Stambolic and became Serbia's president.[78]

By 1989, Milošević had engineered leadership changes in Montenegro, Kosovo, and Vojvodina that gave him control of the collective presidency.[79] He rejected reform proposals from Croatia and Slovenia, setting those republics on a path toward secession from Yugoslavia.[80]

In June 1989, Milošević made a speech on the six-hundredth anniversary of the Battle of Kosovo Field. The event drew Serb multitudes and galvanized Serb commitment to a Greater Serbia concept.[81] That concept encompassed Serb populations in the republics of Bosnia, Croatia, Montenegro, and Macedonia. In Bosnia the Greater Serbia movement envisioned the "creation of a seamless expanse of Serb-held and Serb-inhabited territory on either side of the Drina (River). Along the Sava (River), the strategic aim was to forge a link with the Serb-held Krajina region in Croatia."[82] Brčko and the Posavina corridor provided that link.

During this period, Slovenia began taking steps toward secession, including constitutional changes that ended one-party governance within the republic.[83]

The leaders of the republics of Slovenia (Milan Kučan), Croatia (Franjo Tuđman), and Serbia (Slobodan Milošević) decided among themselves that Yugoslavia would dissolve.[84] Kučan was content to take Slovenia out of Yugoslavia as it was. Both Tuđman and Milošević desired something more for their republics. With one-quarter of ethnic Serbs living outside Serbia's borders, Milosevic desired additional territory in both Bosnia and Croatia.[85] With many ethnic Croats living in the Herzegovina region of Bosnia, Tuđman desired Bosnian territory.[86] Both national leaders were willing to take territory from others by force and to summon the revenants of the Second World War in priming their followers for the effort. The implications for Bosnia-Herzegovina, the republic stuck between Serbia and Croatia, would prove staggering.[87]

As the 1990s dawned, the international community failed to comprehend the forces brewing within Yugoslavia and the willingness of some Yugoslav leaders to use mass violence to enhance their own political prospects and the country's dissolution.

In January 1990, the fourteenth Congress of the League of Communists of Yugoslavia failed when the Slovene and Croat delegations walked out.[88]

That February, Croatian Serbs formed their own political party, the Serbian Democratic party (SDS in Bosnia).

In May, a party of Democratic Action (SDA) formed in Bosnia. Alija Izetbegović, a prominent Bosnian Muslim, was chosen party leader.[89] That month elections in Croatia swept the Croatian Democratic Union (HDZ) and its leader, Franjo Tuđman, into power.[90]

In July a Bosnian Serb political party (SDS) formed, electing Radovan Karadžić as its leader. That month Slovenia declared its sovereignty, but not (yet) its independence from Yugoslavia.

The following month, ethnic Serbs in the Krajina region of Croatia declared their sovereignty and autonomy following a referendum.[91] Ethnic Serbs represented thirteen percent of Croatia's population.[92]

In November and December, elections were held in Bosnia. The three national parties, SDS (Bosnian Serb), SDA (Bosnian Muslim), and HDZ (Bosnian Croat), captured 202 of 240 parliamentary seats and formed a governing coalition.[93]

In May 1991, Croatia held a popular referendum on independence. The vote in favor (93%) was overwhelming.

In June, Slovenia declared independence. Croatia followed suit on the same day.[94] A brief war between the Yugoslav People's Army and Slovenia's Territorial Defense Force ensued. After ten days, the Yugoslav army withdrew from Slovenia to go on the offensive in Croatia.

That September, Bosnian Serb leader Radovan Karadžić declared Serb Autonomous Areas (SAO in Bosnian) in Bosnia-Hercegovina, and established parallel government institutions.[95] The national army (JNA) secretly armed Serb populations within the SAOs and developed plans for a military takeover of Bosnian territory.[96] Implementation of these plans awaited political developments within Yugoslavia, including testing the international community's support and commitment to an independent Bosnian state.

The following month, Bosnian Serb representatives boycotted the Bosnian Parliament.[97]

In January 1992, the international community brokered a cease-fire in Croatia. At that time, Croatian Serbs controlled twenty-five percent of Croatian territory.[98] The Yugoslav People's Army (JNA) withdrew from Croatia and prepared for military action in Bosnia. Bosnian Serbs declared an independent Republic of Bosnia-Herzegovina on January 9, later changing its name to Republika Srpska.[99] That month the European Union recognized both Croatia and Slovenia as independent states.[100]

In March, Bosnia held a referendum on independence that was boycotted by the Bosnian Serb party (SDS). The SDS prevented voting in Serb Autonomous Areas. Those voting elsewhere overwhelmingly (ninety-nine percent) approved independence. Following the vote, sporadic violence began to break out in Bosnia.[101]

That April, Serb paramilitaries went into action in Bosnia. Bijeljina was sacked,[102] and a campaign of ethnic cleansing began.

On April 7, 1992, the United States recognized Bosnia-Hercegovina, Croatia, and Slovenia as independent states.

On April 30, 1992, the bridge connecting Brčko, Bosnia, and Gunja, Croatia, was destroyed with severe loss of life. The Bosnian War had arrived in Isak Gaši's hometown of Brčko.[103] By the war's end in November 1995, many Bosnians had perished.

In January 2013, the Research and Documentation Center of Sarajevo, in conjunction with the ICTY, published the *Bosnian Book of the Dead,* an exhaustive attempt to document casualties from the Bosnian War. Their figure of 97,207 is considered a minimum. There are many unidentified from mass graves, with mass graves still being found. Of the confirmed dead, the ethnic breakout was sixty-two percent Bosniak, twenty-five percent Bosnian Serb, and eight percent Bosnian Croat. The figures for civilian deaths were eighty-two percent Bosniak, ten percent Bosnian Serb, and six-and-a-half percent Bosnian Croat. In Brčko, the casualty figure was 1,667, including both civilian and military deaths.

REFERENCES

- Andrić, Ivo. Bridge on the Drina, trans. Lovett F. Edwards, Belgrade: Sezam Book, 2014.

- Bildt, Carl. Peace Journey: The Struggle for Peace in Bosnia. London: Orion House, 1998.

- Borger, Julian. The Butcher's Trail: How the Search for Balkan War Criminals Became the World's Most Successful Manhunt. New York: Other Press, 2016.

- Cohen, Roger. "Bosnians Angry at U.S. and UN as New Battle Looms." The New York Times, 7 May 1994.

- Coll, Steve. "Bosnia in the Shadow of the Holocaust." Washington Post Magazine. 25 September 1994, 7-28.

- ICTY Case number IT-02-54, the Prosecutor versus Slobodan Milošević, transcript of hearing on 11 September 2003, pages 26430-26469 (htpp://www.icty.org/x/cases/slobodan_milošević/tran/en/030911ED.htm), accessed 3 February 2015.

- ICTY Case number IT-03-67, the Prosecutor versus Vojislav Šešelj, transcript of hearing on 10 March 2010, pages 15761-15825 (htpp://www.icty.org/x/cases/šešelj/trans/en/100310IT.htm), accessed, 3 February 2015.

- ICTY Case number IT-95-5/18, the Prosecutor versus Radovan Karadžić, transcript of hearing on 15 July 2011, pages 16647-16705 (htpp://www.icty.org/x/cases/karadžić/trans/en/110715IT.htm), accessed 3 February 2015.

- ICTY Case number IT-95-5/18, the Prosecutor versus Radovan Karadžić, transcript of hearing on 14 July 2011, pages 16606-16646 (htpp:// www.icty.org/x/cases/karadžić/trans/en/110714ED.htm), accessed 3 February 2015.

- ICTY Case Number IT-00-39, the Prosecutor versus Momčilo Krajišnik, transcript of hearing on 4 February 2004, pages 374-480 (htpp://www.icty.org/x/cases/krajišnik/trans/en/040204ED.htm), accessed 3 February 2015.

- ICTY Case number IT-00-39, the Prosecutor versus Momčilo Krajišnik, transcript of hearing on 5 February 2004, pages 481-583 (htpp://www.icty.org/x/cases/krajišnik/trans/en/040205ED.htm), accessed 3 February 2015.

- ICTY Case number IT-94-1, the Prosecutor versus Dusko Tadić, transcript of hearing on 15 May 1996, pages 697-761, (htpp://www.icty.org/x/cases/tadić/trans/en/960515it.htm), accessed 3 February 2015.

- ICTY Case numbers IT-99-36/2 and IT-04-79, the Prosecutor versus Stojan Župljanin and Mico Stanišić, transcript of hearing on 21 October 2009, pages 1775-1851 (htpp://www.icty.org/x/cases/župljanin_stanišićm/trans/en/091021IT.htm), accessed 3 February 2015.

- ICTY Case numbers IT-99-36/2 and IT-04-79, the Prosecutor versus Stojan Župljanin and Mico Stanišić, transcript of hearing on 20 October 2009, pages 1760-1774 (htpp://www.icty.org/x/cases/župljanin_stanišićm/trans/en/091020IT.htm), accessed 3 February 2015.

- Kaaber, Lars. "On Escape from the Memories." Politiken. Copenhagen, Denmark, 18 October 1993.

- Koff, Clea. The Bone Woman: A Forensic Anthropologist's Search for Truth in the Mass Graves of Rwanda, Bosnia, Croatia, and Kosovo. New York: Random House, 2004.

- Moore, Adam. Peacebuilding in Practice: Local Experience in Two Bosnian Towns. Ithaca: Cornell University Press, 2013.

- Selimović, Meša. The Fortress. trans. E.D. Goy and Jasna Levinger. Evanston, Illinois: Northwestern University Press, 1999.

- Silber, Laura and Little, Allen. Yugoslavia: Death of a Nation. New York: Penguin, 1997.

ENDNOTES

1. Silber and Little, Yugoslavia: Death of a Nation, p. 215.
2. Silber and Little, Bosnia: Death of a Nation, p. 252.
3. Andrić, p. 191.
4. Balija is a derogatory term used against Muslims.
5. www.worldpressphoto.org/people/bojan-stojanović.
6. Meša Selimović, The Fortress, trans. E.D. Goy and Jasna Levinger, (Evanston, Illinois: Northwestern University Press), 1999, p. 137.
7. The United States eventually made special provisions and allowed 168,644 Bosnian War refugees to emigrate. [Tara Zahra, The Great Departure: Mass Migration from Eastern Europe and the Making of the Free World, (New York: W.W. Norton, 2016), p. 274.]
8. Lars Kaaber, "On Escape from the Memories." Politiken, Copenhagen, Denmark, October 18, 1993.
9. Steve Coll, "Bosnia in the Shadow of the Holocaust." Washington Post Magazine, September 25, 1994, 7-28.
10. https://wikileaks.org/plusd/cables/92ZAGREB2532_a.html
11. Margaret Thatcher, "Bosnia and the Future of Ethnic Cleansing." World Affairs, v. 156, no.2, Fall 1993, p.104.
12. Roger Cohen, "Bosnians Angry at U.S. and UN as New Battle Looms." The New York Times, May 7, 1994.
13. Carl Bildt, Peace Journey: The Struggle for Peace in Bosnia, (London: Orion House, 1998), pp. 6-7.
14. Adam Moore, Peacebuilding in Practice: Local Experience in Two Bosnian Towns, (Ithaca: Cornell University Press, 2013).
15. In his book The Butcher's Trail: How the Search for Balkan War Criminals Became the World's Most Successful Manhunt, journalist Julian Borger details the fourteen-year effort to bring the 161 individuals indicted by ICTY prosecutors to The Hague (New York: Other Press, 2016).
16. www.wikileaks.org/plusd/cables/08THEHAGUE56_a.html.
17. I obtained an H-1B visa as a skilled guest worker in 2001, and Jasminka, Adna, and I moved to Washington State in 2001.
18. www.icty.org/x/cases/krajišnik/trans/en/040205ED.htm and www.icty.org/x/cases/krajišnik/040206ED.htm.
19. She had two children, ages twelve and nine at the time. They had been sent from Brčko to relatives earlier, as the nurse and her husband were worried about their safety.
20. Joseph Conrad, Heart of Darkness, (Penguin: Middlesex, England, 1986), p. 116.
21. http://pescanik.net/contexts-don't-burn.

22. www.nanticokeindians.org/tale_of_two_wolves.cfm.

23. LIFE magazine, 18 Oct 1963, Vol. 55, No. 16, p. 92—ISSN: 0024-3019.

24. Noel Malcolm, Bosnia—A Short History (Washington Square, New York: New York University Press, 1996), p. 2.

25. Malcolm, Bosnia—A Short History, p. 6.

26. Malcolm, Bosnia—A Short History, p. 9.

27. Malcolm, Bosnia—A Short History, p. 10.

28. Malcolm, Bosnia—A Short History, p. 11.

29. Mazower, The Balkans: A Short History, pp. 42-3.

30. Malcolm, Bosnia—A Short History, p. 14.

31. Malcolm, Bosnia—A Short History, p. 17.

32. Malcolm, Bosnia—A Short History, p. 20.

33. Cohen, Hearts Grown Brutal, p. 211.

34. Malcolm, Bosnia—A Short History, p. 20.

35. Malcolm, Bosnia—A Short History, p. 43.

36. In 1990, their descendants inhabited Croatia's Krajina region and attempted to break away from Croatia.

37. Laura Silber and Allan Little, Yugoslavia: Death of a Nation, pp. 93, 104.

38. Malcolm, Bosnia—A Short History, p. 53; Mazower, The Balkans: A Short History, p. 46-7.

39. Malcolm, Bosnia—A Short History, p. 50.

40. Malcolm, Bosnia—A Short History, p. 94.

41. Malcolm, Bosnia—A Short History, p. 89; Mazower, The Balkans: A Short History, p. 17.

42. Malcolm, Bosnia—A Short History, p. 133.

43. Mazower, The Balkans: A Short History, p. 30.

44. Mazower, The Balkans: A Short History, p. 94; Robert D. Kaplan, Balkan Ghosts: A Journey Through History, p. 54.

45. Mazower, The Balkans: A Short History, p. 95-7; Malcolm, Bosnia—A Short History, p. 134.

46. Mazower, The Balkans: A Short History, p. 100.

47. Malcolm, Bosnia—A Short History, p. 141.

48. Malcolm, Bosnia—A Short History, p. 137.

49. Robert D. Kaplan, Balkan Ghosts: A Journey Through History, p. 63-4.

50. Mark Mazower, The Balkans: A Short History, (New York: Modern Library, 2000), p. xxxix.

51. Malcolm, Bosnia—A Short History, p. 150; Robert D. Kaplan, Balkan Ghosts: A Journey Through History, p. 62.

52. Mazower, The Balkans: A Short History, p. 106; Malcolm, Bosnia—A Short History, p. 155.

53. Robert D. Kaplan, Balkan Ghosts: A Journey Through History, p. 65.

54. Mazower, The Balkans: A Short History, p. 110.

55. Mazower, The Balkans: A Short History, p. 110.

56. Mazower, The Balkans: A Short History, p. 129.

57. Robert D. Kaplan, Balkan Ghosts: A Journey Through History, p. 66.

58. Malcolm, Bosnia—A Short History, p. 170.

59. Malcolm, Bosnia—A Short History, p. 173.

60. Mazower, The Balkans: A Short History, p. 123; Malcolm, Bosnia—A Short History, p. 175.

61. Robert D. Kaplan, Balkan Ghosts: A Journey Through History, p. 5

62. Steven L. Jacobs, Confronting Genocide: Judaism, Christianity, Islam, (Lanham, Maryland: Lexington Books, 2009), p. 158-9; Laura Silber and Allan Little, Yugoslavia: Death of a Nation, p. 93; Cohen, Hearts Grown Brutal, p. 139

63. Cohen, Hearts Grown Brutal, p. 31

64. Malcolm, Bosnia—A Short History, p. 176; Cohen, Hearts Grown Brutal, p. 36

65. Malcolm, Bosnia—A Short History, p. 177

66. Malcolm, Bosnia—A Short History, pp. 178, 179, 187, 188.

67. Malcolm, Bosnia—A Short History, p. 181.

68. Malcolm, Bosnia—A Short History, p. 184.

69. Mazower, The Balkans: A Short History, p. 131; Laura Silber and Allan Little, Yugoslavia: Death of a Nation, p. 29.

70. Malcolm, Bosnia—A Short History, p. 193.

71. Mazower, The Balkans: A Short History, p. 140.

72. Malcolm, Bosnia—A Short History, p. 210.

73. Malcolm, Bosnia—A Short History, p. 205; Laura Silber and Allan Little, Yugoslavia: Death of a Nation, p. 34.

74. Cohen, Hearts Grown Brutal, p. 105.

75. Laura Silber and Allan Little, Yugoslavia: Death of a Nation, p. 29.

76. Robert D. Kaplan, Balkan Ghosts: A Journey Through History, p. 75.

77. Laura Silber and Allan Little, Yugoslavia: Death of a Nation, p. 119.

78. Laura Silber and Allan Little, Yugoslavia: Death of a Nation, p. 47.

79. Malcolm, Bosnia—A Short History, p. 213.

80. Robert D. Kaplan, Balkan Ghosts: A Journey Through History, p. 75.

81. Mazower, The Balkans: A Short History, p. 141; Laura Silber and Allan Little, Yugoslavia: Death of a Nation, p. 71

82. Cohen, Hearts Grown Brutal, p. 205

83. Malcolm, Bosnia—A Short History, p. 214; Laura Silber and Allan Little, Yugoslavia Death of a Nation, pp. 75, 149

84. Laura Silber and Allan Little, Yugoslavia: Death of a Nation, p. 117

85. Malcolm, Bosnia—A Short History, p. 215; Cohen, Hearts Grown Brutal, p. 139

86. Malcolm, Bosnia—A Short History, p. 218; Laura Silber and Allan Little, Yugoslavia: Death of a Nation, p. 86.

87. Laura Silber and Allan Little, Yugoslavia: Death of a Nation, pp. 131-132, 144, 190-191.

88. Laura Silber and Allan Little, Yugoslavia: Death of a Nation, p. 80.

89. Malcolm, Bosnia—A Short History, p. 218.

90. Malcolm, Bosnia—A Short History, p. 215.

91. Malcolm, Bosnia—A Short History, p. 224.

92. Laura Silber and Allan Little, Yugoslavia: Death of a Nation (New York: Penguin, 1997), p.87.

93. Malcolm, Bosnia—A Short History, p. 222.

94. Malcolm, Bosnia—A Short History, p. 225.

95. Laura Silber and Allan Little, Yugoslavia: Death of a Nation, p. 214.

96. Malcolm, Bosnia—A Short History, p. 227.

97. Laura Silber and Allan Little, Yugoslavia: Death of a Nation, p. 216.

98. Malcolm, Bosnia—A Short History, p. 230.

99. Laura Silber and Allan Little, Yugoslavia: Death of a Nation, p. 218.

100. Malcolm, Bosnia—A Short History, p. 230.

101. Malcolm, Bosnia—A Short History, p. 231.

102. Malcolm, Bosnia—A Short History, p. 236; Laura Silber and Allan Little, Yugoslavia: Death of a Nation, pp. 222-226.

103. Laura Silber and Allan Little, Yugoslavia: Death of a Nation, p. 232.

CPSIA information can be obtained
at www.ICGtesting.com
Printed in the USA
LVOW03*0155080318
569076LV00004B/4/P